THE ART OF WHITETAIL DECEPTION

CALLING, RATTLING, AND DECOYING MAKE BIG BUCKS HUNT YOU!

OUTDOORSMAN'S EDGE®
GUIDES

The Art of Whitetail Deception

Calling, Rattling, and Decoying Make Big Bucks Hunt You!

Kathy Etling

CRE**A**TIVE
OUTDOORS™

TABLE OF CONTENTS

P R O L O G U E

Some deer hunters may seem perfectly content, on their yearly trek into the deer woods, to merely loll about and enjoy nature. Such hunters will gladly take the occasional 'gift' deer that wanders by within range, but will rarely exert himself or herself to do so. This book is not for fair-weather or once-a-year hunters.

Rather, it was envisioned as an advanced text conceived and executed in such a way as to take the truly dedicated hunter of whitetails a good distance farther down the trail toward consistent deer hunting success.

"Be all that you can be" is a great slogan, one whose words ring as true for deer hunters as for professional warriors. Anyone who aspires to greatness as a hunter of white-tailed deer must endure a long apprenticeship in one of three ways: 1.) Actually learning by doing while out in the deer woods where one builds directly upon each lesson previously learned; 2.) Learning directly from one or more premier deer hunters who have years of experience and are willing to spend the time to impart their store of knowledge; Or, 3.) through a willingness to study the thoughts, actions, and results obtained by experienced and successful deer hunters and which are recorded in a text like this one. The hunter who opts for choice #3 will be able to learn at his own pace. He will be able to take that which has been so generously offered and adapt, if necessary, those strategies and tactics he feels will work best in his situation. By examining the core of knowledge so unselfishly tendered by those who have come before, the readers of this book will find themselves being led up new and hitherto unexplored trails that will undoubtedly culminate in improved deer-hunting success the very first time they step back into the woods or prairies.

Calling, rattling, and decoying will work on all deer some of the time. What you must learn to do is make it work consistently during the times when you're out hunting. Modern business practices sometimes keep us out of the woods during those times when we would most like to hunt. Become proficient in calling, rattling, and decoying, while also learning how to make the most out of your time spent afield, no matter when that time may be.

These tactics will work not only on resident deer. They will work equally well—if not better—on the transient buck out searching for hot does or, perhaps, even spoiling for a fight. In either case, learning how best to call, rattle, and/or decoy could mean more venison in your freezer, as well as more—and better—deer racks for your family room wall.

Why start from scratch when there is a book—this one—that will spell out what no hunter, ever before, has had the luxury of learning in his own home? Enter the upcoming deer season well-equipped to deal with every eventuality tossed your way by the wary whitetails where you hunt. To do any less is to sell yourself—and your abilities —short.

Reading this book will provide a thorough grounding in white-tail biology, physiology, behaviors, and body language, as well as the nuts and bolts of calling, rattling, and decoying. You will be privy to scientific research rarely, if ever, read by white-tail hunting afficionados. The most minute detail has been attended to. The decoying section, for instance, deals not only with effigies of deer placed about in various tantalizing poses and why they are placed that way, but with the use of the extremely mobile and easily-made 'mock' deer tail, both moveable and stationery, the common sense that led to the creation and use of mock scrapes and rubs, and even the placement of various mock food sources.

Only hunters well-acquainted with every nitty-gritty detail involved in calling, rattling, and decoying have been consulted during the compilation and writing of this book. Each contributor has earned his or her reputation as an expert in one or more of these selected tactics, as well as accolades as a superior deer hunter. Each has been plying his or her deer hunting for many years, and each has the trophies—and anecdotes—to prove that he knows what he's doing, and that he can also teach by the mistakes that he's made. Even more importantly, each has given generously of his time and shared his precious photos to let you participate vicariously in the excitement of many different hunts.

Calling, rattling, and decoying work on a white-tail's keenly developed social sense. The tactics appeal to the animal's curiosity. In some situations they may even threaten its rank within the resident white-tail population's hierarchical structure. That hierarchy is in a constant state of flux, so each deer will try to manipulate circumstances to increase its relative position in the herd. And that, dear readers, works to YOUR advantage.

By learning all there is to know about calling, rattling, and decoying deer hunters are taking a quantum leap forward into the 21st century. The hunter who uses these tactics in the proper way and at the optimum time will elevate his hunting to another level: He or she will no longer simply be hunting deer; the deer will be hunting THEM!

A hunter thoroughly versed in calling, rattling, and decoying's finer points will not only know which tactic to use when, but how often the tactic should be used—a particular calling sequence, for instance—as well as the circumstances in which a particular call will work best. The text provides advice on how best to deceive whitetails right up until the moment you loose your bowstring or squeeze the trigger.

The art of calling, rattling, and decoying doesn't end at the instant when a deer's attention has been seized. The true art of your deception lies in being able to wait, perfectly still, as you battle nervous tension, vagrant winds, and other variables right up until the moment the ever-cautious white-tail makes that final, fatal step. Such a feat may sound easy until one sets about accomplishing it. For once you have set into motion the process that leads to a white-tail's hunting YOU, you also have set yourself up for failure since each of that deer's formidable senses will be focused on YOU and you alone. After all, the deer now believes that you are another 'deer' and its intention now shifts to finding out who that other deer is.

Calling, rattling, and decoying sometimes will work so well as to seem almost foolproof. I would be less than truthful, however, if I said these tactics were foolproof, all the time. They aren't. Like us, each deer is an individual. As such, they can be thoroughly unpredictable. Reading this book, however, and studying the many incredible hunting and bowhunting tips contained within will provide the serious hunter with knowledge enough to turn his or her deer hunting world upside down. Calling, rattling and decoying can conjure up whitetails quicker and more reliably than any other deer hunting tactics used today. Far from being mere 'smoke and mirrors,' these white-tail Special F/X will transport the hunter willing to suspend disbelief into a brave new world where YOU control your deer-hunting destiny. What hunter could ask for anything more?

—Kathy Etling

ACKNOWLEDGEMENTS

White-tailed deer are one of my passions. I love to watch them, photograph them, and simply learn more about their behaviors under varying circumstances. I also love to hunt them, whether with bow, muzzleloader, modern rifle, or shotgun. Whitetails are the complete game animal. They are intelligent and cunning, beautiful as well as unpredictable. Adding to my fascination with these creatures are their antlers; antlers that grow in many amazing–and sometimes humongous–configurations. Antlers that might be wide or high or wide and high, many-tined or not-so-many tined, drop-pointed or sticker-pointed, bleached pale or rubbed russet, mahogany, or a shade in between. I will love whitetails always, and hunt them until old age prevents me from doing so. I pray that the latter circumstance never happens!

My love for whitetails has manifested itself during the past twenty years and more in the tremendous number of articles I've written about them. As I researched these articles I became aware of the vast amount of in-depth research that dedicated biologists have contributed to the scientific literature. This research represented a vast and untapped resource as I set about to document what was known to be the truth about whitetails versus what had been suspected by those of us who simply observe and hunt them. In many cases, what was known to be fact dovetailed neatly with what was suspected to be true. In other cases, though, what was suspected by hunters was, in truth, merely fallacious or the product of many years of old hunters' tales. Reconciling the truth about whitetails with the suspected became one of the objectives of my writings about these magnificent animals.

To get to the crux of any matter concerning these deer, I have always had my best success when interviewing those hunters who pursue these deer in many different states for most of every season, as well as when I consult with the finest research minds that have studied the white-tailed deer and all its diverse behaviors. The list of people who have contributed to the writing of this book is long and varied. I wish to thank everyone for the time and effort and thought they put into the answers they provided to my sometimes pesky questions, and also to the generosity with which they supplied me with videotapes, research studies, and other data that they had accumulated during their own years of fascination with whitetails.

As always, I wish to thank Bob Zaiglin, manager of the vast Harrison Ranches in south Texas, for his intuitive knowledge of whitetails. His tried-and true methods of calling and rattling, which he has used for many years to bring in trophy bucks for his hunters, are explained in detail in these pages. Bob is also one of the finest outdoor photographers in the business. I wish to thank him for allowing me to use many of his photos of the beautiful south Texas country that he knows and loves so well.

I'd also like to thank Dr. Steve Demarais, who together with Bob Zaiglin authored a four-year telemetry study on the home range habits of bona fide trophy whitetail bucks.

Thanks are also due Mickey Hellickson of the King Ranch. Mickey very graciously consented to allow me to use two of his groundbreaking rattling studies as chapters in my book. The studies have been presented in much the same format as that in which they were originally submitted. What you will learn as you read these chapters may change everything you ever knew – or thought you knew – about antler-rattling and buck response to that rattling. Mickey has my thanks, as well, for the wonderful photographs he has so graciously shared with me and the readers of this book.

Thanks are due, as well, to Brian Root, author of a landmark Missouri telemetry study on the home range habits and movements of deer both before and during firearms hunting seasons.

M.R. James, bowhunter extraordinaire and editor emeritus of *Bowhunter Magazine,* really went the extra mile with his well-thought-out answers to a seemingly endless stream of questions, a wealth of great field shots, and diagrams.

Peter and Kate Fiduccia have my thanks as well. This book was Peter's idea and, at first, I must admit I wondered where I would find enough to write about if the subject was limited to rattling, decoying, and calling. By the time I put the book together, however, I discovered I could easily have written another 50,000 words, although I am sure that both Peter and Kate are very glad I stopped when I did. This manuscript quickly became a labor of love as I realized how much knowledge so many hunters were willing to share. One of those hunters is Peter Fiduccia. Until I interviewed him I had no idea how long he'd been calling, rattling, and decoying successfully, even in eastern states where so many other hunters believe rattling won't work. He is a credit to hunters and lovers of the outdoors everywhere because he has the gumption to not only try new tactics, but to devise strategies that no one else has even thought to try.

Jim Holdenried, Mel Dutton, Brad Harris of Outland Sports, Don Kisky, Holly Fuller, and Jerry Shively of Flat Iron Outfitters in Thompson Falls, Montana, were all extremely generous with their time and in explaining their hunting techniques, which, among hunters, is almost unparalleled. Each also supplied photos to be used in the book.

A special thanks is due Darren Thornberry and everyone at Buckmasters Whitetail Magazine for their gracious consent in allowing me to use their spectacular photographs of Mike Beatty with his amazing record-book whitetail.

So many others contributed to the writing of this book, as well. People like Brian Murphy of the Quality Deer Management Association in South Carolina, Dr. Karl Miller of the University of Georgia's School of Forest Resources, Dr. Larry Marchinton, retired whitetail researcher who once worked with Dr. Miller and others to learn more about these deer, Dr. Tom Atkeson and Dr. Harry Jacobson, two of the first to investigate the various whitetail vocalizations, T.R. Michels, Jay Cassell, Tom Storm, Dave Berkley, Mark Drury of M.A.D. Calls, a division of Outland Sports, Ernie Richardson, the late Terry Kayser, Billy Macoy of Southern Sportsman's Hunting Lodge in Hayneville, Alabama, Dennis Smith of Outdoors South radio and TV program fame, Dale Carter of Carter's Hunting Lodge in Pittsburg, Illinois, Ronnie Robison, Butch McElwain of Whitetail Creek Outfitters in Cadiz, Kentucky, Angel Vogel, Bob Shepard, Billy McDonald, Jerry Peterson of Woods Wise Products, Will Primos of Primos Wild Game Calls, Bill Jordan of Realtree and Advantage Outdoors, Mark Higdon of Higdon's Motion Decoys, and Spike Stacey.

Without the help of these generous people this book would not be what it is today. Thank you, one and all!

—*Kathy Etling*

1

The Surprisingly Vocal Whitetail

It was a miserable day. Light fog combined with a bone-chilling drizzle to thoroughly dampen my spirits and soak my gear. The only bright spot in this otherwise dismal day stood on the hillside directly in front of my stand. Through my binoculars I watched as a small spike buck timidly trailed an estrous doe. Every now and then, the doe would look behind her and then twitch her white tail, as though annoyed at the hopeful youngster's pretensions. The time was 11:00 A.M. on the second day of Missouri's firearms deer season, and I was doing my best to hold out for a good buck. *Why couldn't that spike have bigger antlers?* I thought.

I shifted around to get more comfortable on the flat, narrow tree stand platform. As I did so, the buck grunter on a lanyard around my neck caught my eye. With that spike following so closely on the doe's heels, it just might work, I reasoned.

This anecdote took place many years ago, during my third season using deer calls. The call I'd decided to use that long-ago day was one that imitated a buck's tending grunt. I had nothing to lose by trying the grunt call. I didn't want to take the spike; if he skittered away in fear at the sound of another buck's tending grunt, it wouldn't bother me at all. But by making such a grunt, as the spike trailed closely behind the doe, my hopes ran high that a larger buck might show himself, if for no other reason than to teach the impertinent spike a lesson in manners.

I'd become enthralled with the concept of deer calls two years prior to that damp November day.

When rainy weather lowers a whitetail's guard, try calling. Author poses with a nice 8-pointer. Credit: Bob Etling.

On that occasion, I called in two small bucks the first time I used a grunt tube. The following year I added some rattling horns, and soon afterward rattled in two more bucks. These experiences were not only thrilling, they were addictive. You might say I became hooked on deer calling.

The spike continued to wend his way slowly up the hillside, unwilling to let the doe get more than a few feet away. It was now or never. I pulled out the buck grunter and blew on it three times. A low, guttural sound punctuated by a slight clicking noise emanated from the tube. I found it amazing that the call was able to make a vocalization that so closely resembled the real thing. I paused and

The author nailed this heavy-antlered buck when it charged from some brush after she'd used her buck grunter. Credit: Bob Etling.

then blew the grunt tube again, this time much louder, making certain the tube's open end was facing in the buck's direction. And it worked, even from two hundred yards away! As I watched in astonishment, a heavy-antlered buck charged down off the hilltop from where he had been lurking in a thick tangle of brush. With his ears laid flat back, the larger animal rocketed directly at the spike and knocked the smaller buck off his feet. As the spike scrambled back up, I dropped the call, picked up my rifle, and found the big buck in my scope. I fired just as the spike squirted out of my field of view, his plans for the doe forgotten.

The bullet from my rifle found its mark. The buck went down in a heap, then rolled end over end off a twenty-foot bluff. When I finally reached the spot where he'd come to rest, I still couldn't believe I'd managed to lure this big deer out of hiding in such a spectacular manner.

A BRIEF HISTORY OF DEER CALLING

Long ago Northwest coastal tribes used primitive calls to lure Sitka black-tailed deer within range of their bows. It is presumed that most other Native American people called whitetails and mule deer, too, even though thousands of miles separated the various tribes. Hunting tactics, like trade goods, were disseminated near and far by this country's indigenous peoples. But then calling as a tactic vanished within just a few centuries of European settlement upon the continent, along with most of the country's whitetails. It would be many years later, when whitetails were once again plentiful, that calling would again come into its own.

After the animals had been market-hunted into near oblivion, the first modern American hunters took to the forests and fields. Since deer were still few in number as well as widely scattered, the animals were incorrectly perceived as being silent creatures. For decades, only a few people realized that deer produce a wide array of sounds. To be honest, some hunters probably heard whitetail vocalizations but were unable to identify them as such. Yet whitetails are anything but quiet. Deer not only emit many different vocalizations to communicate with one another, they also signal each other with antler-clashing and hoof-stomping. The savvy whitetail

M.R. James shot this east Texas buck at twelve yards when it responded to his buck grunts. Credit: M.R. James.

hunter should reserve a place for all three tactics: calling, rattling, and hoof-stomping.

Calling provides some of the most exciting whitetail action. Hunters proficient with calls have for years issued vocal invitations to flocks of geese and ducks and then watched with anticipation as they cupped their wings and dropped down to within range of waiting guns. The same applies to hunters who take to fields and forests with slate, cedar box, or diaphragm, minds set on fooling gobblers with their own inimitable style of turkey talk. But in my opinion, the biggest hunting thrill of all is when a white-tailed buck, one of the most cunning animals on earth, comes looking for you because of a call you made. Calling works, and it works well, in all sorts of situations and under most conditions. Calling is definitely a premier "go-to" tactic to use whenever you're in the woods trying to score on a whitetail.

My husband, Bob, discovered calling soon after I did. Of course we couldn't keep the news to ourselves, and our daughter, Julie, soon became hooked on the tactic, as did our son-in-law, Rick Ply. Every successful whitetail hunter of my acquaintance now carries one or more calls in his or her pack and never leaves home without them. As my good friend Brad Harris of Outland Sports says, "Deer calling has resulted in more deer being taken, during the years since it was rediscovered, than any other hunting tactic, bar none!" Those are heady sentiments, indeed.

Let's return to my husband. One extremely hot autumn day, Bob, who had been bowhunting, was growing bored. It was almost noon. The sun was at its zenith and shade was in short supply. Bob had decided to go back to the house for lunch. But when he heard distinct walking sounds— rustling leaves—on a nearby but hid-

den trail, he blew on his grunt call instead. The walking sounds stopped. Bob grunted again. There was no mistaking the animal's immediate reaction. It turned around and made a beeline for the sound of the grunt, passing within ten yards of Bob's stand as it did so. The big buck felt compelled to find out what other deer was making that grunting noise and why, even on a hot, muggy day. Although this wasn't the first buck Bob had called in, it remains, years later, one of the largest he's ever taken with his bow.

Later that same year, on the first day of firearms season, Bob grunted in—and subsequently passed up—a dandy 8-pointer because he thought an even larger buck might respond later in the season. Bob learned the hard way that calling can make a deer hunt easier, but ponder long and hard whenever you

When a buck hears a tending grunt, he thinks he's hearing another buck and that a hot doe might be near. Credit: Bob Etling.

find yourself in the position to decide to pass up a trophy-caliber buck.

Whether you are reading these words in the dead of winter, well after all hunting seasons have closed, during springtime's first blush, or in the weeks just prior to the whitetail rut, delay no longer. Now is the perfect time to formulate a strategy for next season. Let us begin with a capsule course in whitetail rut physiology.

ALL ABOUT THE WHITETAIL RUT AND HIERARCHY

In August, the rut's peak is still more than a month away, but whitetails are already becoming restless. Whether from the effects of decreasing amounts of sunlight upon the pineal gland, or a slow, gradual decline in daily ambient temperatures, or from the combined influence of both of these factors, deer have started to alter their everyday habits. The lethargy displayed during the long, hot summer now morphs into a spurt of autumn activity. The bucks' antlers, although they may still be partially covered in velvet, have almost completely *ossified,* or turned to bone. As the rut approaches, each new day brings with it an increase in a buck's blood testosterone level. Blood testosterone levels signal the antlers to harden, the blood—which had nourished the still-growing bone—to dry up; and the velvet to wither and curl. Bucks test their new, hardened headgear against small saplings or by whacking a cedar's soft, lowermost branches. The astute hunter will be in the woods whenever possible, perhaps not in his opening-day stand, but out there just the same, watching and learning. Understanding the whitetail is paramount before attempting to master tactics, such as calling, that will lead to consistent hunting success.

More than twenty years ago two whitetail biologists began studying the vocalizations of these fascinating animals. These two researchers, Dr. Harry Jacobson and Larry Richardson, identified eight distinct vocalizations. More recently, research studies made by then-graduate student Tom Atkeson, together with Drs. Larry Marchinton and Karl Miller, all of the University of Georgia's School of Forest Resources, identified twelve different whitetail vocalizations. Each of these calls could further be categorized as either *dominant-subordinate* or *cohesive* in nature.

What do those terms mean? Well, white-tailed deer are herd animals. And while each "herd" may be composed of many loose-knit groups of individuals, within any given herd's structure, each individual will occupy its own niche. Let's say that fifty whitetails of various age classes—ten bucks and forty does—live in an area of four square miles. The area's *buck-to-doe ratio,* therefore, is 1:4—which means there is one buck for every four does. In any hunted population of deer, one older, *dominant* buck may survive to, perhaps, $5\frac{1}{2}$, $6\frac{1}{2}$, or $7\frac{1}{2}$ years of age. Suppose, as well, that the population also includes one or two bucks between $3\frac{1}{2}$ and $4\frac{1}{2}$ years old, three bucks $2\frac{1}{2}$ years old, and that the balance is divided equally between doe fawns and button bucks (the young-of-the-year), and yearlings (spikes, forked-horns, and other eighteen-month-old bucks). While the oldest, wiliest buck may be the herd's dominant individual, this isn't always the case. For the purposes of this discussion, though, we will say that it is true. If so, that buck would have little tolerance for bucks that are younger or weaker than he is. The *whitetail hierarchy*—where each individual deer ranks on the social scale or pecking order—determines how much leeway an old monarch will provide a subordinate animal. An old buck may be quite unforgiving of an interloping $2\frac{1}{2}$-year-old male, yet be more tolerant of a $4\frac{1}{2}$-year-old that might easily mortally wound him or challenge his supremacy. If a hot or *estrous* doe is at stake, though, the dominant buck might throw caution to the wind and come out fighting mad, whether his opponent is the $4\frac{1}{2}$-year-old or the $2\frac{1}{2}$-year-old. Luckily, *whitetail hierarchical standing* is almost always determined well before the rut, at a time when velvet-clad antlers are incapable of causing significant damage. This is probably nature's way of assuring that the fittest individuals will survive to breed in autumn. Surprisingly, whitetail social standing is usually determined not by head or antler-butting, but by foot-flailing—contests where two deer stand erect on hind legs and flail at each other with their forelegs until one of the combatants yields. Does also engage in foot-flailing, and yes, each doe maintains her own distinct place within the hierarchy. An old doe may attain an even higher ranking in the social strata than the dominant buck, yet even she will back down when the buck is sporting his impressive head-gear. Should she fail to do so, the buck might become aggravated and give her a good thwacking with his antlers. That thwacking could result in a mortal wound, a fact of which old does seem well aware.

Once antlers harden, bucks become more aggressive. Such aggression is the result of increased levels of blood testosterone. The animals channel these aggressive tendencies into activities such as rubbing the bark off trees, particularly those of fragrant species such as pine, cedar, sumac, and cherry; slashing low-lying limbs with their uppermost tines; rubbing their antlers into early season territorial scrapes; and sparring with their fellow bucks. These activities aren't just for show. Each helps to build up the buck's neck and shoulder muscles. After long, lazy summer months of doing little but feeding and sleeping, a buck is not extremely fit, at least not in whitetail terms. He's been lolling about, doing nothing, and if he's to compete for the attention of willing does, it behooves him to get into shape. The sparring starts off gingerly as each buck tests his respective headgear. Since bucks are unable to look into mirrors to see how large their antlers really are, this sparring activity helps each individual to familiarize himself with his antlers as well as recognize what he's able to do with them—and, more important, what he's not able to do. Attitudes are formed, for better or worse, and each buck arrives at a sense of how far he can reasonably go should a fight actually materialize. In one month or less, the sparring sessions will become less frequent and may actually cease. The clash of antlers that may be heard near or at the rut's peak could very well be the sound of a mortal struggle. Although it is rare for one buck to gore and kill another, it is not unheard of. Neither is the unfortunate circumstance in which two or three bucks lock antlers and are unable to pull apart. Unless a human comes along to free them, death is almost a certainty.

THE VOCALIZATIONS

According to Dr. Miller, each of the twelve whitetail vocalizations can be put into one of four general classifications: *agonistic* (the word means exactly what it sounds like—an antagonistic call that is one step short of a battle), *maternal, mating,* and *contact.* Calls are also classified as either *cohesive,* meaning that the deer wants to be social, or *noncohesive,* meaning that the deer is not seeking companionship and, indeed, is seeking recognition by other deer of its dominance within the hierarchy. Maternal, mating, and contact calls are cohesive calls. Agonistic calls are noncohesive calls.

Understanding the differences in these classifications will help you to get the most out of your calling experience. For example, an old, dominant buck used to being the "king of the mountain" can become quite incensed should he suspect a younger or unknown buck is nosing around a doe in estrus. Any buck—dominant or subordinate—interested in an estrous doe will signal its intentions as it chases her by grunting in low, guttural, rhythmic tones known as the *tending grunt.* The tending grunt is a social call and also a mating call, and thus is cohesive: The buck is trying to convince the doe to stand still for breeding. The noise he makes sounds something like a low *burp, burp, burp, burp,* with a distinct background clicking noise. Hunters who have never heard this call before may confuse it with the grunting of a distant pig. A few hunters have stated that they have heard squealing noises in conjunction with the tending grunt, although such squealing has not been scientifically documented.

When you climb into your stand and use a buck grunt call, you are telling any buck within earshot that 1) you are a buck, and 2) a hot doe is nearby. Should the old, dominant buck hear your call, he may respond because 1) he doesn't know which deer is making the grunt, but since he's the top deer in the area, he feels sure he can whip him, and 2) he, too, is interested in finding that hot doe.

Should a younger buck hear you, he might respond because if he is lucky, the grunting buck will be smaller than he, and he can then steal the hot doe.

Should a doe that is ready to be bred hear you, she might respond because 1) she wants to see exactly which buck is chasing that other doe, or 2) she is curious about what is going on. Early each season does will commonly respond to grunt calls. Once the peak of the rut has passed, however, a tending grunt will sometime inspire does to flee. So much for the romantic skills of the whitetail buck.

Another buck grunt you should know about is the ***trailing grunt.*** A buck that has had a whiff of a doe that is either about to come into estrus or already is in estrus will wander through the woods, grunting occasionally, thinking of possible thrills yet to come. This trailing grunt sounds like a simple *burp,* (pause a while), *burp,* (pause a while), *burp.* A buck will sometimes grunt with each step he takes. Should a hunter make a similar grunt when the trailing buck is within earshot, the animal will often respond immediately. Hearing another "buck" simply verifies that the doe he is trailing is nearby, and that this second "buck"—you—is with her. Curiosity—and amour—will win out, and you could easily be the beneficiary.

A simple ***buck grunt***—*burp!*—made every five minutes or so can also pay huge dividends. This grunt can be made in either a high or a low pitch. Dr. Miller has found, rather surprisingly, no correlation between the deep, guttural grunts supposedly made by old, dominant bucks and the higher-pitched, softer grunts many hunters believe are made exclusively by younger bucks. Phil Liddle, who hails from New York State and is the two-time National Deer Calling Champion, disagrees. Liddle believes that there is a definite and recognizable difference in pitch between an older buck's grunt and that of a younger buck. While arguments could be made on both sides, it's probably better to be safe than sorry. The trophy hunter should concentrate on making deep, guttural grunts, while the meat hunter—or someone who just wants to take a buck—may see more deer when producing softer, less aggressive-sounding grunts.

All three of the above grunts are termed cohesive because each is made for the purpose of initiating social contact with another deer, the doe. The tending grunt and trailing grunt are further classified as mating calls, while the buck grunt is simply a contact call that can be used to locate another deer, buck, or doe.

The highest level or most extreme agonistic call is the buck's ***grunt-snort-wheeze.*** This call is used by one buck to challenge another. It is a strange-sounding call; should a novice hunter hear a grunt-snort-wheeze while out in the woods, it is doubtful whether he or she would even recognize the sound as emanating from a deer. It sounds like this, although this is a very rough approximation of an extremely harsh and threatening sound—*burrrrp . . . whew . . . fffffooooo!*—made loudly and aggressively. It is a definite challenge to another buck, seen or unseen, to either battle or back down. The buck's entire demeanor changes when he makes this call. His intentions are visible in his eyes and his body language. His head is thrust out upon his neck. His movements become stiff and somewhat stilted. His hackles may be raised. He may swing his head from side to side. The grunt-snort-wheeze is a great trophy hunter's call. Should an area's dominant animal hear this call, you can bet he will come in to investigate the bold interloper daring to challenge him to a fight on his own turf.

The ***grunt-snort*** is less aggressive or agonistic than the grunt-snort-wheeze.

And, just to confuse you further, a low buck grunt by itself can sometimes be classified as agonistic. This low grunt, unlike other grunt calls, is quite prolonged. To make it, blow one low grunt on your grunt tube without varying its pitch. Hold it anywhere from several seconds to many seconds in length. It could almost be termed a **buck bawl** except for the fact that the tone remains the same throughout the call.

Other cohesive calls include both **maternal** calls and **contact** calls. The **fawn mew** sounds almost like a cat's meow. It is a low-level call, and does not sound very intense. *Mew,* the fawn cries whenever it wants to attract its mother's attention. This sound is made more by newborn fawns than by older ones. Fawns are born without an identifiable scent. When a young fawn beds down, it does so at some distance from its mother. This is probably a survival strategy. Predators searching for a meal will key in on the doe's scent and leave the scentless baby alone. The doe, of course, can escape on her fleet legs. When she returns, the fawn's large ears detect her presence and the youngster mews to bring her closer.

The **fawn bleat** is another cohesive vocalization. It sounds like *baaa . . . baaaa,* and is repeated every ten minutes or so. Fawns bleat when separated from their mothers or when hungry. A fawn bleat sounds radically different from the doe bleat, another call often used by hunters. The fawn bleat is more intense than the fawn mew, and sounds something like a calf's bleat, but is less intense than the **fawn bawl** (or **fawn distress bleat**) a call with a real sense of urgency or danger. While the fawn bleat is asking the doe mother where she is so the fawn can go to her, the fawn bawl is saying, "Mama, come quick!" It's an aggressive-sounding call similar in pitch and cadence to the squeal of a terrified cottontail rabbit: *baa-AAA! baa-AAA! baa-AAA.* Each vocalization begins on a slightly lower, less intense note and culminates in a tone that's both louder and higher. The fawn bawl is an ideal call to use when you're trying to attract a doe to your stand site. Repeat the call three times every half hour. And whenever you succeed in attracting a doe, a buck may not be far behind.

The **nursing whine,** a cohesive call made by the fawn, resembles the contented noises made by an infant human sucking on its bottle. It can best be described as a throaty, whiny sound that signals satisfaction.

The **doe bleat** is used to communicate with other deer. A dominant doe may use it to express her dominance over a subordinate, or a subordinate may use it to show her subordination to a dominant doe. Buy an audio or video tape to learn the difference. Does may sometimes bleat to attract bucks, in which case the bleats are actually being used as mating calls.

The **doe grunt** can be either a maternal or a contact vocalization. Strictly speaking, it could also be classified as agonistic when used by a dominant doe to bully a subordinate. It is higher-pitched, softer in tone, and shorter in duration than a

Peter Fiduccia has been sold on calling as a way to lure whitetails in to his gun or bow since the mid-1960s. Credit: Peter Fiduccia Enterprises.

buck's grunt. Imagine how a doe would grunt to her fawn to prevent it from proceeding farther and try to imitate that sound. On the other hand, if a doe sees a familiar deer and wants to attract its attention, the grunt she makes would sound more inquisitive. Abrupt and to the point would categorize a grunt used by a dominant animal to a subordinate other than a fawn. Some hunters further classify this vocalization into doe bleats and doe *blats*, although researchers do not recognize the difference between the two sounds.

As for *snorts,* never fall into the trap of believing these important vocalizations express only alarm. The snort conveys many things: Deer snort when they're curious; to say hello to each other—particularly to an unknown deer; during the heat of rutting activity; and when they are unsure exactly what is going on. This last type is used when something, they may not be sure what, happens that seems out of place or is somewhat troubling to them. They snort, but aren't yet sure that the snort is warranted. Use this snort to your advantage if you spook deer that you believe have not yet smelled you. Snorting in return, as though you are simply a noisy deer ambling through the woods, can often stop deer in their tracks and calm them to the point where they don't flee the area. Finally, an agonistic snort, when combined with other whitetail battle sounds, can be used to bring deer in closer by making the auditory components of the fight seem more realistic.

Antler-thrashing or *rattling,* while not classified as a vocalization, is used by bucks as an auditory signal to other deer in the vicinity. Depending on the mood you are trying to impart, the antler-clashing or tickling sounds that you make should be some of the most important sounds in your whitetail-hunting repertoire. The visual cues provided by an antler-rattler who whacks his horns against a small sapling, causing it to bend and sway, lend even more credence to the mini-drama you're creating to entice a buck into shooting range.

Finally, don't forget *hoof-stomping.* Although hoof-stomping can provide a subtle auditory clue to nearby whitetails in many situations, it is best used in conjunction with rattling and calling. Pummeling the earth with your antlers is often the added attraction that will drive listening whitetails crazy.

And that, after all, is the reason hunters continue to be sold on calling as one of the most important weapons in their whitetail-hunting arsenal.

2

More on Vocalizations

In Chapter 1 we examined whitetail vocalizations from a wildlife biologist's perspective. Here, in Chapter 2, we will delve somewhat deeper into the subject, only this time from a *hunter's* point of view.

IDENTIFYING DEER VOCALIZATIONS

While it is true that wildlife researchers have year-round access to whitetail deer kept in enclosures, and that they study them under these controlled conditions, it's possible that not every whitetail vocalization has as yet been catalogued. Bona fide turkey researchers have not, to my knowledge, arrived at anything approaching the numbers of calls identified by Missouri's dean of turkey hunters, Leroy Braungardt. Does this mean Braungardt has falsely inflated the number of different turkey sounds he's isolated and identified? Or does it mean, instead, that researchers either are unable to differentiate among sounds as easily or as well as Braungardt or have yet to hear the same wide array of sounds as he has? No one knows for certain, just as no one really knows for certain whether all whitetail vocalizations have been heard or properly categorized.

I do know this: As a long-time deer hunter, I have heard whitetails make vocalizations not included in either of the most widely known scientific studies. I'm not the only one, either. Many other hunters have identified additional yet hitherto unreported whitetail vocalizations. Whether a hunter needs to be able to duplicate all of these sounds when hunting remains uncertain. But knowing what they are, should you hear them, as well as knowing the basics of reproducing them, should you desire to do so, could help you out in seasons to come.

DOE BLEATS AND BLATS

Let's begin by discussing the difference between **bleats** and **blats.** Peter Fiduccia, a noted whitetail authority as well as the host of the *Woods N' Water* television series, is not the only hunter convinced that there is a significant difference between the two vocalizations. He may, however, be one of the most influential, as well as one of the most well-respected. Fiduccia spends weeks, sometimes even months, each autumn and winter hunting white-tailed deer. It is his contention that blats are made by *all* adult deer, while bleats are the domain of yearlings and fawns.

Jay Cassell with a 10-pointer he took in New York's catskill Mountains. He used a fawn bleat to keep some does in the vicinity of his stand; this buck came along to investigate. Credit: Jay Cassell.

"A bleat is much higher pitched than a blat," Fiduccia said. I agree because I, too, have heard deer, usually does, blat, loudly and clearly. I can see why hunters would categorize a blat as something other than a bleat since a younger animal's bleat sounds distinctly different. The *adult* or *social blat* sounds much like a sheep's or goat's baa-ing—*baa-baaaaa... baa-baaaa* . . . . The call should be blown gently, tapering off to a soft whine as it ends.

"The blat is a very effective call, but don't make it too often," Fiduccia said. "Once every thirty to forty-five minutes should be enough. If you notice a deer approaching, stop calling. When the deer hears no additional calls, the animal may become curious and decide to seek out the unseen 'deer' that has been vocalizing. A deer displaced while feeding and trying to locate others in its group will often blat. A lone individual separated from its family unit or bachelor band by a predator or a scare may blat to find its lost friends. Young adults of both sexes, confused after having been kicked out of the whitetail family unit by the doe as she prepares to enter estrus, may blat in dismay and misery.

"The blat is the most social of all deer calls," Fiduccia said. "In different situations, deer will blat to locate, attract, or warn away other individuals." Depending on how the blat is used—if Fiduccia's contention is correct—the call could be considered both cohesive and noncohesive. Improper use, however, could result in a spooked whitetail if your intention is to attract but you

Hunters wise to the ways of whitetail vocalizations, like Peter Fiduccia, use calls to talk the deers' language and bring them in close. Credit: Kate Fiduccia.

Peter Fiduccia has been calling in deer like this tremendous non-typical since the mid-1960s. Credit: Northern Wildlife Ventures.

Hunters like Jay Cassell have their best success when using a doe bleat or "blat" and a fawn's distress mew, especially during the pre-preseason. Credit: Bob Etling.

inadvertently warn away approaching deer.

Fiduccia further states that a solitary doe in or nearing estrus will make a long, urgent, whiny-sounding blat to attract bucks that have not yet picked up her scent. The call is made at average volume, never too loudly, to create a drawn-out *baaaaaaah . . . baaaaaah!* Hunters should make this call once every fifteen minutes or two or three times each hour.

Jay Cassell, a whitetail authority who has written innumerable magazine articles and four books on the subject, has hunted across the country. He lives in the Northeast, and that's where he does most of his calling. "I've used many different calls, including grunt calls, doe blats, and fawn bleats," Cassell said. "They all work, depending upon the situation, but I generally have the most success with the fawn bleat. When you use this call, you'll often have does come right in, and often quickly. They just can't help themselves—they hear a fawn in trouble, and they want to investigate. Perhaps they want to help the fawn, I'm not sure. But when you have a doe coming in to your call, there is always a chance that you'll pull in a buck with her."

SNORTS

Various **snorts** are also used by whitetails to communicate their fears and their moods. Unfortunately, researchers don't differentiate too much between these snorts. The exceptions to this unwritten rule are the **grunt-snort-wheeze** and the **grunt-snort.** The reason these two are broken out as separate vocalizations seems to rest in the fact that each is more complex than a single snort. When one examines the various situations in which a whitetail will snort, four possibilities come to mind: when the deer is alarmed but is not quite sure why; when a deer is alarmed and runs in a state of near panic; when a deer is confronting an unknown deer in a social situation; and when a deer is somewhat unnerved by nearby noises but is reluctant to leave the area.

The first of these snorts, the ***alarm snort,*** was discussed in Chapter 1. This is an easy snort to identify: The deer may blow a single snort—*whew!*—then run a short distance, stop, and blow a second single snort—*whew!* The deer runs a short way to try to provoke a reaction from whatever it is that disturbed it. If it is a predator, it will probably give chase, and the deer is alert enough to bound off immediately. If it is another deer, the alarmed deer has given it fair notice to reveal itself. If it is a person, the deer is counting on the human not knowing the proper way to respond. By running off a short distance, the deer may also get a whiff of whatever it was that provoked the reaction.

The **alarm-distress snort** consists of many quick, aggravated snorts, each individual snort separated by an extremely brief pause from the next. It may sound like this: *whew-whew-whew-whew-whew-whew-whew*. Or, the deer may start off pausing between the first three or four snorts; then, as its distress grows, the final snorts may be jumbled closely together: *whew— whew—whew—whew-whew-whew-whew-whew!* The alarm-distress snort will almost always start off loudly, then steadily fade as the whitetail places distance between itself and the source of its distress.

The **social snort** is used by deer in social situations. It says, "Hi! Who are you?" The deer that is the recipient of the snort-greeting may sometimes respond with a snort of its own. This social snort is less intense and lower in pitch than an alarm snort or an alarm-distress snort. This snort is a simple *whew!* If you are hunting and hear one lone snort, but don't hear a lot of pounding hooves as deer scatter to the four winds, this is the snort you are probably hearing.

Finding fresh buck sign helps M.R. James pinpoint likely calling and rattling areas. Credit: M.R. James.

To illustrate how valuable the social snort can be, Peter Fiduccia shared the following anecdote. "I was bowhunting in New Jersey," he said. "As I waited in my tree stand in a woodlot, I watched a buck feeding on acorns. Every few seconds, the buck would prick up its ears and stare behind him. Then he'd put his nose down and go back to searching for acorns. I waited until his head was down to feed, then I turned away and blew a single, soft snort. The buck lifted his head and looked in my direction. A few minutes later, he went back to feeding. But now he was moving closer with each step. Within no more than two minutes of my first snort, that buck was under my tree stand. Had I not snorted, I believe, I never would have had a chance to shoot him. But because I was able to get the buck to forget whatever was concerning him and making him look behind himself prior to my snort, I didn't give him the opportunity to move away. The social snort relaxed that buck. And that made all the difference on that particular day."

The **tentative snort** is similar in sound to the social snort, but it is used under different circumstances. This is the snort a whitetail uses when it knows it is probably safe, but it hears or sees something, perhaps in the distance, that is somewhat unsettling. Say, for instance, that a deer is browsing in a small clear-cut surrounded by large timber. The deer approached the clear-cut with three companions, but the other three deer remained in the forest, feeding on acorns. There is no scent of danger on the wind, but the deer can hear something moving around in the woods. It believes the noise is being made by its companions, but it is somewhat concerned because they are not revealing themselves. The deer snorts as a way of asking, "Is that you? Tell me that's you and I will calm down." I have watched a deer blow like this on a number of occasions. The animal will pick up its head, stare at whatever it is that is piquing its interest, blow once in a low tone, stare some more, then return to whatever it was doing.

Whitetail vocalizations are extremely expressive. Each sound made by a whitetail cuts straight to the chase. When another whitetail hears these sounds, a fairly strict interpretation applies. Knowing what each call sounds like, when to use it in a hunting situation, if ever, and how to counteract the alarm calls with soothing calls or clever tactics is what deer calling is all about. And yet some hunters are slow learners. After all, Olt Game Calls and Herter's both sold deer calls for many years before the current calling craze hit the deer hunting public.

Brad Harris, a long-time deer call aficionado as well as vice president of Outland Sports, laughs when he tells the story of giving the very first deer calling seminar at the Missouri Deer Classic. "People actually laughed at me because I had the nerve to stand up there in front of them and tell them they could call deer," he said. "I really believe they thought I'd lost my mind." Harris, who probably spends as much time each season chasing after white-tailed deer as any hunter in the country, was sold on the snort call as a way of calling in bucks years before most other hunters had considered it an option. Harris, though, is not afraid to take chances, not when the reward is as great as a big whitetail buck high-stepping it out into his shooting lane.

UNKNOWN WHITETAIL SOUNDS

"I've heard a number of sounds while hunting that I would almost swear had to be whitetail vocalizations," Harris said. "But I've never read anything to substantiate this feeling. One is a high-pitched whistling sound that I've heard on several different occasions. It's much higher in pitch than a snort-wheeze, and although I've done my best to associate it with a mature whitetail buck, so far I have been unable to do so."

Don Kisky, an Iowa farmer and bowhunter with enough big bow-killed bucks to turn you green with envy, has, on more than one occasion, heard mature bucks make "popping" sounds. "I've not heard this often," Kisky said. "But when I do, it's when a big buck is accompanying a hot doe. I think the buck is trying to grunt, but is so excited or short of breath that only a pop comes out."

Texas whitetail biologist Bob Zaiglin, manager of the state's vast Harrison Ranches, believes that hunters hear a lot of deer vocalizations without realizing what they're listening to. "I'll be standing there and hear the most distinct snort-wheeze, and the hunter I'm with that day won't even pick up on it," Zaiglin said. "He can't, since he doesn't know what he's hearing. This failing is similar to that of the guy who's out there every day, picking apart brush with his eyes until he finally finds the hiding buck. If your eyes know what they're looking for, it's going to be a lot easier to find what you're after. It's no different with whitetail vocalizations. If your ears are attuned to your surroundings, you'll be amazed at how much you'll hear and at how many different whitetail sounds will be a part of the mix. The key to this puzzle is simply to remain open to the possibility that some sounds you're hearing, even the strange ones, might be made by whitetails."

Zaiglin has also heard vocalizations that are not yet strictly categorized. "There's a definite *running snort-wheeze* that a dominant buck will use when confronting a subordinate animal. Deer will often cough, too, but this is more a function of trying to rid themselves of bot larvae that have hatched in their nasal passages than a means of communication."

Zaiglin is fortunate in that he was able to meld his passion with his occupation by becoming a certified whitetail biologist for some of the most extensive private landholdings in the country. His passion is white-tailed deer, and the first objective of his job is seeing to it that Harrison's deer population is the best that it can be, both in quantity and in quality. His second objective is seeing to it that anyone lucky enough to hunt on these properties has a good chance of taking home a real wall-hanger buck. Zaiglin thinks about deer so much, I sometimes believe he thinks *like* a deer. "I wouldn't be surprised if deer were a lot like people," he said not long ago. "People have distinct accents depending on what part of the country they are from. Is it that much of a stretch to wonder if a deer from a more northern clime sounds slightly different from one from the South? I know a grunt is a grunt, no matter where the deer may be that is making it. But I also know a grunt sounds slightly different here in Texas than it does anywhere else." It's ruminations like these that keep Bob Zaiglin enthusiastic about his work every day of his life.

Who knows how many more whitetail vocalizations exist, just waiting to be identified? The one vocalization that continues to fascinate me is one that I've been lucky enough to hear on a number of occasions. What's more, I've been able to see the animals that made it. I've told a number of call manufacturers about this vocalization, but they all seem to think I'm somewhat daft. I feel confident, though, that this vocalization could easily be the most productive of all, particularly for a trophy hunter who understands when and how to use it. The first time I heard it, I could not imagine what the sound was. It sounded something like, but not exactly like, a snorting deer. The sounds started off faint, but then quickly became louder. Also, it seemed to be moving extremely rapidly through the woods in front of my tree stand. Here is what I heard: *whew-whew-whew-whew-whew-whew* in rapid-fire succession—one *whew* piled on top of the next, with no letup whatsoever. Each *whew* was extremely high-pitched, and there was only the slightest pause between them. As the sound came closer, I occasionally heard another distinct burst of *whews: whew-whew-whew-whew!* Suddenly, three deer erupted from the woods and bounded through a grassy opening. I had no time to do anything but sit there, jaw agape, and stare as two big bucks raced past only a hundred yards away. Between the two, running slightly faster than either, was a doe. All three animals were bunched so tightly together that I doubt whether a piece of paper could have been slipped between their bodies. They were running rapidly, yet at the same time leaping upward with each bound in an almost joyous attitude. The entire lot was gone in less than three seconds. Even after they'd disappeared, I still could hear the *whew-whew-whew-whew* echoing off the hills behind me. With my ears I tracked their speeding progress as they raced over one hill, down a hollow, along the river, and out of earshot. Had they only ventured into range at a slightly slower pace, I would probably have been able to wait for one to split apart from the crowd and then take a shot. As it was, there was absolutely no opportunity for doing so. One of those bucks was a superb trophy in the 160-plus Boone and Crockett class.

The season ended and I forgot about this incident. Then I had an almost identical experience the following season. This time I was unable to tell how big the bucks were, but everything else was the same: the series of *whews* beginning softly, when the deer were still far away, but increasing in amplitude, volume, and pitch the closer the animals came and the blur of bodies pressed tightly together as the trio leaped and lunged past the spot where I waited and down to the mouth of the hollow, then turned downstream and raced along the river in the same direction as the animals of the previous season had. After the woods stilled again, I suspected I was really onto something.

Unfortunately, no one else seems to think so.

I've heard the sounds several times since then and was lucky enough to see the excited deer race past once more. I think this call would work, and work well, if a call manufacturer could be convinced to give it a go. Perhaps one of Lohman's snort calls would work; trying one next season is the crux of my latest plan.

I relay this anecdote only as a way of reminding whitetail hunters to keep their eyes and ears open. The next whitetail behavior you identify or strange vocalization you hear could be the answer to your hunting prayers!

After all, it wasn't that long ago when people laughed at the mere thought of calling in a deer. But it's we deer callers who are having the last laugh now.

3

Matching the Calls to the Season

Whitetail hunters are fortunate to have three distinct periods during which they can attempt to lure deer with calling, rattling, or decoying. Calling, in particular, is extremely period-sensitive. The pre-rut hunter should definitely use different calling strategies than one who calls during the post-rut period. And the peak-of-the-rut hunter might easily have better luck using completely different tactics altogether.

CALLING DURING THE PRE-PRE-RUT AND PRE-RUT

The pre-rut period is many archers' favorite hunting time, simply because animals are more predictable than they will be later in the season. Undisturbed deer move about fairly freely. Almost a year has passed since they have heard calls or smelled bottled

Calling during the pre-rut nets deer that are less likely to be suspicious. Credit: Mark Drury.

scents. No hunters have been busting them from their beds or flinging arrows or bullets their way, so resident whitetails have gradually lowered their guard. This is why the pre-rut, or preseason, is a superb time to practice deer calling. Undisturbed deer are less likely to be suspicious. Someone using calls now has an excellent chance of having numerous deer respond. Poor calling skills are less likely to prove negative now than later, when whitetails have become so wily they will respond only to the most realistic-sounding calls—if they respond at all. The pre-rut period provides hunters with a learning curve. Even if hunters screw up, which they probably will, they'll still learn something and call in deer while they're at it.

Deer are more susceptible to calling during the pre-rut not only because they have been left alone for almost a year but because does are still actively with fawns. Does that gave birth in the late spring may even be accompanied by suckling fawns. As we've learned from previous chapters, does are extremely social animals for much of

A whitetail hunter should use different calling strategies during the post-rut period than during the pre-rut period. Credit: Jim Holdenried.

the year. Most feed, bed, and travel in family groups. These maternal groups consist of a doe matriarch, her offspring, and the fawns of her offspring. If fawns are still suckling, button bucks and sometimes even spikes or forked-horns are also included in the group. Some groups include individuals from other generations, too. That's why in some areas it's not uncommon to see eight, nine, or even ten does feeding together. Spikes and forked-horns are banished at around eighteen months of age, probably to prevent inbreeding with siblings and mothers. An estrous doe will leave her maternal group only until she has been bred. She will then return.

An intact maternal group will be attracted to the sound of a bleat or a blat, particularly if one or two of its members have wandered away for the time being. Cohesive doe grunts can also work wonders, as can dominant doe grunts. Fawn distress calls or fawn bleats will work well, too, especially in areas where archery seasons open in September. In most areas, even as hormones are beginning their slow, steady rise in whitetail bloodstreams, deer will remain, for the time being, in maternal and bachelor groups. Doe vocalizations can be used to attract other does, fawns, and bucks from both groups of animals. Bucks are not quite ready to go searching for does yet, but should they hear a nearby

doe bleat or blat, they will sometimes become so curious they will respond to find out who made it and why.

Should you see a group of does feeding, try your technique on them. Stick with one particular call instead of throwing everything at them at once—or at least stick with one call at a time until you thoroughly understand what each of your calls is saying. Bleat or blat to them—*baa-baaaa! baa-baaaaa!* If one or more of the animals raises its head and peers in your direction, you have

An intact maternal doe group will be attracted to the sound of a bleat or a blat if one of its members has wandered away. Credit: Kathy Etling.

Matching his calling techniques to the period of the rut helps Peter Fiduccia consistently take trophy whitetails.

succeeded in getting their attention. Do not call again unless the deer lose interest. When you do call again, call just enough to pique their interest. Don't overdo it. The object is to engage their curiosity enough so that they will feel compelled to check things out. A doe bleat or blat used toward the end of the pre-rut period serves another purpose, too: Any doe enticed to within shooting range might be accompanied by a buck nosing about before the rut begins in earnest.

For a foolproof method of attracting one or more does, turn to the fawn bleat or fawn distress call. Hunters and bowhunters intent on getting a head start on their winter meat supply often rely solely on these two calls during the early weeks of hunting season. Venison from deer that have not yet run for long periods or been chased all over the countryside may taste less gamey than meat from stressed deer. If population ratios are heavily skewed in favor of does, the fawn bleat or fawn distress call provides an incredibly effective solution for hunters seeking to lower doe numbers. It's not unheard of for one or more bucks to respond to these calls, either. Doe bleats, doe blats, fawn bleats, and fawn distress calls make excellent sense during the earliest pre-season because they will attract almost any deer in the woods.

"I've brought in does with bleat calls and with fawn distress calls, but that fawn distress call is going to get every deer's attention and bring them to high alert," said M.R. James in a word of warning to those who are thinking of relying solely on a fawn distress call. James, a world-renowned bowhunter from Montana, is the founder and editor emeritus of *Bowhunter Magazine*.

The most overlooked stage of the whitetail's cycle, as it relates to hunting, is the pre-rut period, according to noted whitetail authority Peter Fiduccia. But Fiduccia also believes the pre-rut is the least likely hunting period to be exploited. In his opinion, the day you start discovering fresh scrapes in many locations is the day on which the pre-rut is finally in full swing. This correlates roughly to early October in most parts of the country. Bleats, blats, fawn bleats and fawn distress calls will work as well as they did earlier in the preseason, but as the rut nears, it's time to increase both the number and the variety of the whitetail calls you use.

"I get extremely vocal," said Brad Harris of Outland Sports. "I rely on both bleating and contact grunts." A short *burp,* whether imitating a doe's softer, higher-pitched grunt or a buck's deeper grunt, will appeal to whitetail bucks. "The buck hearing such a grunt knows something is going on," Harris said. "His only unanswered question is whether he should come over to investigate. If he thinks it's a doe, well, he's not sure whether she's looking for the company of a buck. Yet the buck is nearing the stage where he's downright eager for doe company, in hope of breeding yet to come. Should the buck think the grunt has been made by another buck, his aggressive nature might compel him to seek out the source of the call. This is true whether he's already alone or just ready to depart his bachelor group. If a doe responds, I don't mind either, because she may pull in a trailing buck with her.

"For the past ten years I've kept a hunting diary," Harris continued. "Each day

Calling is the first tactic Brad Harris will use during the pre-rut period. Credit: Brad Harris.

I've hunted I've jotted down the events that took place that day. My entries confirm that I've taken a higher percentage of good bucks during the pre-rut period than at any other time. I believe a good part of my success can be attributed to it being easier at this time to pattern or link a big buck to a particular scrape-line, rubline, or core area. Whenever I hunt the pre-rut, calling is the very first tactic I'll use. It is the pre-rut's number one tactic, in my opinion, if your objective is to attract a nice buck to within bow range."

Legions of whitetail addicts are hooked on pre-rut calling, including one of the country's finest outdoor editors, Jay Cassell. Cassell, who's been hunting whitetails for more than two decades, swears by the

Call softly and don't call too often are the two rules Peter Fiduccia follows when hunting wary whitetail trophies. Credit: Fiduccia Enterprises.

fawn bleat in the early season. "As the season progresses, I'll switch to the estrous doe blat," he said. "As for my favorite brand, it doesn't seem to matter. They all work well enough to call in deer. But to be perfectly honest, I use my mouth and vocal cords more than any store-bought call. I just make a *baa—aaaaa!* sound with my mouth, quavering the sound somewhat in the middle tonal range, and that seems to work as well as anything else. The best thing about relying on my voice is never having to dig around in my pockets when a deer appears, or worry about a call or lanyard hanging up at an inopportune time."

"My very favorite time of year to call deer is during the pre-rut," said M.R. James. "I'm especially enamored of the two weeks prior to the primary rut, before bucks go crazy chasing does and mostly ignore calls and rattling in favor of the real thing. I prefer one of those cold, quiet mornings when sound carries well and you can hear a buck coming from a long way away. I'll use a doe bleat, but I will also use a grunt call if I jump a buck out of his bed. If I do, I'll drop to one knee, stay real still until the buck relaxes, if I can see him, and then grunt. You can actually tell if the buck hears you. He will often turn around and come back, searching for the grunt he heard. As unbelievable as it may sound, I was even able to shoot with my bow at one such buck, even though I was on the ground and he was looking for me."

Bob Zaiglin, in his capacity as manager and wildlife biologist for literally hundreds of thousands of huntable Texas acres, spends most of each fall and winter guiding hunters and hunting himself. Zaiglin is one of the country's finest trophy whitetail hunters. He spends an inordinate amount of time trying to think like a whitetail so he can become a better hunter and biologist. Through the years he's come up with some excellent tactics and interesting twists that have enabled his hunters to take more and better whitetails.

"During the pre-rut period I usually rely on short grunts," Zaiglin said. "I don't grunt a lot. What I'll do is slip close to a food plot or stock tank [pond] using the wind to my advantage. As I'm slipping into position, I'll be making a few grunts. I then position myself on any nearby mound, slight elevation, or brush pile where I have a good view of the food plot or stock tank. Surprisingly, I don't blow many deer out of the country when I'm slipping along, making an occasional grunt. Deer seem to give me some slack because I'm grunting; maybe they think I'm another deer.

"The pre-rut is a sensitive time, especially here in Texas," Zaiglin continued. "Deer are well fed. They don't have to move very much. Since our weather is extremely warm, that cuts down on deer movements, too. And while I use the grunt call to calm down deer as I'm moving into position during the pre-rut, and may even have called a number of bucks in, the pre-rut is when I'm setting the stage for my favorite hunting period, the primary rut."

Calling has helped Peter Fiduccia take big bucks at different times of the season for more than thirty years. No wonder he has so much good advice to share. "I've found that one of the best grunt calls to make during the pre-rut is the trailing grunt," Fiduccia said. "The trailing grunt is simply a series of soft, short, burp-like sounds a buck makes as he searches for a doe. The buck may make only the occasional grunt as he's traveling. His nose may or may not be locked onto the ground. He may zigzag back and forth so he doesn't lose the scent, but could also be traveling in a straight line, as though being pulled by a string. During the pre-rut, it is unlikely that every buck with its nose to the ground is on the scent of an estrous doe. Instead, the buck is probably excited about a scent that reveals that a particular doe may be nearing her estrous cycle. Bucks seem to possess a sixth sense that cues them early on into low-level pursuit. They may never exceed a no-nonsense walk. But they seem to sense that if they can catch up with the doe, they can stay with her until she comes into estrus."

To make the trailing or "burp" grunt, simply blow on your grunt tube at middle to low pitch and volume—*burp, burp, burp, burp, burp, burp*. Fiduccia has dubbed this call the "burp-o-matic" and, indeed, that is exactly what it sounds like. The buck may emit a constant stream of quiet grunts, or he may grunt only when he takes each step. Some trailing bucks may make a grunt only every ten seconds, others only every thirty seconds, and others may emit only an occasional grunt a minute or more apart. Remember that each buck is an individual. It is unlikely that any two will sound exactly alike.

24

Trial and error will teach you how much to call, as well as how loudly or softly. Credit: Kathy Etling.

That provides you with a lot of latitude for mistakes and experimentation. There's no telling what will work from one day to the next, or from one set of weather conditions to another. Keep the volume low, follow each burp with a second or two of silence, and try not to sound too aggressive. Make a series of low burps, or a trailing grunt series, then wait thirty minutes before repeating the series. "I do this every thirty minutes, like clockwork, until I leave the woods," Fiduccia said. "Should I see a deer respond, I'll stop calling. Not only do I watch for interested deer, though; I'll also listen for them. The wise hunter keeps his ears as well as his eyes attuned to his surroundings. Sometimes you may hear a deer grunting in response. Should this be the case, remain at high alert. The deer is probably coming in to see what's going on."

Hunters who consider calling vital to their success are quite specific about when the tactic works best. "If it's windy, I won't use a grunt call," Zaiglin said. "Even if you blow loudly, the sound just doesn't carry very well."

"I find that calling works best in the pre-rut if there's a slight breeze," Harris noted. "I'll get excited on a cool, sunny morning with a five-mile-per-hour breeze. Should a deer respond, the breeze will stir leaves and brush just enough to conceal my movements. Sound will still carry extremely well. Dead calm days are all right, but in my experience deer are much spookier then. Obviously, success improves dramatically right after a storm or cold front has moved through an area, or after extended periods of bad weather, no matter if it's wind, rain, or cold. I try never to miss going out on such occasions."

CALLING DURING THE PEAK OF THE RUT

The flurry of excitement that occurs during the whitetail's primary rut affects hunters as in no other season. The actual dates may vary somewhat depending upon a number of variables: latitude, the state in which you're hunting, the subspecies of deer you're hunting, and even, to a limited extent, the weather. In some places, transplanted

Larry D. Jones grunted in this big Colorado whitetail and arrowed him from a tree stand overlooking a well-traveled trail. Credit: M.R. James.

whitetails rut at a different time than native varieties, really gumming up rut forecasts. But in most areas of the continent the whitetail rut occurs sometime between the last week in October and the first or second week in February, with rutting deer in all parts of their ranges wearing themselves down in their quest to breed and perpetuate both their species and their own lineage. On some not-yet-totally-understood biological cue, does enter their estrous cycles. In well-balanced whitetail populations—those with buck-to-doe ratios of 1:1 or 1:2—it's amazing how does will enter estrus at nearly the same time. With hot does racing everywhere, bucks lose all caution. If they aren't chasing hot does, they're trailing them. And if they're not trailing does, they're out trolling the woods for them. That's the very best time to be out hunting.

In 1996, for instance, on the Thursday before that year's first shotgun season, Dale Carter, of Carter's Hunting Lodge in Pike County, Illinois, was feeling under the weather. He'd almost decided not to go hunting that afternoon, but changed his mind at the last minute. He decided to try a new stand, one he'd just recently hung. To reach this stand, Carter had to walk down a long ridge and well back into a stand of thick timber. He climbed into the stand and waited, wondering if he'd made a mistake going out when he was feeling so ill.

At about 4:00 P.M. a buck entered the hollow about 150 yards from where Carter was waiting. The deer stepped down into a ditch that sliced through the hollow, then stepped back out and headed toward him. "I hadn't yet taken my bow down," Carter said. "I'd forgotten my binoculars, so I was unsure whether the buck was a 'shooter.' By the time the buck had closed the distance to fifty yards, Carter had seen all he

needed to see. He removed his bow from its hanger while the deer kept coming. The buck walked into a shooting lane, and Carter blew his grunt call. The buck stopped, quartering away, and presented the archer with a perfect shot.

That buck, a big 10-point, grossed 162 Boone and Crockett points. When Carter got his hands on those antlers, he quickly forgot he'd ever been sick.

Dale Carter hunts some of the best whitetail locations in the country. Lush vegetation covers the hills and bluffs that stand at the edges of fertile crop fields. Slow, meandering streams flow through the area. Pike

Here are just a few of the big bucks taken by bowhunters at Carter's Hunting Lodge near Pittsburg in Pike County, Illinois. Credit: Bob Etling.

County, in fact, is part of Illinois's "Golden Triangle," a northern delta of sorts, where the Illinois River and weathering glaciers have, through the eons, piled up the mineral-rich silt and loess responsible for the many spectacular antlers taken in this region.

Carter, who is guide and outfitter as well as hunter, uses deer calls not only to stop bucks where he can get a clear shot, but also to bring deer within archery range. Although Carter's Hunting Lodge once catered to both firearms hunters and bowhunters, the Carters eventually switched to an all-archery operation. One reason for the change was to keep whitetails reasonably undisturbed and thus moving about more freely for a longer period of time. Anyone who runs such an outfit relies a great deal on the magic of deer calling.

Bob Zaiglin believes, based on deer movements, that the whitetail's actual breeding activity peaks well before what the peak of the rut. Credit: Bob Zaiglin.

So does Bob Zaiglin. "I prefer not calling until deer are moving extremely well during the rut," he stated. "We know fairly well when each year's rut will begin. And by the rut, I mean when deer *appear* to be most active, not necessarily when most breeding occurs. Personally, I believe actual breeding activity peaks well before what we hunters call the peak of the rut, based on deer movement. But it's deer movement that gets hunters excited. An abrupt change in temperature from warm to cold or a big storm usually stimulates the whitetail activity that we call the peak of the rut. Calls can be very effective now, but seldom do I rely on just a call. I prefer, instead, to both grunt and rattle. If I'm rattling and a buck comes in, I'll use the grunt call to hold him there. The grunt call adds an incredible touch of authenticity to the combat scene. Bucks will look and look, maybe even leave completely, and then return to see who's grunting. That's critical when you're hunting in the brush. Usually when you rattle alone [without calling], a buck will bust in through the brush and give everyone an adrenaline rush, but it's not an effective way to hunt on its own. When you use the grunt, though, the animal may pause, may even turn and give the hunter a chance to look him over and decide whether to shoot."

While Carter opted to use the grunt to make a buck stop, Zaiglin prefers including the call as part of his rattling sequence. Rattling, which will be covered in greater depth in a later chapter, is highly effective when hunters spice it up with grunts, snorts, and hoof-stomping. Zaiglin, through years of trial and error, has experimented with the grunts he produces to determine what type works best. What he's discovered is important enough to be included in this section: "When I'm done with a particular rattling sequence, I'll end up by making some very lengthy, really guttural grunts. A buck, like a person, moans when it's hurt, sometimes producing a tremendous amount of noise. This moaning sound seems to be extremely attractive to bucks. Bucks are incredibly curious. If they hear the sounds of battle, they can't help themselves. Like people who race or run to the sounds of a car crash, a buck will run in to see what is going on and who is involved. Simple curiosity leads to more hunter-taken bucks than any other factor."

Ohio bowhunter Mike Beatty used a doe bleat canister on November 8, 2000, while he was hunting a mix of corn fields and woodlots in Greene County. The corn was still standing and Beatty was almost as wet as the surrounding countryside due to a steady, drizzling rain. The bowhunter figured that the rut's peak was just kicking in, so he set out three containers of estrous doe scent in a triangular pattern around his tree stand. Beatty had positioned his stand eighteen feet up in a pin oak, about ten yards from the edge of the corn.

A slight breeze was blowing toward the tree stand. After an hour of not seeing or hearing any deer, Beatty used the bleat canister to make three bleats, with a pause after each. Five minutes later, he detected an 8-point buck moving through the woods, about 150 yards out. He thought he'd seen this buck while scouting during the summer with his son Andrew. As luck would have it, there was a shooting lane cleared in the buck's direction. Nerves did the rest. Even though Beatty managed to turn around very quietly, he started shaking so badly that he feared he would not be able to get off a clean shot. But then the big buck solved Beatty's problem by simply turning around and walking away in the same direction he'd come from. Beatty assumed that since the deer had been behind him—and the wind was blowing in Beatty's face—that the buck had winded him.

Still shaken, Beatty pulled out his grunt tube. He made a few calls and added some light rattling sounds to the mix. A short while later, he made three plaintive bleats with the doe bleat canister. When he checked behind himself a few minutes later, he saw another deer coming from the same spot the 8-pointer had just vacated. He stood up and grabbed his bow. This time, he didn't worry about trying to sneak or hide his movements. It was quickly getting dark, and he knew this would be his last opportunity of the day.

"I could see that it was a different deer," Beatty said. "I put the tree I was standing in between me and the deer's head so I couldn't see his rack and get nervous. I followed his rump around until he reached a thorn tree that was my fifteen-yard marker."

The buck quartered toward Beatty, who hit his release as the animal ducked under the thorn tree. The buck immediately spun around and raced away.

Although Beatty spent a long, nervous night wondering if the steady rain that had begun falling would obscure any blood trail after failing to find the buck right

Buckmasters' Russell Thornberry awards Mike Beatty the prestigious Golden Laurel citation for his tremendous Ohio buck that scored 286⁴/₈ BTR system. Courtesy Buckmasters.

after his shot, all turned out well. The following morning, Beatty and Andrew returned to the search before the boy had to be at school. "It was about the break of day, and still overcast," Beatty said. "We went across a cattle pasture to where I'd lost the trail the night before."

Halfway across the pasture, Andrew tugged on Beatty's shirttail. "Dad! There he is!" The deer was only thirty yards from where Beatty had stopped looking the night before.

Beatty's huge buck is perhaps the largest whitetail ever to be taken with the aid of deer calls. With 286⁴/₈ inches of antler mass using the Buckmasters Trophy Record (BTR) scoring system, the Beatty buck unseated Dale Larson's 1998 Kansas whitetail as the No. 1 Irregular in BTR's compound bow category. Although the letoff of Beatty's bow will probably prevent it from being listed in the Pope and Young Club's record book, it will undoubtedly score well up in the Boone and Crockett Club's record book and rank as the world record taken by archery tackle. Not bad for one night's work with a few deer calls in a drizzling rain.

Jim Holdenried, who has called in nearly all of his trophy whitetails—including two Boone and Crockett bucks—said he's grunted in hundreds of deer through the years. "That doesn't include the ones that walked by that could have been attracted to my grunt," he said. "If I see a smaller buck, one that I'm not interested in bagging, I won't grunt. I already know how well this tactic works. I don't want to educate the little guys. That way, maybe they'll be more willing to come to a call after they've grown to trophy size."

Holdenried generally hunts whitetails in several states each fall. He's a good observer, too. He pays close attention to details that might escape other hunters. "This past season in Kansas I was hunting from a tree stand when I saw a buck that probably would have scored about 115 heading into a dense thicket," Holdenried said. "I didn't grunt to him because I didn't want to educate him, nor did I want him to come in. I thought I'd wait and see what happened. Many times if you see one buck, another, better one may be lurking nearby.

"About twenty minutes later, a good buck appeared in the same area where the smaller one had been," Holdenried continued. "I grunted to get his attention, but while he looked my way, he never made a move toward me. I grunted again. This time, I pulled him in at an angle.

"The buck started walking along the thicket's edge toward me. As he did so I knew I'd get a thirty-five-yard shot. But then, instead of continuing straight in my direction, he went into the thicket for about ten or fifteen yards. I could barely make him out as he put down some scrapes, made a few rubs, rubbed his suborbital glands over brush, and licked branches. Almost every whitetail behavior he could think of, it seemed like this buck was doing. All the while, I kept grunting constantly. I varied the mix to keep it interesting. First, I'd make some aggressive power grunts. I'd wait a while, then make some soft ones. Instead of coming out where I might get a shot, the buck went farther into the thicket. When I lost sight of him completely, I pulled out a different brand of grunt call and hit it loud three or four times. I stopped, and then blew on the first grunt tube for a while.

"Suddenly, I heard something pop. I looked straight ahead, and there was the buck, moving purposefully out of the thicket and coming straight for me, downwind

Jim Holdenried packs three brands of buck grunter so that he's sure he has the perfect-sounding grunt call for every occasion. Credit: Jim Holdenried.

of my position. He never grunted in reply. When he left the thicket he was thirty-five yards distant. I knew he would probably spook as he circled downwind of my position, but I kept grunting anyway. I don't know how I got away with it, but that buck came in directly downwind of my position and I shot him as he stood right under my tree stand! When he was standing beneath me, he picked up his head and sniffed the air to try to scent the other 'buck.' I'd picked up my bow when he was thirty or thirty-five yards away, but I just knew I'd never get a shot. So when he was under my tree, he'd lifted his head, put it back down, then looked behind him to the left. When he did that, I wondered if he saw another, bigger buck behind him. I looked, just to be sure there wasn't, and then I shot him. This is one buck I don't think I would have bagged had it not been for using those dueling grunt tubes."

Holdenried's Kansas buck's rack eventually netted in the mid-140s in the Boone and Crockett scoring system.

Holdenried has seen this type of big buck behavior before. "Many times when bucks are tending does, they'll go into a thicket and just stand in there with the doe," he said. "I've watched them hanging around in thickets for an hour and more. The doe will just be standing there, so the buck stands there, too, watching her every move. When she moves, he will, too. In my opinion, if he's acting interested in the doe— tending but not chasing—you may be able to lure him out of there if you set up properly and convince him there's something he needs to be aware of not too far away."

Holdenried has tried many deer vocalizations, but the grunt remains his favorite. Why? "I have faith in it," he said. "It's like a fisherman tying on his favorite lure. During my worst season out of the past ten, I called in perhaps ten or twelve bucks. Think about that. I called in that many and that wasn't a good year! During an average season I'll call in anywhere from twenty-four to thirty-six bucks. Over the years, I have called in hundreds and hundreds of deer. I knew they were coming in, too, because these were all deer I watched coming in to the grunt, not deer that I *think* were responding to the call.

"I use the tending grunt most of the time," Holdenried continued. "If a buck is chasing a doe on a hard chase, I'll use an aggressive grunt along with a soft grunt. The loud, aggressive grunts are indicative of a big buck chasing a doe on a hard run. She'll be running hard and he may lose sight of her, so he'll be grunting loudly so she doesn't forget he's on her trail. On a day when bucks are running does hard, I might be able to grunt in four or five bucks."

Here, in Jim Holdenried's own words, is how he makes grunt tube music for a big buck's ears: "First, I'll make three or four soft grunts—maybe as many as six or seven soft grunts, but never any more than that. I'll wait a second or two. Then I'll softly grunt twice more. I'll wait three or four seconds, then grunt another three times. Now, I'll wait ten or fifteen minutes, just to see if the first grunt sequence will pull in any nearby bucks. If no bucks respond, then I may do one of two things. I may do another soft sequence just like the first one. Or, I may do the entire sequence using loud, aggressive grunts. When I'm through, I'll again wait quietly for ten or fifteen minutes to see what shows up, if anything. This is my favorite tactic for use during the hard rut. This works especially well when you've seen a big buck chasing a doe, but he hasn't come close enough for a shot."

Unlike some advocates of rattling, Holdenried doesn't normally switch calling locations. "My theory is simple: Let the deer come to me."

Surprisingly, Holdenried has had tremendous luck hunting from tree stands positioned not far off the forest floor. "I had a great deer season last year [2001]," he said. "I took a Missouri buck that scored in the mid-140s with my bow, a Kansas buck with my bow that scored in the upper 140s, and a Boone and Crockett Illinois buck with my shotgun. Two of those bucks—including the Boone and Crockett—were taken from tree stands positioned only three feet above the ground. The other buck was taken from a stand eight feet above the ground. As I've gotten older, I've gotten wiser. You don't have to get nosebleeds from the altitude to take good deer from tree stands."

Nosebleeds are definitely not an option when you're hunting the way I was during the past season. I've sometimes gone several years without taking a whitetail from our Missouri farm. I'm after big bucks or no bucks. I don't have a problem with this philosophy, either. My husband, daughter, and her husband all hunt there with me. If we're to maintain any semblance of a good buck-to-doe ratio, that means someone will have to refrain from shooting smaller bucks. Those someones are usually Bob and me, since Julie and Rick both work full-time and can often only get away to hunt on weekends. This past November, I'd already been rifle hunting from dawn until dark for the first eight days of the season. I'd seen lots of bucks, including two that, in hindsight, I probably should have taken. But I hadn't shot, and buck sightings had tapered way off as deer became more nocturnal in their habits.

Bob had told me about his favorite spot, but I had my own honeyholes that I preferred to hunt. After sightings declined, though, I thought that going to Bob's out-of-the-way ground blind might make sense. I arrived early in the morning, when it was still dark. I settled in so that a small tree was at my back. The spot was in a thick grove of small pines. To my left was an overgrown cedar glade. Mature pine-oak forest surrounded me on other sides. The rolling terrain dumped into a gulch in front of me, while a ridgetop crested gently to my rear.

Early on, I saw no deer. But it was cold and quite still so my hopes remained high. I'm an inveterate user of binoculars, so when it appeared as though nothing was moving, I decided to start poking through the brush to see what I could see. I scanned slowly, left to right, looking for anything that might suggest a whitetail. Imagine my surprise when I inadvertently detected a doe that I'd had no idea was there, standing like a statue only about a hundred yards away. She was staring back over her left shoulder. I couldn't make out much of her body, but I could see her head and ears clearly. Since she was watching behind her so intently, I knew there was a chance that a buck was with her. As my eyes tired, I lowered the binoculars. I kept watching, though, and when I saw movement, I immediately raised them again. The doe was gone! I kept the binoculars trained on the spot where she'd been standing, but no other deer appeared. I began scanning the rest of the area. Nothing. Finally, about five minutes later, a spike buck with one long horn popped out where the doe had been standing. He stood there, testing the air with his nose, stretching out his neck first forward, then upward. The small buck seemed unsure of himself. He stood there for a long time before he, too, moved out of sight and up the hill.

The woods were extremely thick, and I could see very little through the brush where the spike had gone. But I kept looking, and eventually I caught glimpses of something moving about through the trees. Then that movement died down, too. Fifteen minutes elapsed before I heard a slight noise directly behind me. Since I was sitting on the ground, I moved my head slightly to try to see what it might be. Not six feet from me stood the doe! She didn't have a clue that I was there, either. Again, she was peering intently over her right shoulder. I carefully twisted around a little more, and almost came unglued when I saw a big buck only about two feet behind her. There was nothing I could do! My gun was on my lap.

As I watched, the doe twitched her tail and loped off. The buck put his nose to the ground briefly, then loped off behind her. As the deer put distance between us, I remembered the grunt call hanging around my neck. I quickly blew several series of grunts. I blew fairly loudly, because I knew the deer would be making quite a bit of noise as they ran through the understory. The grunts didn't seem to make a difference, and both deer soon vanished from my sight.

I waited there, dejected, for five minutes before I noticed movement out of the corner of my eye. I moved slightly in the direction of the movement. The big buck had reappeared. His head was high, and he was looking toward me. He began walking, head erect, eyes bright, and with a stiff-legged gait. The path he was on was very indistinct, but I knew it angled up the hill toward me. Closer and closer he came. I could see flashes of antlers between the trees. He was thirty yards away, then twenty, then ten. He paused only a moment before turning and heading right for where I sat on the ground. When his head went behind a tree, I raised my rifle. His antlers were at least as large as one of the earlier bucks I had regretted not shooting. He emerged from behind the tree and seemed to tower over me from where I was sitting on the ground. Five yards, then three, and it was almost a self-defense situation. He still had not seen me when I fired the .300 Weatherby. The 8-pointer lunged to his right, then fell to his knees and toppled to the ground. Although not record-book class, his rack was high, nineteen inches wide, and fairly heavy. But I didn't care how big he was, to be honest! It was unquestionably the most exciting experience I'd ever had when calling deer!

Brad Harris loves to call deer, but he doesn't just amble out into the woods and begin calling. "During the peak of the rut I'm always looking for good places to set

Grunting in this nice Missouri buck was the author's most thrilling calling experience to date. Credit: Bob Etling.

up," he said. I think choosing the place from which you plan to call is an important part of the equation. Look for heavily used travel routes, particularly any close to definite big buck sign. I certainly like to see big rubs and, if distinguishable, large tracks. In the rocky Ozarks, seeing tracks isn't always easy. What makes the peak of the rut exciting for me is simply knowing there will be more opportunities to see—and possibly take—bucks during daylight hours. This is the time to start using doe bleats. Mix in a few loud, aggressive-sounding grunts, too. Any buck hearing these sounds will assume that some unknown buck is behaving agonistically toward another buck, and it very well might be over a doe. If an area's dominant buck hears the commotion, he may be fooled into thinking his territory has been invaded, and a fight or breeding is going on right on his home turf. Some bucks won't tolerate this and will come in readily. Others may take their time, but will eventually come in. During the rut's peak I rely on my calls to a tremendous degree. Bucks are actively engaged with does. They're already trailing or tending or chasing them, and they are less dependent on rublines or scrapelines, at least for the time being. This is when it pays to increase the volume, frequency, and aggressive nature of calls.

"I love hunting the rut," Harris concluded. "This is the time when even the monster bucks will make an occasional mistake. That's what you're always hoping for. The largest deer I've ever seen killed was one my son took a few years ago. That buck grossed 195 Boone and Crockett points. The buck had been hot after a doe. We grunted to stop him, but for all we know he and the doe had been attracted to our earlier grunting sequences. Anyway, the buck stopped and that was that. In all my years of

Brad Harris likes to call near heavily used travel routes, especially if they are close to big buck sign. Credit: Brad Harris.

hunting, I've taken my biggest bucks during the rut when I've either caught them alone or they were between does and spoiling for a fight."

"About three years ago, I was in a tree stand about a mile from my home in New York," recalled Jay Cassell. "It was the peak of the rut, and I could hear a buck grunting from the swamp behind my stand. I first attempted to call him in with grunt calls. He'd answer me, but he wouldn't come in. So I decided to try the estrous doe blat. As soon as I made a few blats, the 6-pointer I'd heard grunting came in close enough—about twenty-five yards—so that I was able to swivel around in my stand and shoot him with my bow. He wasn't a monster deer, but I didn't really care. It's just so exciting when you can call them in like that."

To make the estrous doe blat, Cassell simply blows a short blat on his doe bleater two or three times. "If you listen carefully when does are walking past your stand, you might hear them making this noise," Cassell said. "When you see a

Use the tending grunt with some doe bleats, or rattle with passion to fool a dominant buck into believing its territory has been invaded by an outsider.

36

Brad Harris grunted this buck to a standstill after it chased a doe past his son's tree stand during the peak of Missouri's rut period. Credit: Brad Harris.

buck chasing a doe, tune out his grunting and try to concentrate on the noises *she's* making. That's an estrous doe blat."

Mel Dutton, another hunter who's sold on calling, has been hunting South Dakota whitetails for longer than he cares to remember. Dutton, who owns a large ranch that his family operates, is responsible for reviving the practice of decoying white-tailed deer and pronghorn antelope. His packable, mobile decoys can be used by themselves, or a bowhunter can crouch behind one until an animal gets close enough for a shot. Since the animal, be it antelope or whitetail, actually thinks it's seeing another one of its kind, it's expecting movement. If the archer rises from behind the decoy and shoots in one fluid motion, the animal should remain still for as long as it takes to get off a good shot.

Dutton is also sold on deer calling. "I use doe bleats during the rut," he said. "I'll bleat very softly, perhaps three or four times, then wait for about four or five minutes. I'll use either a commercial call or one of those bleat canisters."

Dutton also uses doe bleats during rut. "I bleat very softly, maybe three or four bleats in a row. Then I wait about four or five minutes. But I personally feel the buck grunt works better for me."

As for which brand of call works best, Dutton is unmoved by advertising claims. "I think any call will work," he said. "If you've got four grunt calls, I think each will get about the same results. I can't see one having any big advantage over another."

If it's the peak of the rut, 90 percent of the time Dutton will use the buck grunt. "I blow on it two or three times in a row, then pause if I don't see a deer," he said. "It's wide-open country here in South Dakota. If you're set up in a good location, you can see several drainages that feed some of the tributaries to the river. I'll get back into one of the little wooded pockets where most of the deer in a given area spend a lot of time, and call. Then I'll just start grunting. Sometimes I'll grunt quite a lot.

Dutton has had many successes hunting like this. "Last November I grunted in one good buck that came all the way in, and then I decided not to take him. I was in a tree stand near a heavy use area where deer were feeding. The cottonwoods in this particular drainage were spaced out fairly dramatically, and the rest of the terrain was open. I noticed this buck about two hundred yards away. I tried rattling, but he'd just turn his head and look. He didn't seem the least bit interested. So I grunted, and that got his attention. I continued to grunt, probably about twenty times in all. The buck started trotting toward me and didn't stop until he was twenty yards away. He looked around as though trying to locate the other deer, then he circled my tree. There was a slight breeze blowing, but he never caught my scent. This was a pretty respectable buck, too. He probably would have scored about 120. Grunting is just a real effective tactic. If you aren't using it, it's about time you try it for yourself."

All breeding bucks are stressed by the rigors of the primary rut. Bucks put on fat all summer while in their bachelor groups. As the pre-rut period approaches, they break away from each other to become loners. At this point, the bucks are solely interested in finding hot does to breed. This is their biological imperative, and they will literally wear themselves out to accomplish it. They rub the bark off saplings and small trees, an intense exercise that strengthens neck, shoulders, and back; they lose interest in food and rarely feed; and they'll often move all day and all night, particularly when they can detect no hunters in the woods. In the early stages of whitetail courtship, bucks often race several hundred yards after nonreceptive does before losing interest, and they may do so several times each day. Later in the season, when does start their estrous cycles, bucks still chase them, but eventually the does will stand to be bred. The estrous period for each doe lasts about twenty-four hours and, when possible, a buck will usually stay with a doe for that entire time.

After tending one doe, the buck is soon looking for another. If a smaller buck is tending a doe and is intercepted by a larger buck, the smaller animal will usually have to leave or fight to keep his doe. With so much going on in the deer woods during the rut period, it's no wonder so many mature bucks wear themselves out.

The rigors of whitetail breeding are so intense, according to research conducted at Texas A&I University by wildlife researcher Charles DeYoung, that about 25 percent of all bucks will die each year even when no hunting is allowed. We don't notice a lot of dead and dying deer in the woods once the season has ended simply because hunters take so many bucks that would have died anyway, regardless of the legality of hunting. This study provides another excellent reason that hunting whitetails simply makes good biological sense.

CALLING DURING THE POST-RUT PERIOD

Every now and then, the north wind gusted so hard it made my eyes water, my nose numb, and my teeth chatter. If it hadn't been for the sun's pale rays burning feebly through my coveralls that mid-December morning, I don't know how long I would have lasted out on stand. I'd seen deer, and was glad I had, because if I hadn't seen them I might already have made a beeline back to the house. But so far, all I'd spotted were a few feeding does.

During one of the wind's lulls, however, I heard a familiar sound. A buck was grunting somewhere behind my tree stand. There was a rustling of leaves that soon got louder and louder, and then I saw two deer running right beneath my stand. The second one, a buck, was trailing so closely behind the doe that his antlers seemed to be slapping her flanks with each stride. The two animals streaked past so quickly that I didn't even have time to draw my bow, much less shoot. They were moving so rapidly that I wouldn't have attempted a shot anyway. When they finally topped the next ridge—the buck still glued to the doe's heels—I knew I was witnessing the whitetail rut the second time around.

When both the pre-rut and the rut are just fond memories, you have to take your hunting up a notch for the second rut, sometimes called the second season. Many hunters give up when the primary rut draws to a close. They know the late season's bad rap, and many believe that rap is well deserved. Whitetails aren't stupid. Pressure them even slightly and some bucks become almost totally nocturnal. Because of this, you'll almost always see more animals during the primary rut than during the second rut. But don't count the second rut out too soon. Bucks—including big ones—will be up and moving then. Hardy hunters who force themselves to leave their warm beds and get out in the field will have a good chance of success the second time around.

Even if only one or two does in your area begin their estrous cycles and initiate a second rut, it will be well worth your while to go hunting. Everywhere that hot doe travels, she'll leave her own hot doe scent upon the ground. Whenever a buck crosses her trail, he'll immediately be interested, especially if few other does are cycling at the time. One hot doe can lead a lot of bucks past your stand, even if you never actually see her yourself. If she passed by in the dark, well before you even got to your stand, you could still reap the benefits hours later. How often have you seen a buck, nose to the ground like a bloodhound, intently following a trail where no other deer have gone? Smart money says that buck is tracking a doe that traveled there before you ever arrived on stand.

Peter Fiduccia believes that deer are especially edgy in the late season. They have been heavily pressured, and have probably been called to repeatedly. Because of this, he recommends using a short series of calls to lure out deer that may be holed up in brush or thick cover. "Give them time to listen and look for a while before making up their minds," he said. "Deer are curious. They want to find out what's going on.

The post-rut provides deer callers with a second or third chance to take a deer. Credit: John Phillips.

But after the main firearms hunting seasons have closed, they will be much more cautious than just a few weeks earlier.

During the post-rut, does that have not yet been successfully bred will again come into estrus. Late-born fawns from the preceding spring may also experience their first estrous cycle in the early weeks of winter. Grunting can be effective in various areas even well into January and February, especially if there is a visible resurgence in deer activity. Does may be seen urinating while rubbing their hocks together in a dead-on imitation of a buck freshening a scrape. They may be heard emitting soft grunts, too. These cohesive or contact grunts are made for the purpose of attracting a nearby buck. This is a good time to use such a grunt in the hopes of doing the same.

Does also make a dominant-subordinate grunt to reprimand fawns and yearlings as well as to warn off young bucks or does from other subdominant family groups. A dominant doe will even use the dominant-subordinate grunt to threaten dominant bucks, particularly when these animals have cast their antlers. Researchers have made note of a wide array of doe grunts, ranging from high-pitched squeaks to deep, throaty grunts quite similar to those of bucks. A post-rut doe grunt, though, is a more demanding vocalization. The doe expects a buck to answer, and if a buck isn't forthcoming, she actively attempts to seek one out. Alert hunters may discern her steady grunts as she wanders through the woods. Although such doe grunts are usually higher-pitched than those of bucks, this isn't always true. To imitate the late-season estrous doe grunt, simply make two or three long, drawn-out, middle-tonal-range burps in a row: *buuurp . . . buuurp . . . buuurp.* Wait fifteen or twenty seconds and repeat. Then wait several minutes before repeating the sequence. The call is insistent, but not loud. If made properly, it should sound like a soft cry for attention.

The post-rut buck grunt is as excited a sound as you're likely to hear in the woods. The buck that gets on the trail of one of the few remaining hot does seems to realize that this may be his last time to breed this season. He is vocal in his desires. But this is the time when younger bucks, animals that have not yet been worn out by the rigors of fighting, running does, and mating, can pull off a big upset by whipping a more dominant animal and claiming a hot doe's favors for himself. The post-rut buck grunt isn't so much a *burp* as an *eeerp*. Draw out each syllable of this grunt, while making it slightly louder and higher pitched than the buck grunt you made just one month earlier. Make three long, high-pitched grunts, pause a few seconds, and repeat. Wait several minutes before making another series of grunts. Should this not work, make an extended series of excited post-rut grunts. This is one time you might want to throw caution to the winds. Don't worry about calling too much. Try moving your head as you grunt, or cup your hand over your call to vary the sounds, as though the buck is moving through brush and behind trees. Continue grunting for one, two, or even three minutes. When you stop, pay close attention to nearby terrain for even the slightest indication of a curious whitetail.

The post-rut period is ideal for using both buck and doe grunts. You can grunt slightly more during this time than any other period of the whitetail rut. You can experiment a little more freely during this time by grunting louder, too. Sounding excited during the post-rut is a good thing.

Many successful hunters rely a great deal on this second season. It provides them with a second or third chance to take a deer. "Evidence of the second rut is never as distinct as that from the first," explains Missouri's Mark Drury, founder of M.A.D. Calls, a division of Outland Sports. "One reason is that the number of does entering a second estrous cycle may vary from year to year." Drury, together with his brother Terry, nevertheless agrees that it's still an excellent time to kill a big buck.

When Mark hunts the second rut period, he heads back to those places where he keyed in on deer earlier in the season. "I'm looking for core areas with lots of rubs and scrapes, or thick, brushy, bedding grounds. I believe thicker cover attracts and holds bucks not harvested during the firearms season. Bucks hide in areas they know best. I call these areas their "comfort zones." Whenever I hunt comfort zones, I'm extremely careful of buck feeding or bedding areas. Since bucks have recently been subjected to intense hunting pressure, they're much spookier now than at any other time of the year."

During the late season, Mark reexamines old, untended scrapes. "During the late season a buck will often re-open scrapes you'd earlier written off as being totally unproductive," he said.

"I took a nice buck on December 7 one year," Mark continued. "To zero in on a feeding area, I'd placed my stand in a triangular patch of timber alongside a river. That timber served as a funnel for deer using a nearby crop field. I saw some awesome behavior that year, including a good 9-point buck that was grunting after and chasing seven does all over the place. He eventually came close enough for a shot. His rack gross scored 128 Pope and Young points."

According to Mark, rattling and calling will both work during the second rut. "Both tactics will work well in the early season, but may fall off somewhat during the rut," he said. "But I've found that they will both come on strong again later in the season. Since fewer does are in estrus during the late season, competition is intense among remaining bucks for those does that are. This intense competition makes rattling and calling pay off. The tending grunt, doe bleat, and doe grunt will all produce now."

"I believe that short, continuous grunts are just as effective during the late season as rattling is during the rut," added Bob Zaiglin. "These grunts don't have to be as loud, or as long, or as intimidating as the grunts you made just a month or so previously. All you want a listening buck to know is that he may be missing some action. And if the grunts attract does, so much the better. A buck might trail a doe right into where you've set up."

Zaiglin continues to rattle and grunt even during the post-rut period. "I carry on some of the darnedest ruckuses with rattling horns and grunt calls you've ever heard. I do so despite the great 1:1.2 buck-to-doe ratio that exists on our ranches. But even with this great ratio, some does will recycle. When they do, you'll see bucks schooling around them. It's not uncommon to see six, eight, or even ten bucks hovering around one hot doe. When that happens, confrontations are bound to take place. If one does, the sound of that confrontation will be very attractive to other bucks. Even bucks that aren't fluttering around a hot doe are looking for some action. Whenever the sounds of a fight reach their ears, they'll come in looking for the hot doe that's probably at the bottom of the ruckus."

After Zaiglin rattles, he'll grunt and stomp his feet on the ground for several minutes. "I'm trying to create an illusion of a buck hazing a doe after an altercation with another buck," he said. "Those sounds seem to attract bucks, particularly if they're schooling around a doe. The sound might not be nearly as appealing to bucks that have worn themselves out during the rut and are trying to regain their strength. Such bucks will remain near food plots, trying to regain their strength. After the rut's peak, some bucks have had it with fighting, at least for the time being. What I do is grunt and stomp for several minutes, like I'm a buck hazing a doe after the rattling. That seems to be very attractive to a buck, particularly when they're schooling."

"It's sheer accident if a hunter ever kills a good Alabama buck before January," according to noted guide Billy Macoy. Credit: Billy Macoy.

In some areas of the Deep South, hunters aren't even able to take advantage of the second whitetail rut. "It's a sheer accident here in Alabama if a hunter ever kills a good buck before January," claimed Billy Macoy of Lineville. "I guide deer hunters at Southern Sportsman Lodge in Hayneville, and our deer just don't start moving in their rutting patterns until January at the earliest. Our season ends on January 31, and I know good bucks are killed in auto/deer accidents well into February. That makes me think our second rut occurs after our hunting season is over."

Dennis Smith of Alabama, host of *Outdoors South*, hunts the Alabama hills about an hour west of Atlanta. "Where I hunt I'll see scrapes everywhere during the first week of December," he said. "Bucks will be chasing does all over the woods. During the last week of January and well into February, bucks go wild again. I found fresh scrapes everywhere late last season. This doesn't actually seem to correspond with a second rut, as I understand it, since so much time has elapsed between those two observable rut periods. That leads me to think that in some areas, two distinct rut periods occur because these areas may be populated by two different whitetail subspecies."

Smith could be right. Many areas in the United States lost most of their native deer populations back in the late 1800s or early 1900s, for a variety of reasons, so wildlife managers stocked these depleted areas with deer from other areas that still had strong populations. For that reason, for example, descendants of northern whitetails now roam Georgia and rut at a different time than their southern cousins. Some hunters who think they are hunting a second rut might actually be hunting a second *primary* rut with a completely different cast of whitetail characters.

Peter Fiduccia had a tremendous 2001. "I shot a big buck in New York state," he said. "After that my wife, Kate, and I traveled to Saskatchewan, where it was bitterly cold and windy. I didn't even see a deer for several days. Then, everything broke loose in the span of a couple of days. On this occasion, I'd set up near a field. I soon noticed a doe that would run out to the edge of the same field I was hunting, race into the middle of that field, and then run back to the field edge. I thought this was strange behavior, but then I realized that she was probably flirting with a buck in the woodlot at the field's edge.

"The preceding day, I'd scared a nice buck in the 150 to 165 Boone and Crockett class," Fiduccia continued. "I'd thought I'd be safe grunting to a buck that big, but I wasn't. Perhaps he'd been beaten up by bigger bucks. Who knows? In any event, the buck ran off, so I wasn't about to try grunting now, not after spooking the buck the day before. I decided to try the doe blat on her. I blatted, and she became very interested in the sound. She started moving my way, coming within forty or fifty yards of my stand.

"As she came closer, I watched the surroundings carefully. I noticed that two bucks in a nearby woodlot paralleled the doe's course as she made her way toward me. The first buck was an extremely heavy-beamed 10-pointer. His rack was symmetrical, and I thought he would probably score in the 155-point range. I kept my eyes on him, while he kept his eyes on the doe. As I watched, the second buck appeared from behind the 150-class animal. He, too, stood there looking at the doe in front of me. Had I not used the blat call, I doubt whether I would have seen this buck at all.

"I blatted again," Fiduccia said. "The doe stared up at my tree stand, then trotted behind my stand and through an open pasture. I can only guess she was trying to get a better look at what was making the sound, or she was trying to get downwind of me. As the doe moved away, the larger of the two bucks must have become concerned that the doe was leaving. He broke out of the woodlot and entered the pasture only about forty yards from where I was waiting. I steadied the Leupold Vari-X III®'s crosshairs upon the buck's vitals and pulled the trigger. The Thompson Center 30/06 roared, and the buck fell to the ground."

Fiduccia had scored on one of Saskatchewan's regal nontypical whitetails. The buck's massive rack grossed 207⅜ using the Boone and Crockett system. It is a hunt that neither Fiduccia nor his videographer wife, Kate, is ever likely to forget. Would it have been possible without the judicious use of the proper deer call? No one really knows. But can you really afford not to learn all you can about this superior whitetail hunting tactic, no matter what the season may be?

Whenever you choose to hunt—pre-rut, primary rut, second rut, or all three—you can't go wrong with calling. As you've learned from the anecdotes related here, each season features its own brand of calling excitement. But no matter what the season, the more time you invest in learning how to call whitetails, the greater your chances of hanging a trophy on your wall while filling your freezer with venison.

Whether you choose to hunt the pre-rut, the peak of the rut, or the post-rut periods, you can't go wrong with calling. Credit: Brad Harris.

4
Advanced Deer Calling

Many hunters rely on deer calling no matter when or where they hunt. Old, reliable calls, such as those covered in the preceding chapter, remain their bread-and-butter choices, but they can also see the wisdom in expanding their calling repertoire to include calls most other hunters can't imagine using no matter what the circumstances.

One such hunter is Peter Fiduccia of New York State. Unlike many big buck hunters, Fiduccia is eager to share the keys to his calling success. If you are interested in becoming a more well-rounded deer caller with tricks you can pull out of your hat no matter what the situation, learning about these calls is worth your while, too.

Fiduccia truly believes in the power of deer calling. For that reason, he feels it's imperative that anyone who uses deer calls get a firm grounding in what deer vocalizations sound like. Whether you learn by watching a TV show such as Fiduccia's *Woods N' Water*, rent or buy a hunting videotape such as the excellent *Grunt, Snort, Wheeze,* which is sold by the Quality Deer Management Association, or

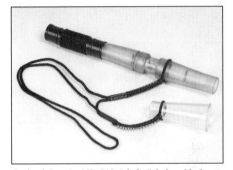

Outland Sport's MD 512 Inhale-Exhale with Snort-Wheeze®. Credit: Outland Sports.

invest in a cassette-style audiotape, learning how deer really sound will give you confidence in your own calling ability. "Confidence is the secret to calling success," Fiduccia said. "Knowing your calls sound authentic, and then believing that they are going to work, is critical to your eventual success."

ONE HUNTER'S CALLING STRATEGY

Fiduccia is a confident caller because he's used the method to score on whitetails for nearly forty years. He prefers blowing calls softly most of the time. Only occasionally will he resort to a louder, more aggressive tone. "I'm convinced that you will often chase off smaller, less dominant animals," he said. "Even if they'd already started to respond to your calls."

Fiduccia has other calling tips, too:

When whitetails race off snorting in alarm, try snorting to them to calm them down and call them back.
Credit: Kathy Etling.

- Don't call too much. After all, you've put the ball in the buck's court, at least in a figurative sense. Most deer don't call excessively. Why mimic an abnormal deer behavior that could rouse a whitetail's suspicion?
- Don't call when you can see or hear that a buck has responded and is making his way to you. This is the time to make the buck's curiosity work for you rather than against you.

Fiduccia joins the ranks of hunters like Bob Zaiglin and Brad Harris, both of whom are fearless when it comes to using a snort call. "The snort is the most misunderstood call of all," Fiduccia explained. "It doesn't only signify flight and alarm. A deer will use various snorts, either alone or in combination with other vocalizations, to spice up its vocabulary. Any hunter who wants to become a proficient deer caller must be able to reproduce these sounds, because they can pay big dividends for those fearless enough—and wise enough—to use them when the right opportunity arises."

THE ALARM SNORT

The alarm snort has been covered in a previous chapter. To review what we covered, this is probably the snort a deer will make when a hunter on his way to a deer stand inadvertently spooks the animal. If you feel certain that the deer has not winded you, wait until it snorts a second time. Then imitate the snorts the frightened whitetail has just made: *whew . . . whew!* Blow hard a single time either on your snort call or with your mouth. Wait for about two seconds. Blow again. Should the deer respond by snorting again, answer it with the same kinds of snorts and in the same cadence. Keep doing this as long as the deer is snorting. Many times the deer will be circling back to where you are standing. If conditions are perfect, you might even get a shot.

"I snorted at one buck fifty-seven times," Fiduccia recalled. "Each time I'd snort, the buck would answer me. I was positive I was communicating with a wary old patriarch. Instead, a small 6-point emerged from a nearby stand of pines." Still, snorting a frightened deer back is a thrill every hunter should get to experience at least once in life.

Fiduccia's wife, Kate, has also successfully snorted in deer. Kate had been

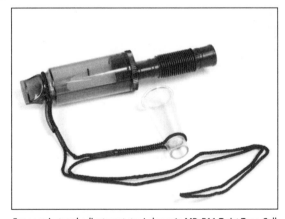

For ease in tonal adjustment, try Lohman's MD-511 Twist Tone Call with Snort-Wheez®. Credit: Outland Sports.

still-hunting through a climax forest when she inadvertently stepped on a dead branch. The branch cracked loudly, spooking a nearby buck. The animal ran off, snorting. Kate snorted in reply. This cat and mouse game went on for several minutes before the spike finally stepped out from behind a copse of cedars and Kate was able to down it with one shot.

Peter Fiduccia is one of the country's most inventive deer callers. Although I've never hunted with him, I've been using a snort call for years, usually in conjunction with antler-rattling. Fiduccia, though, actively looks for deer on which he can use the alarm snort, particularly when he's bowhunting. "I'll walk through heavy cover with the wind in my face, occasionally snapping twigs or kicking leaves," Fiduccia said. "If all goes as planned, I'll alarm a buck into jumping up from its bed. If the buck responds with an alarm snort, I know there's a fairly good chance I'll be able to call him back. I'll alarm snort in return, making sure that before I do I'm well hidden in heavy brush or pines. The buck will usually walk past me in search of the other deer. I've shot several nice bucks at ranges less than ten yards while using this tactic. As the buck gets closer to you, blow the call more softly and in the opposite direction of his approach. This makes it seem as though the 'other deer' is walking away."

THE ALARM-DISTRESS SNORT

The alarm-distress snort can be a dynamite call when used by a hunter who's aware of its potential. "Of the four recognizable cadences of snort, the alarm-distress snort is my favorite," said Fiduccia. As someone who is also always seeking to learn more about whitetails—and how to put that knowledge to good use while I'm hunting—I'm impressed with the many ways in which Fiduccia has made this call pay off. "One of most effective is to use the alarm-distress snort to aggressively roust a bedded buck from heavy cover," Fiduccia continued. "I use it when I'm hunting thick cedar swamps, laurel thickets, and standing corn. I've had my best luck when I've been able to climb above large areas of thick cover—like onto a rock shelf or other vantage point. Once I'm in such a position, I'll blow my alarm-distress snort—*whew . . . whew . . . whew-whew-whew!* When a whitetail makes this snort, the volume trails off as the deer runs away. Okay, so let's say I'm on a ledge looking down into a tangle of laurels below. The first thing I'll do is drip about four or five drops of commercial interdigital scent, so that it's exposed briefly to the air. I'll start stomping my foot, and then I'll begin to blow or snort. Rather than convincing whitetails to lie low, this display seems to have the opposite effect. I can't begin to tell you how often a buck has picked up its head from some thicket to stare in my direction. Or he might start sneaking away, and you'll be able to nail him. Once you blow that call, instinct takes over. From the second the buck was born, his doe instilled in him that this sound means real trouble—leave the area now! The buck doesn't wait to find out why it should leave the area. Its gut instinct is to get up and then get out. I used the alarm-distress snort to successively take a 14-point buck in Montana that grossed 168 Boone and Crockett points. I use the interdigital scent simply to make the entire scenario seem more realistic."

Fiduccia has given this topic plenty of thought. "Another good way to use the alarm-distress snort is to locate thick cover where whitetails are sure to be holed up,

like a cedar patch or swamp, and then post hunters along deer escape routes. Hunters should set up on the outermost fringes of the cover. Once they're on stand, wait about half an hour for things to settle down, then walk into the middle of the thickest cover. Don't even try to be quiet. Once you get into a place that looks like it would be a good bedding area, follow the steps listed above. Start with the interdigital gland scent. Stomp your feet. Then make the alarm-distress snort: *whew . . . whew . . . whew . . . whew, whew, whew, whew!* Hesitate for a second or so between each of the first three snorts, then finish by making the next four in rapid succession. If deer are hid-

Use an alarm-distress snort to aggressively roust a bedded buck from heavy cover, then shoot it as it sneaks out or pauses to look back.

ing, they should make a beeline for escape routes."

Fiduccia told of another good use for the alarm-distress snort. "I'll use it to roust deer from cattails, out from under ledges, from brush piles or small woodlots, and from crops still standing in fields," he said. Fiduccia knows how often nice bucks bed down in the safety of standing corn. To nail such a buck, Fiduccia will pick a corner of the field where the last two rows in each direction converge. "Hunker down in any nearby cover so that the wind is blowing toward you," he advised. "Put out several drops of interdigital scent, then follow with foot-stomps and alarm-distress snorts. Sometimes, after making the first call, you'll hear deer slipping around in the corn looking for a safe exit. When they find what they think might be a good escape route they may poke their heads out of the corn to look both ways before heading to the nearest cover. This is when you'll usually get your best opportunity for a shot."

THE GRUNT-SNORT-WHEEZE

Jerry Shively, an outfitter from Thompson Falls, Montana, is a big advocate of M.A.D Calls' Grunt-Snort-Wheeze®. "This is a phenomenal call, especially if you know you're in an area being frequented by a big buck. It can be used any number of ways, too. It's a great buck grunter, number one. But if you see a good one coming in—or know he's in the area—use it as a grunt-snort-wheeze, the most dominant of all buck vocalizations. I guarantee: If he can hear you, any dominant buck will be coming in. If you can see the deer, so much the better. You'll be able to see him get all agitated as he tries to peg where the sound is coming from. It won't be long and he'll be on his way. If you don't see him, just rely on your gut feeling. It's amazing how often some sixth sense will tell you how much to call and when. But if you see just a mediocre buck, don't give him the full treatment. A wheeze will probably scare him off."

Anything goes when deer calling. It's reconciling yourself to the fact that any call—a grunt, snort, blat, or bleat—when used at the right time can result in the most spectacular whitetail hunting action you've ever known.

5
Whitetail Body Language

An individual deer will behave in a manner consistent with its ranking in the whitetails' social hierarchy. Most encounters within groups of deer could be termed aggressive interactions. Higher-ranked animals dominate subordinate animals, which is simply the way nature operates. A subordinate animal, on occasion, may actually be driven from the group. It's far more likely, though, that the animal will simply be required to put space between itself and the aggressor. When subordinates learn the value of avoiding dominant individuals, aggression within the group is minimized. All of the group's deer benefit when this occurs. Less energy is expended, and the risk of injury is reduced.

SOCIAL RANK

A whitetail's social rank is based mainly on size and age. Larger bucks usually dominate smaller bucks, while older does generally dominate younger does. (Since adult does are all about the same size, age is a better determinant of rank.) Adult bucks dominate does, although, except for the mating season, there is little interaction between the sexes.

It is easy to confuse *dominance* with *leadership.* Consider the fact that one doe in a group may clearly dominate the others. Sometimes that animal is younger than other does in the group. The older matriarch, however, is always the group's leader. Research studies have concluded that it is difficult to pick out the leader of a group of bucks simply by observing them.

Whitetails play by a rather rigid set of hierarchical rules. Lower-ranking members not only learn to avoid dominant animals, they also shun direct eye contact with them. This may result in a strange juxtaposition when deer bed

When a subordinate buck, such as the one with the lowered head, learns the value of avoiding a dominant buck, social aggression is minimized. Credit: Bob Etling.

near each other. Group members may bed so they all face in the same direction, or they may bed in an outward-facing circle, but they will never bed facing each other. Avoidance of direct eye contact may even provide deer with a survival advantage. If deer aren't totally engrossed in watching each other, they'll be looking elsewhere. This can provide tangible benefits when any such animal detects approaching danger.

GROOMING

Before whitetails bed down, groups of does and their offspring will often spend between several seconds and a few minutes grooming each other. Such grooming is usually directed toward the head, neck, ears, or thighs. The behavior outwardly communicates to other deer that these deer are relaxed and possibly getting ready for a nap.

DOMINANCE POSTURES

Aggressive intentions may also be signaled by a whitetail's various postures. The lowest level of aggression is a direct stare, or *hard look.* The dominant individual will supplement this stare by laying its ears back along its neck. Its posture signals to others that it is peeved by something. In many encounters, the hard look is all that's needed for a dominant individual to put a subdominant in its proper place.

Moving up the scale of aggression, we encounter both *head-high* and *head-low* threats. These two postures seem to be of equal importance in revealing the level of aggression still to come. A head-low seems to indicate that to get its way, an animal is willing to chase after another. Before giving birth, does may chase away yearlings. When they do, they will often strike with a foreleg at the younger animals' flanks. A head-high threat seems to signify a willingness to rear up or foot-flail at an offending animal. When deer of equal rank refuse to back down from each other's threatening postures, both may rear up and flail at each other for five or ten seconds at a time. When it comes to foot-flailing, does will behave as aggressively as non-rutting bucks.

RUTTING BEHAVIOR AND POSTURES

Although not really classified as a behavior per se, it's interesting to find out that older bucks lose their antler velvet sooner than younger bucks do. When velvet disappears, *sparring* begins. Early in the season, when bucks show no interest in does, their sparring matches qualify as low-level aggressive encounters. Such a sparring match typically begins when one buck lowers his antlers toward another buck that may feeding nearby. If the second buck accepts the first buck's challenge, he'll engage antlers with the animal. A shoving match ensues. The smaller of the two bucks is usually pushed backward and withdraws from the contest. Since the contest takes place when bucks are not yet extremely aggressive, each animal is able to assess its own level of strength compared to that of its opponent. The most vigorous sparring occurs between males of similar size. In all but the smallest bucks, sparring has ended by the time breeding begins. Most sparring contests take place between bucks of yearling, two-year, and three-year age classes, maybe because they remain less assured about their relative places within the whitetail hierarchy. Biologists believe that antlers serve as visual indicators of a buck's position in the hierarchy

After scenting a doe's urine, the buck may curl its lip in what is known as **flehmen**. Credit: Bob Etling.

because their size closely reflects an animal's body size and physical condition.

Courtship or doe chasing begins four to six weeks after sparring commences. Mature bucks travel alone once buck groups break up. No one is yet certain whether this change is precipitated by an increase in male hormones or a scent change in does and their urine as estrus approaches—or a combination of the two. Early in the season, a buck will trail for a brief period behind a particular doe. The doe will run hard to prevent the buck from catching her. This discourages the buck, and he'll soon leave her to seek a more willing partner. A buck finally allowed to

I shot this big buck as he lagged a full ninety minutes behind a smaller buck hot on a doe's trail. Credit: Bob Etling.

get closer to the doe later in the season will follow her in a courtship posture with his neck extended and lowered and his chin slightly elevated. The doe may pause to urinate while being pursued. The buck stops frequently to sniff the urine. After scenting the urine, the buck may curl his lip in what is known as *flehmen.* When a buck performs flehmen, he lifts his chin into the air at a forty-five-degree angle, then curls back his upper lip.

During courtship, bucks are no longer so tolerant of each other. If several bucks are shadowing a doe, the largest buck will follow the closest behind her. Should the large buck turn to stare at the smaller animals, they will quickly turn away. When a larger buck joins a chase in progress, smaller bucks drop farther back in the pack.

It is not unusual for the largest buck to stay on the track of an estrous doe, yet remain forty-five minutes or more behind the buck or bucks doing the active chasing. Whether or not these laggard bucks have learned through bitter experience that staying on a hot doe's trail is dangerous, it appears, at least to this observer, that each year more big bucks are trailing from a distance.

Bucks signal their aggression by a hard look and laid-back ears during the courtship period. Most subordinates will turn away in submission. If they do not, the dominant buck may bristle his hair, lower his antlers, and advance slowly in a stiff-legged walk. If the subordinate buck still refuses to submit, antlers may be met. Antlers are touched in this threatening way only when bucks are closely matched.

The bucks then may charge at each other from a short distance (usually three to six feet away), or they may circle each other before coming forcefully together. A hard pushing match ensues, with both bucks shoving for all they are worth. Clods of dirt, forest debris, and grass may be pitched up by the contenders' hooves. The loser will suddenly bolt away, and while the winner may chase his adversary for a short distance, he has something more important on his mind: The estrous doe.

In open areas, a doe group may consist of as many as ten or twelve individuals. A single dominant buck may try to ride herd over the entire group. Should other, smaller bucks try to move in on him, the dominant animal will often wear himself out trying both to court does and run off subdominant bucks.

THE ESTROUS PERIOD

A doe's estrous period lasts only about twenty-four hours. At this point, does no longer run from courting bucks. Pairs isolate themselves. The buck *tends* the doe by standing behind her, nosing her rump. The buck will feed and bed with the doe until she consents to stand still, thus letting him determine that she's ready to be bred. After the pair mates, the buck will remain with the doe anywhere from several to as many as twenty-four hours. While the buck remains with the doe he will continue to chase off other bucks.

A doe that holds her tail straight out and slightly off to one side reveals that she is accepting breeding bucks. Credit: Kathy Etling.

A doe that holds her tail straight out and slightly off to one side is in full estrus. Her posture reveals that she is accepting breeding bucks. Such a doe is almost certainly being followed by a buck. When an estrous doe approaches an open area, she may proceed across it with little regard to safety. A large buck, however, may hang back at the edge of the cover, allowing the doe to cross first and then giving any subordinate buck hangers-on time to cross the opening, too.

Always remember that a whitetail's tail is like a semaphore: It's used by deer to signal other deer. A deer standing completely still, so that not even its tail is moving, is highly alert. The deer wants nothing to interfere with its early warning system of eyes, ears, and nose. The slightest twitch of its tail might compromise the quality of external information reaching its incredible sensory system, especially its ears. Since its peripheral vision is capable of viewing a large area arcing to each side— which, depending on how the deer is standing, may include its tail—the animal keeps its tail still so as not to interfere with motion that may be out of place and thus be dangerous.

OTHER WHITETAIL POSTURES AND SIGNALS

It's no great secret that a doe that *stops and looks behind* her is looking at or for another deer. If the doe appears to be alone during the rut, it's quite possible that she is looking for a buck. A doe will also look behind her for her fawns or traveling companions, so this isn't always a surefire signal. It works well enough, though, especially during the peak of the rut.

Should a doe have her *ears cupped backward*—even only one ear—she is either not alone or she hears something behind her. If it is the peak of the rut, a buck could be following her.

If a group of deer scatters, pay attention to the deer that are not displaying white tails. *Flagging* is a behavior more commonly associated with does and fawns than with bucks. If a group of deer bounds away, the deer that doesn't flag its tail is most likely the buck. Flagging is used by does and fawns to stay in touch with each other. A doe flags her tail so that fawns know where to run if danger materializes. A doe will lift her tail in possible warning before heading for the hills. This tells you that the entire group may be about to bolt. An estrous doe may also flag a buck so he is better able to see where she's gone.

A deer that *flicks its tail from side to side* is signaling its intention to move. Most likely, it will continue onward at whatever pace it was using when it stopped. The side-to-side tail flick is sort of an all clear message. Be aware, though, that on rare occasions a deer may flick its tail like this before bounding from sight.

Deer are attuned to every rock and tree within their home range. It is not uncommon for one of these alert animals to spot something that seems out of place. The deer may continue feeding toward any such troubling object, at least for a while, as it keeps its eyes firmly fixed upon the source of its consternation. When it can no longer take the suspense, it may stop, stare at the object for long minutes, then pretend to take another bite of forage. What the deer does instead is lower its head and then lift it up again quickly. A deer may execute this ***head-bob*** once, twice, or as many as twenty times, trying to trick or fake out the troubling object into revealing itself as a predator, human, or another deer. If a deer that has been watching you intently for some minutes suddenly pretends to lose interest, beware! Chances are it's trying to deceive you into moving, at which point it will bound away. Hunters who aren't aware of the whitetail's propensity to play games with them may move, in which case the deer will immediately retreat.

A hunter can outwit the head-bobbing deer, but only by remaining perfectly still *no matter what the animal does.* If it circles downwind, all bets are off unless you are wearing a suitable scent-locking garment. If it returns to feeding, remain still until you are certain that this is not another ploy to get you to reveal yourself. Only when the deer (usually a doe or young buck) has neglected to look in your direction for some minutes and has resumed feeding or has started staring somewhere else can you feel safe in relaxing or in moving.

Whitetails reveal their intentions not only through their vocalizations and other nonvocal sounds such as antler-rattling and hoof-stomping, but by the way they carry themselves, the way they move, and the behaviors they exhibit. Whitetail bucks, in particular, use other, more complex behaviors to communicate with other deer, but these actions are important enough to a hunter's eventual success to deserve chapters of their own.

6

Whitetail Travel Patterns
Where Do Bucks Go?

As the hunter trudged wearily into camp, he saw the old man standing by the gate. The old-timer owned this farm. Each evening of deer season, he waited for his hunters to return. Although the farmer longed to hunt the land he loved so well, he realized those days were behind him now. So he just watched and he waited.

"Well?" he asked, his breath steaming in the cold November evening. "See anything?"

"Not a thing," the hunter replied. "Those darned deer are really laying low."

"Laying low?" The old man snorted. "Not a chance! They're at the Widow Thompson's place, makin' fools of us all." He turned stiffly and looked toward the widow's farm. "Yep, they're enjoyin' themselves all right, like minnows in a spring hole. The widow don't allow deer hunting, and on opening day, every whitetail in the county heads there. And that's where they stay, 'til the last hunter's gone home."

From that day on, whenever deer got scarce later in the season, the hunter remembered what the farmer had said. When the old man died, the hunter began looking for land of his own. He discovered some next to a seasonal wildlife refuge run by the state. If deer were smart enough to hide at the widow's, surely droves of the creatures would be running through here once the shooting started. Finally, the hunter felt he had a good chance of solving the case of the disappearing whitetails.

For years, wildlife biologists have tried to provide deer with scattered safe havens during firearms seasons. They believed refuges would help some deer survive no matter how hard an area was hunted. Thirty years ago, one well-known conservation department established refuges at a number of public hunting areas for that very reason. During gun season, the agency declared these refuges off-limits to all human activity, not just hunting. Wildlife managers believed that if deer weren't harassed in a particular location, that is the place they would go once the shooting started. When they got there, they'd be protected. Yet for years, no one knew for certain whether those refuges actually did the job.

No one but hunters, that is. If you asked hunters, they'd readily state that local whitetails make tracks for any refuge or unhunted property as soon as they hear the first gunshots on opening morning.

Yet despite what most hunters believed, wildlife managers had nagging doubts.

Ask any hunter, and he or she will readily agree that local whitetails make tracks for unhunted property as soon as they hear the first gunshots on opening morning. Credit: Holly Fuller.

Did refuges really attract local whitetails? Did they keep these deer safe? Norb Geissman, a biologist with the Missouri Department of Conservation (DOC), wanted to know. He recruited Brian Root, at the time a University of Missouri graduate student, to conduct a research study designed to find out what—if any—effect these seasonal refuges really had on deer.

During this study, Root worked closely with his university adviser, Dr. Erik Fritzell, and other department and university personnel. The study site was the 3,900-acre northern unit of Deer Ridge Wildlife Management Area (WMA) in Lewis County, which is located in the extreme northeastern part of the state. The refuge portion of Deer Ridge totaled 1,739 acres: 200 acres permanently closed to hunting plus 1,539 acres declared a "no trespass" zone during the firearms deer season.

Rolling hills thick with oaks and hickories dominate Deer Ridge's landscape. Fallow fields, pastureland, and row crops comprise twenty percent of the area. Outside the DOC's holdings, much of the county is fertile farmland. So in many ways, Deer Ridge resembles whitetail habitat in other areas of the country. The hunting pressure is similar, too. During firearms season, more than a hundred hunters per square mile—about one for every six acres—flood the area. Hunting pressure is more than three times greater than what whitetail researcher Don Autry termed "particularly harassing" to deer during his landmark southern Illinois study.

To find out where whitetails went and why, researchers decided to keep tabs on both the humans and whitetails that were using the area. The biologists needed to know how many people entered the area—and for what reason—to determine human impact on resident deer. They also trapped and radio-collared twenty-four deer so they'd be able use radiotelemetry to track the animals' daily movements.

Root and his colleagues followed these deer for two years—during the preseason, firearms season, and postseason periods—twenty-four hours a day. Armed with this information, they would then be able to compare the differences, if any, in the deers' daily movements based upon the amount of human activity the animals were subjected to. By plotting each animal's location on a map, researchers would learn whether pressured deer traveled to the refuge where they would be safe.

"When we looked at how does moved when subjected to hunting, we discovered that they moved a significantly greater distance during firearms season," stated Root. "During the preseason, radio-collared does had been traveling between two and two and one-half miles per day. Once firearms hunting began, they immediately increased that by twenty-five percent. In response to all the hunters in the woods, these does were traveling more than three miles per day, making them much more vulnerable to hunting pressure."

Unhunted does (those with home ranges completely inside refuge boundaries) did not travel more. But *all* does, whether they were hunted or not, *stayed within their original home ranges*. None wandered into unfamiliar areas, even when hunting pressure became extremely heavy.

The bucks were expected to behave like the does. But instead of moving more, bucks traveled less. During the preseason, each radio-collared buck had been traveling an average of about five miles each day. But during both the firearms season and the postseason, they moved only about four miles per day, *twenty percent less than normal.*

"Four miles is still quite a bit of movement, more than most hunters probably expect a buck to move," said Root. "Bucks seem to have a one-track mind during the rut, which is at its peak during firearms season." Abundant hormones in the blood seem to rob bucks of much of their native caution, which in turn compels them to travel long distances, regardless of potential danger.

Stay out all day, every day, and there's a good chance you'll solve the case of the disappearing whitetails.

When the shooting started, radio-collared bucks whose home ranges lay partially inside the refuge shifted almost all their activity to refuge areas. These animals stuck like glue to refuge portions of their ranges once hunters had infiltrated non-refuge portions. These bucks would leave the refuge on occasion, but only at night.

Discovering the difference in home range size between northern Missouri bucks and does was one fascinating highlight of the study. The size of the study bucks' average home range was 1,576 acres, more than three times the size of the 502-acre average home range of the study's does. Once firearms season started, the bucks' seasonal home range size decreased, probably in response to hunting pressure.

Researchers were able to glimpse just how cagey a hunted buck can be. "One unhappy hunter passed within twenty feet of an 8-point radio-collared buck lying in a brushy fencerow," Root recalled. "We were about three hundred yards away, watching through binoculars. The buck's antlers were clearly visible through the undergrowth. After the hunter had passed by, the buck remained hidden another ten minutes. But two hours later, the animal was more than one mile distant."

The results of this study do not substantiate the general beliefs of most hunters. Deer do not run for a known refuge as soon as they're aware of danger. At Deer Ridge WMA, only deer whose home ranges lay partially within refuge boundaries used the refuge to a greater degree during firearms seasons. Once firearms seasons began, deer whose home ranges lay outside refuge boundaries did not travel to the refuge. These deer stayed put on their own home ranges where they dealt with hunters to the best of their ability.

This study seems to prove that if a refuge is to protect deer, those deer must have prior, personal knowledge of it. To be of value, the refuge must currently be or at some point in the past have been a natural part of a deer's home range. Since deer family units break up when yearling bucks disperse or migrate, fawns will be as familiar with their dam's home range as she is. If this home range included a safe haven such as a refuge, these dispersed animals will probably remember it. These will be the only deer that may travel long distances to reach refuge areas.

When the study ended, the DOC eliminated Deer Ridge's refuge area. Today, the DOC manages this area under the regular statewide quota system.

Deer hunters should consider the Deer Ridge study whenever they start thinking that the grass is always greener somewhere else. "Hunters needn't worry about deer moving into areas closed to hunting," concluded Brian Root. "Most deer will stay right where they've been all along."

The evidence is in. Stay out all day, every day, and the chances are good you'll solve for all time the troubling case of the disappearing whitetails in your own neck of the woods.

7
Wind, Scent, and the Whitetail

The whitetail buck moves steadily along the trail, head burdened beneath a huge set of antlers. As he travels, he occasionally pauses to sniff both ground and air, searching for danger. All is well, so the buck continues onward. A twig snaps, and the animal's cupped ears pick up the sound. He halts, every muscle tensed for flight. But when a squirrel begins chattering, the buck twitches his tail and plods ahead. Later, the buck's eyes catch a flash of movement. He stops. Suspicious, he drops his head to scope out the terrain. Again it's nothing, just a turkey trying to locate its flock. He relaxes and moves forward. Then the air currents deliver something his ever-alert senses will absolutely not accept: the smell of a human.

Knowing that his survival depends on an immediate decision, the buck springs into action. He pivots and bounds back the way he just came. He could have snorted, but larger bucks often won't allow themselves the luxury of making noise. This particular buck just disappears, like smoke, back into the forest. Two hundred yards ahead, a lone hunter sits in his stand, oblivious to the fact that a record-book whitetail was so close just a few short seconds ago.

Such is the way of the wary whitetail. We may sometimes fool its ears, occasionally fool its eyes, but only rarely, if ever, can we fool this animal's incredible sense of smell. Some of the best whitetail hunters have given up even trying. Instead, they make what they know about air, wind, and whitetails work for them. Before taking a look at how some super whitetail hunters do this, along with some facts recently discovered by researchers, let's first examine the basics.

Successful hunters like Peter Fiduccia bank on being able to fool the whitetail's eyes, ears, and nose. Credit: Peter Fiduccia Enterprises.

HUMAN SCENT

A human must smell pretty repulsive to a whitetail. But is it really our smell? Or is it what wild deer associate with it—danger! In either case, even the faintest whiff is enough to send deer into a panic. If they smell humans, most of them run away or hide.

Human scent, or body odor, consists of several components: sweat, breath, *pheromones* (similar to the whitetail's), and faint smells released by other bodily secretions like those from our sebaceous (oil) glands. Many individual scents combine to form an odor that would probably be as identifiable to each one of us as a whitetail's is to him, *if* our sense of smell were as acute as a deer's. Even though it's not, pheromones and our own personal scent are what makes us attractive to prospective mates, or so scientists tell us.

How each of us smells depends, in good part, on our personal hygiene and habits. We can avoid meat, strong spices, alcohol, and tobacco and bathe with unscented deodorant soap to minimize our natural scent. But it's doubtful that we will ever be able to eradicate it completely. Human scent is a problem, but when it comes to hunting deer, it's only a small part of the problem. The real problem lies in how that scent is dispersed.

AIR

Air is the culprit here—the air all around us. No matter where we may move, our bodies must travel through air. Even when the atmosphere around us appears to be dead calm, ever-present air molecules combine with the gaseous scent molecules given off by our bodies, so as we move, our scent is left behind. Even if we don't move at all, our scent certainly does. Unfortunately for those of us who hunt, the air is never perfectly still.

WIND

Wind is simply air in motion. It is pure energy that constantly moves across the earth's face. It may move so slightly we can't even feel it, or it may blow in tornado-like gusts. The weight of the air, or *air pressure,* is the driving force behind wind. High-pressure areas around the globe are continuously shifting as they rush to fill low-pressure voids. Wind results. Think of a balloon. If you fill the balloon with air and hold the end shut, all is well: The air is contained. But release your grip on the balloon just a slight degree, and the high-pressure air inside surges violently outward to join lower-pressure air.

As the earth rotates, its motion affects both wind speed and direction. And when wind skims over topographic features such as mountains, forests, and deserts, the friction produced also influences wind speed and direction. Tremendous problems confront anyone, whether meteorologist or hunter, attempting to predict what the wind in a given area will be doing in an hour, a day, or a week.

THERMALS

Most hunters have had deer smell them when deer seemingly shouldn't have been able to do so. *Thermal currents* were almost certainly to blame. Thermal basics are simple in that, as with wind, thermals aren't always totally predictable. Meteorologists call them *thermal slope winds.* According to theory, as air warms each morning, it flows upward from valley floors to ridgetops. Warm air rises because it is lighter and less dense than colder air. As warm air rises, it carries scent along with it. At sunset, the reverse is true. Ridgetops cool swiftly, while the valley floor remains warm. But while this warmer air continues to rise above the valley, the ridgetop's heavier, colder air displaces it as it flows down the slopes. The result is simply this: each evening, scent should drift downhill, while each morning scent should rise. Even with the prevailing wind in your favor, though, these thermal slope winds can occasionally give you away.

Thermals are especially unpredictable when they contribute to what are popularly known as "swirling" winds. When winds swirl, friction is usually a contributing factor. Try for a moment to imagine a southwesterly wind (one that blows *from* the southwest) as it gathers speed over an open field. The wind gains speed because nothing exists in that field to slow it down. Imagine that wind now slamming into a forest at the field's northeast edge. The resulting friction forces much of the wind up and over the treetops, but some will find its way through the trees. If field and forest are both located in a valley, hunters in the woods near the field's edge would logically believe that when the wind comes over the field like this, their human scent will be dispersed toward the forest. Should they hunt in the morning, they'll think rising thermals will carry their scent up to the ridgetop beyond the forest. But here's the catch: When thermals are confronted by friction, they may do the unexpected. Thermals influenced by friction might carry scent aloft, then drop it back onto the valley floor in the opposite direction from where the wind is blowing. The invisible air eddies thus formed may hold hunter's scents in places they least expect them to be.

Missouri's Jim Holdenried can confirm this. An accomplished bowhunter and firearms hunter, Holdenried has experimented with wind and its currents. To do so, he tosses handfuls of baking soda into the air simply to observe the ways in which it drifts. "You can actually see air currents swirling," he said. "From years of experience, I know deer will readily move when winds are strong. I firmly believe that they gather in spots where air eddies form. They feel safe there, because eddies will concentrate and hold most of the scent in an area."

Holdenried discovered one such spot that seems to attract deer whenever wind conditions are right. To keep deer from detecting him before climbing into his stand, Jim refuses to hunt this stand unless everything is perfect. Because of this, he may only hunt this spot two mornings a year. Yet every time he does, he sees three or four bucks. "One morning I saw two huge bucks, but the wind gave me away before I could draw on either one," he said. Later that morning, however, he killed a nice 6-pointer.

"The bucks that I spooked had approached my stand site from downhill, so the thermals should have been in my favor," Holdenried recalled. "The wind was from the southeast [blowing toward the northwest], while the deer were traveling toward the northeast. No way should they have been able to smell me until they were within bow range, but they did, and I believe it was because of the way the wind was swirling."

Since Holdenried hunts inside a line of woods near the edge of an open field, friction was probably the culprit here. But in the process of investigating the way winds swirl, he learned something else about whitetails: During periods of high wind, deer are often more active than usual.

This fact was verified in the landmark four-year Texas whitetail radiotelemetry study mentioned in previous chapters. "We divided wind speeds into five groups for this study," study co-author Dr. Steve Demarais explained. "These were: 0 MPH to 4 MPH; 5 to 9 MPH; 10 to 14 MPH; 15 to 19 MPH; and 20 MPH and above. We discovered that deer moved quite readily when wind speeds registered from 0 to 4 MPH. Their activity levels then declined as the speed of the wind increased, until they bottomed out when wind speeds reached 15 to 19 MPH."

But surprisingly, when winds exceeded 20 MPH, deer activity was highest.

Dr. Steve Demarais and Bob Zaiglin discovered in their Texas telemetry study that bucks move readily in winds of between zero and four miles per hour. Credit: Brad Harris.

"High winds aren't common here, so we had fewer observations to base our data on," Demarais noted. "Still, this study definitely revealed to us that deer move the most when winds are strongest."

When pressed for an explanation, Demarais made a guess. "I think that when it's really windy deer lose their ability to sense the environment around them. They can't hear, see, or smell as well as they usually can. They move because they're nervous. When winds are highest, deer will even run at strange sounds because they can't figure out what caused them.

"Any reasons as to why deer move more during high winds would only be a guess, but we do have a theory. During moderately high winds, deer probably bed down. They are sound-, sight-, and smell-oriented, and when wind picks up it confuses these senses. They consequently don't move around as much, at least up to a point. But then, when winds really pick up speed, deer get skittish and scared. They get up and move *more,* possibly because they're nervous. Maybe they move more because high winds often accompany weather fronts. But that brings up another item we were able to verify for the big buck hunter: Bucks move best on the day a weather front moves through an area. And, surprisingly, they move just as well the day *after* the front moves through."

Study data such as these prove that dedicated hunters shouldn't give up when the wind is at its worst. They should just plan to hunt *in the wind.* Why? Because that could very well be the best time to bag a buck.

Two other top hunters have turned whitetail hunting in the wind into a science. One of them, Dr. Bob Sheppard, an internist from Carrollton, Alabama, has been hunting whitetails for thirty years. Sheppard's taken many deer, some of them real trophies. He's killed most of them on public land, too, and lets the wind select his hunting location for the day.

To be fair, someone who does as much scouting and planning as Sheppard does deserves to succeed. Still, his methods—even on a small scale—should work for anyone. He first obtains topographic maps of his hunting areas from the U.S. Geological Survey. Then he buys satellite infrared photos of these areas if they're available for that sector. In Alabama, prime sources for these photos include the county office of the U.S. government's Agriculture Stabilization and Conservation Service (ASCS) as well as various timber companies. Old military photos are another possibility. These photos are both big—forty inches by forty inches covers 3,500 acres—and fairly expensive . . . but worthwhile if you can talk someone into selling them. (Sometimes the ASCS will part with them when an updated version becomes available; Sheppard says you just have to keep trying.) At one time, Sheppard used standard aerial photos from the ASCS, and they'll work, too, but he changed to the satellite infrared versions because they're so much more detailed.

Sheppard scouts during February and March in thousand-acre chunks at a time. "I walk back and forth, from east to west, and then from north to south," he said. "I go over as much as I can to find out how the land lays and what the available cover is like. Then I look for any bottlenecks and funnels that could force a deer to use a certain area, and later log that information on my master map. I'll also note any good deer sign near potential stand locations. I use numbered thumbtacks for each spot and position these on my map. Each number corresponds with a place to hunt. Each numbered location is also entered into my computer database along with all pertinent details."

Some of the details Sheppard enters concern the wind. "I decide which way the wind should be blowing for both the best approach to the stand and the best chance of success while hunting it," he said. "Right now, I own six forty-by-forty maps that have a total of about five hundred thumbtacks stuck in them. Before I go hunting, the first thing I do is turn my radio to the weather channel to find out which way the wind is blowing. If it's blowing from the northeast, I type "NE" into my computer and it prints out a list of all the best places to hunt under those wind conditions."

Sheppard uses a portable computer that goes with him to deer camp. Anyone wanting to adapt this system for personal use could start a manual system using index cards, but it would take a bit longer to access than an electronic one.

Another trick Sheppard uses when he's deer hunting is to tie a piece of No. 8 black sewing thread to either his broadhead or the end of his gun barrel while he's in his stand. He also ties a piece of thread to a tree limb down at ground level. By watching both threads, he can tell whether the wind is consistent or whether it's shifting from place to place. If it shifts too much for the stand to be effective, he'll move to a different one.

"It's amazing how much turbulence there is when you're hunting along an edge," he commented. "The air can flow around a steep hill or a clear-cut just like water flows around a rock in a river. The wind may look like it's blowing your scent away from an area when you're twelve or fourteen feet up in a tree. But at ground level, it can be an entirely different story. That's why I use thread, so I'm sure."

One hunter with a less scientific approach—yet one who gets real results—is Angela Vogel of Cottage Hills, Illinois. "Angel" has taken a number of Pope and Young bucks since she started bowhunting in the mid 1980s. "I became addicted to hunting big bucks without even knowing it," she said. "They're what I'm after, and to me they make the hunt worthwhile."

Vogel is another fanatic about wind and her various stand locations. She's been known to spend two hundred hours bowhunting each season, and when she can, she prefers positioning at least twenty tree stands from which she can choose each day. Like Bob Sheppard's, some of Vogel's locations are good only when the wind blows from a certain direction. She got her second Pope and Young buck because she was patient enough to wait for an east wind before hunting a spot that she'd suspected for quite some time had real trophy potential. "I'd found a steep ravine that connected two crop fields," Vogel explained. "It was a natural pathway for deer. But although it was full of sign, I knew the only way I'd be able to hunt it right was if an east wind was blowing. We don't get many east winds, but since I waited until everything was perfect, I shot a big buck the first time I hunted there." Vogel's "east wind" buck scored $159\frac{3}{8}$ points, good enough to qualify as a nontypical for Pope and Young.

Vogel bagged her third Pope and Young trophy while hunting during a forty-miles-per-hour wind. "Terribly windy," she remembered, "but the bucks were tremendously active. I'd been using a grunt call, but in all honesty I can't say that the deer were responding to it. I'm not even sure they could hear it. But first a 6-

Illinois's Angel Vogel won't hunt in a particular stand unless the wind is perfect. Credit: Kathy Etling.

point buck came in, and then an 8-point. Both were acting crazy, so I figured a doe in heat was probably nearby. I kept waiting and hoping, and then this big, beautiful buck came in. I shot him from fourteen yards, and he dropped in his tracks." The buck was Vogel's largest to date, with sixteen scoreable points. It tallied up $174\frac{4}{8}$ nontypical inches of antler under the Pope and Young scoring system.

It's hard to fool a whitetail's incredible sense of smell. But now, perhaps, we can do what these hunters have done for years. We can make what we now know about air, wind, and the whitetail work for us this coming season.

SCENTS AND NON-SCENTS

Before hunters can deceive a whitetail's ears or eyes, they must first understand the many ways they can deceive the animal's nose. Some hunters swear by whitetail scents. Others wouldn't use them if their lives depended on it. What most hunters seem to believe, no matter what their predilection, is that whitetail scents will work *on occasion.* Through both trial and error and paying attention to tips provided here, you should be able to determine the best time and way to fit scents— or the lack thereof—into your own hunting routines.

The first whitetail I ever killed was taken in a spot where I'd sprayed nearly an entire can of apple scent. There were no apple orchards within a hundred miles, so I'm not really sure why the deer was there. Nothing works like success, however, and I, for one, was hooked on scents for years afterward. Other hunters believe that it doesn't really matter if a tasty food source isn't present in a certain part of a whitetail's range. They think that if a food lure smells enticing enough, whitetails will be drawn to it anyway. Whether the smell attracts deer looking to fill their bellies, or simply because the animals are curious, will probably never be known for certain.

What *is* known is this: Should you decide to use scents, choose well-known brands. *Matrix scent,* a combination of urine, glandular matter, and secretions from non-rutting bucks and does, is an all-season scent. It is especially effective during the early season before animals become almost immune to all the new smells wafting through the forest. Other excellent all-season scents include *tarsal gland scent, interdigital gland scent,* and *forehead gland scent,* the latter combining glandular secretions from whitetails' preorbital and sudoriferous glands.

Both *doe-in-estrus scent* and *buck urine* seem to work best just prior to the rut and immediately afterward. Most bucks are so busy chasing does during the rut that bottled scent seems to hold little appeal for them at that time. The exception may occur in an area with low deer densities where bucks are actively seeking does. Enough hunters report success using scent during the rut's peak that many experts put out these scents anyway. They believe that it won't hurt anything, and that it might actually help.

Some hunters will use a *coverup* or *masking scent* such as raccoon urine, fox urine, or coyote urine to mask their human odor, which can linger along the trails they take to get to their stands. Wearing high-topped rubber boots also cuts down on human scent dispersal and may be a wiser tactic. If you are dead set on using a masking scent, however, then use raccoon scent. Not only are raccoons not predators, and therefore not threats to deer, but they also climb trees. A curious deer that follows a raccoon's scent trail won't find it unusual to discover that the "raccoon" has climbed a tree.

I quit using skunk as a masking scent a long time ago, after spooking numerous deer. Once I began thinking about it, I realized that anything that would spook a skunk (and cause it to spray its scent) would probably make a whitetail uneasy, too.

Lures (food attractants) such as apple scent will probably work best in areas where that scent is commonly found. Use acorn scent in a forest of oaks, pine scent in a region of pines, and so on. But never discount the curiosity factor when confronted with the thorny problem of whether or not to use a particular scent. Whitetails may be compelled to check out an unusual or new scent they've never before smelled.

Some hunters carry scent-matching to extremes. They believe that the pine scent contained in a particular bottle may not be the exact same pine scent with which deer in their hunting area are familiar. After all, there are many different species of pine trees. They may all smell the same to us, but what should concern us most is how they smell to a whitetail.

Probably the most valid use of deer scent is for making *mock scrapes.* Mock scrapes continue to be underused tools, probably because they involve so much work. To make an effective mock scrape, scout your locations well before the pre-rut period. A garden claw and long-handled trowel will come in handy, and always wear rubber gloves. Whenever possible, remove and freeze the tarsal glands from the previous season's deer, but if that's not an option, either buy a good grade of tarsal gland scent or use a freeze-dried tarsal gland that can be rehydrated. The mock scrape is, in effect, simply another method of decoying deer, albeit one that attempts to fool a whitetail's eyes and nose. See Chapter 23 for more information on making mock scrapes.

The final deceit is the elimination of most, if not all, human scent. There are several ways in which this can accomplished. The first way is time-consuming but inexpensive—a method I used years ago, I collected leaves, branches, and grasses from the area near my deer stand. I placed this vegetation inside a pillow case, tied the case shut, then tossed pillow case and my hunting clothes into the washing machine. I ran through a plain warm water cycle so that the natural scents permeated all my gear, then dried everything—sticks, leaves, and grass included—in the dryer. Once the clothes were dry, I stored them in a large plastic garbage bag tightly tied shut. I then wore those clothes to my stand and tried my best not to get sweaty along the way. (I sometimes changed into my scented clothing at the stand and stashed my sweaty clothing in the plastic bag to prevent the whitetails' keen noses from detecting it.)

Mickey Hellickson, wildlife manager for the King Ranches in Texas, pays strict attention to the wind whenever he hunts the ranch's vast holdings, whether for himself or with a client. "I'm not a big believer in cover scents or attractants," Hellickson said. "When I'm rattling, I pick positions where I'm able to see downwind openings where bucks may come in. I suppose the closest attention I ever paid to masking my scent was before I'd moved down to Texas from Iowa. Back then, I'd store my clothes in a sack with soil I'd gathered from around an old, rotten stump. That soil had such a rich, heavy smell, I thought it would work perfectly as a cover scent."

Although the technology is expensive, odor-eliminating suits and outerwear are worth the investment. Some garments are made to be worn under hunting clothes but over underwear. Other items have been manufactured as outerwear, complete with a soft, quiet microfiber shell. Such clothing has many small patches of odor-eating carbon integrated into the fabric. The carbon literally blocks human odor from reaching the surrounding air. Of course, for the technology to work best, all your other gear, as well as your hair and exposed skin surfaces, should also be as scent-free as possible. I have worn as many as three layers of scent-adsorbing clothing to try to completely beat the whitetail's almost otherworldly sense of smell. The results are worth the time, effort, and money I've spent. I've had bucks nearly step on me while I was hunting on the ground—even when they approached me from downwind!

When clothing made with carbon technology loads up with too much human odor, deer will start smelling you. They may simply behave in a more nervous manner. They may make low snorts, as though trying to clear the scent from their noses. Keep in mind that most whitetails live in relatively close proximity to human activity. It is not unusual for them to occasionally get a whiff of human scent. What your aim as a hunter should be is to reduce your human scent to an acceptable level. Scent-adsorption clothing does this better than anything else. To make such clothes scent-free once again, simply toss them into a clothes dryer set on high for a minimum of forty-five minutes.

Magicians use smoke and mirrors to perform illusions in our everyday world. In the whitetail's world, you can create your own brand of magic, doing what may seem downright impossible: making whitetails appear by making yourself disappear . . . and tricking their noses in the process.

HOW TO USE THERMALS TO YOUR ADVANTAGE

My favorite tree stand was a top producer for years. It sat high atop the crest of a ridge overlooking a seventy-five-foot-wide power line right-of-way that was cleared of brush every four or five years by the local utility company. From my vantage point in this stand I

I've worn as many as three layers of scent-adsorbent clothing to try to completely beat the whitetail's phenomenal sense of smell. Credit: Bob Etling.

was able to observe a number of whitetail travel lanes. Through the years, I took several high-quality bucks from this stand. It was a wonderful spot, complete with an outstanding view, but I used it for so long that local whitetails became wary of it.

Biologists have noted that cultural knowledge plays a critical part in the survival strategies a whitetail adopts. Simply put, if a deer suspects a place is dangerous, it somehow is able to pass that knowledge along to other deer. I believe that is what happened to my power line stand. Since some of the bucks I shot had been chasing does at the time, I believe those same does later spread the news that my power line right-of-way was a dangerous place for deer.

After several years of consistent success, I realized that the local deer had adopted some annoying—to me—habits. When I first set up my stand, they filtered across the right-of-way all morning long. They stopped—presumably to bed down—during early afternoon hours, then resumed crossing at about 4:00 P.M.

Over time, that all changed. The deer slowly became warier. In the mornings, I combated this increased wariness by wearing a camouflage face mask and sitting very still. Deer still looked my way, but if the wind was right and all else appeared normal, they were usually lulled into thinking no one was about.

Evenings presented a dilemma, however. When I first started hunting there, does, fawns, and small bucks traveled down the hillsides that funneled into the gorge in front of my stand. When evening approached, they climbed back out of the gorge to cross the power line right-of-way en route to nighttime feeding grounds. Nothing bothered them—but then their behaviors changed. After about five years, the whitetails started holing up in the gorge until well past shooting hours. The gorge—which is on adjoining property where no hunting is allowed—is extremely deep and thick with brush and timber. I was unable to see any deer waiting—*staging*—within it, nor would it have been legal to shoot them if I somehow had seen them. But I sure could hear them.

I believe these deer were making good use of the knowledge that late afternoon, when the sun starts its slide toward the horizon, is the ideal time to lie low and wait. Even under totally windless conditions, even when I was scrupulously clean and wearing scent-blocking clothing, these deer often started snorting. Low levels of human scent, which at one point didn't faze them, now sent them into a panic. They waited in the gorge, constantly testing the air, putting to good use the "zero tolerance" policy they seemed to have adopted for even the merest whiff of human scent.

The best bucks I've taken from this stand were all shot during the morning when thermals were rising. The only buck I ever shot there in the afternoon was a 10-point spooked by a hunter on a neighboring farm. Had the buck not been fleeing another hunter, I doubt if I would have seen him.

I finally got fed up wasting every afternoon on a stand that had never been an evening producer. On the third day of that year's firearms season, I began wondering where I could go to make the most of the dwindling afternoon. I went over in my mind the basics we all learn when we first start hunting whitetails. *Why* were deer lurking in that gorge each evening? And not just small bucks, but even the does that might pull into view a lust-crazed larger buck? The answer was simple: The deer knew about my stand and knew about me. They waited until after dark in the lowest spot available, where evening thermals would deliver any scents of danger.

How could I fool them? I had to adapt, as they had.

I realized that I simply could not get these particular deer. Their staging area was not on our property, nor was it legal to hunt there. But since our farm is full of similar steep-sided gorges and rugged hollows, finding another area where whitetails might also be staging seemed like a viable option. I began to plot a strategy.

That year, the acorn crop had been an almost total bust. The deer I had seen in the power line right-of-way had been browsing on oak brush and grazing on open-country grasses and forbs. Since the deer had been reduced to browsing and grazing, I decided to hunt close to a pasture where I'd occasionally seen deer feeding in the evening. This pasture followed a gentle ridge line that, at its terminus, dropped steeply off into a small creek bottom. That small creek in turn dumped into another, larger creek. I set up on the ground at the juncture of those creeks, about as low as I could go and still be downwind of the field, yet able to scan its edges.

I settled into position at 4:00 P.M. I made a doe blat, and within ten minutes I saw several does traveling inside the treeline, just outside the field edge. A small buck followed, nose to the ground. The group milled about where the field cornered with the woods, noses scent-testing the air. I wasn't sure that they had heard my call at all. When I squirted some of my wind-check powder into the air, it swirled down to the ground, then streamed down-hollow, away from the deer. Unable to scent me, the whitetails fed up the hill, browsing inside the woods until they were out of sight.

Then I heard a noise behind me, and I slowly turned my head. At the crest of a saddle stood a fairly good buck. He'd crawled under a fence and was heading down the creek bottom toward my position. I wasn't sure at first whether to try for him. He had good mass and some decent width, but his tine length seemed weak. For several minutes, I wasn't sure I would even have a chance, for when he reached the creek bottom he began scent-checking the air. He stood there for ten minutes tossing his head and sniffing, first one way, then the other. It was obvious that he'd performed this maneuver before. Finally, he started walking—straight down the creek. He veered when he was about fifty yards from me, now angling about ten feet above the hollow's floor. I wasn't planning to shoot—until I saw his antlers going away from me. When he paused, looking around, perhaps for the doe that had uttered the bleat, his nearly white rack suddenly looked very good indeed. I shot and he ran in a circle and fell. My .280 Remington's bullet had pierced his heart.

Deciding to take a buck based on what its rack looks like going away is not a particularly bright thing to do. The 8-pointer was a good buck—sixteen inches wide and sixteen inches high with fairly good mass—but he wasn't a *great* buck. I was grateful, though, for having had the chance to take him after waiting less than an hour on a spur-of-the-moment ground blind. I knew I was onto something important.

Each year I speak to many people about hunting whitetails and hear the same complaint: They have a good morning stand that peters out in the afternoon. Or perhaps they'll see deer in the evening but rarely in the morning. What should they do?

"You've got to really work those thermals," said the late Terry Kayser of Horizons West Outfitting in Dodson, Montana. My husband, Bob, and I hunted with Kayser when he was outfitting in the rugged Cabinet Divide Mountains near Heron, Montana. Each morning, he placed us in lonesome clear-cuts at the top of his world. In the late afternoons he moved us to stands located along river bottoms or in valleys—as low as he could get us. That's how I scored at five o'clock one evening on a really good 10-point buck at the edge of a lowland cedar swamp. At the time, Kayser was rattling for Bob somewhere out of sight of my location. I couldn't hear him rattling, and I'll never know whether the buck could or not. All I know is that the buck came busting out of the bog, stood at the edge of a giant clearing for several minutes alternately scent-checking the wind and refreshing one of his scrapes, then came barreling across a stretch of open prairie. I shot him as he dawdled near a second scrape.

"I learned long ago that whenever you are rattling or calling, or even if you're just waiting in a stand, hunt low in the evenings and high in the mornings," Kayser told me. "If deer are holed up because of bad weather, wait until later in the day and then try working your way downhill, calling as you go, with the wind in your face. That's a good way to jump deer bedded near bottoms, where scent will be swirling on stormy, low-pressure days. You have to learn to work the thermals, because deer always do," he said.

"Hunt high, hunt low" seems like an easy concept to grasp, but it can work against you. First, if you get on stand too early, or if you hunt extremely deep canyons such as those in some western areas, the morning sun may not warm the air fast enough to force thermals upward until eight or nine o'clock.

Second, said whitetail hunting expert Jody Hugill of College Station, Pennsylvania, "You have to watch your scent when you're hunting in bottoms. Scent can sometimes stall in low places. If it seems 'windstill' in a bottom as the air starts to cool, the scent that's already there may actually be pooling. Stay alert to subtle air movement that will carry your scent almost imperceptibly away from any area you plan to watch. Under windstill conditions, scent pools in the deepest spot. If you hunt at the very end of this 'pool,' you might be able to pick off whitetails as they either pass through or stage there before heading to nighttime feeding areas."

Hugill is right. Even in windstill conditions, a good scent-check powder or other wind-testing device (e.g., API's Windfloaters or Pete Richards Wind Detector) may reveal a pronounced air current, often in the direction of the prevailing wind.

"I noticed this tendency of scent to drift on several occasions, even under seemingly windstill conditions when I was sure whitetails would scent me, yet didn't," Hugill said. "Afterward I wondered, how did I get away with that? So I began checking the wind under every possible set of conditions using my own homemade variations of Windfloaters. At summer's end, I'd collect dried milkweed pods or Canadian thistle heads. I broke them open, gripped the seeds between my thumb and index finger, and yanked with the other hand to separate them from the floating silky fibers. I stored these 'floaters' in plastic bags, then stuffed some into a film canister when I went hunting. They worked great and didn't cost a dime."

Hugill said he has often dropped one of his floaters and watched it drift down a creek bottom, make a large circle, and return. "That's why I know pooling scent can contaminate a large area. By understanding this, you can make certain your stand is properly positioned."

"Steep-sided hollows produce more swirling evening thermals than will more open creek bottoms," agreed M.A.D. Calls' master deer hunter Mark Drury. "I'll go low in evenings too, but only if I can locate a consistent wind direction—even if only a subtle one—that helps me take advantage of thermals."

"If there is one thing that is going to negatively affect a hunter who decides to use calls or rattling, that one thing will be not paying attention to scent, wind, and thermals," said Bob Zaiglin. "Even when walking in to a stand site, I'll try always to walk with the wind hitting me in the face. This gives me a chance to walk up on a deer, sure. But it also means I won't be spooking out every deer in the countryside."

"I probably have a different view on the wind than many experts," said Brad Harris. "Other hunters have told me that their deer usually come in from a down-wind direction. Now, calling is my passion; it is the one thing that I do all the time. I know I can't see every deer that responds, but I have had very few deer ever try to skirt me and come in from downwind."

Why does Harris think this is so? "Well, once I have a deer on the string, I'm not about to let up. I continue to call or rattle aggressively, doing everything in my power to get it to come in. I don't want it to have the time to think about the situation and decide, *I have to go downwind.* I firmly believe that a deer will do this when a hunter sees a deer on its way, drops the call, and sets up. Heck, yes, that makes a deer nervous. All of a sudden the deer's thinking, *Where did that noise go? Why did it stop? Uh-oh, I'd better go downwind to check up on it.* If any deer stops to look the situation over, that's when I'm going to call or rattle for all I'm worth. I want to reassure it that, yes, I'm right here. I don't want the deer to think it over. I want it to know I'm here and I'm waiting. As long as I'm calling, I'm in control. If you do what many experts suggest, you risk letting the deer's natural instincts take over. It's a lot like playing a big bass. When you've got it on, your best bet is to keep the line tight and reel it right in to where you are waiting."

The science of air, scent, wind, and non-scents isn't rocket science. It doesn't take an Einstein to be able to figure out how to trick a whitetail's nose as easily as we sometimes trick its eyes and ears. What it does require is the willingness to pay close attention to every detail that transpires in the whitetail woods or plains each time you go out the door. Only knowing what worked and why, as well as when to resort to the same tactics again, will pay off in the end.

8

A Look at the Calls
The Good, the Bad, and the Ugly

After many years of calling deer, using almost every call I could get my hands on, I can relate a plethora of interesting experiences—some good, some bad, some ugly. I'd like to get "down and dirty" and reveal the goods about which calls work the best, as well as which calls aren't worth their salt. That's easier said than done, though. As an outdoor writer, I'm fortunate to receive almost every new deer call that appears on the market well before the rest of the public even knows it exists. The truth of the matter is this: I have never had a deer call that didn't work, and I've never had a deer call that did not sound like the deer vocalization it was supposed to be imitating.

Why is this so? Well, I firmly believe that the field of deer calling is simply too competitive for any slipups. Manufacturers are put under the gun to deliver a call that works and works well. There's nothing stopping Joe Retailer from opening packages from every call manufacturer, then allowing potential customers the chance to try them out. You can see how readily the wheat will be separated from the chaff. Since deer calls are not a high-dollar item, a hunter who is not happy with a particular call will buy another, better call. But he will also tell everyone he sees that he's not happy with the first call, and word of mouth is important. Consequently, sales will eventually drop. Manufacturers who make poor calls will not be in business long.

This lineup of calls from Olt, Burnham Brothers, and Lohman during the early 1980s represents the best that deer calling had to offer. Credit: Bob Etling.

The call industry is full of people who have paid their dues. Most can boast a long and distinguished history in the business. Bob Zaiglin, for example, once designed a fine buck grunter for Eastman's Outdoors. That was before the calling craze really got going, though, and that call is no

Buck grunts or doe bleats will often call in deer, but no call will call in whitetails every single time you use it. Credit: M.R. James.

longer available. I use Zaiglin's name to illustrate the fact that every call manufacturer with whom I am acquainted keeps high-caliber deer hunting experts on staff. It's these experts who provide the input into each call's design, sound, and features. One of the best ways to choose a call is to find out which experts are on the company's pro staff, then decide what you think of their deer hunting acumen, whether by reading outdoor articles or books (such as this one), watching videos or TV shows, or listening to audiocassette tapes. I can truthfully say I've never used a deer call that wouldn't have worked in a hunting scenario. Remember, though, that even calls that work will not always call in deer. But if you want to improve your chances of seeing more and better whitetails than ever before, you must give calling a go. A listing of call manufacturers is included at the end of this chapter.

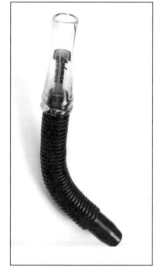

Lohman's Model 1107 Gold Series Triple Grunt Call® is one of the best grunt tubes on the market. Credit: Outland Sports.

Calling deer isn't a foolproof tactic. Not only will you *not* always call in deer—although you will probably see far more than you would had you not used a deer call—you can also, on occasion, frighten deer away when calling. Deer calling is a tactic of trial and error. You will call, and you will learn.

Some of that learning may take place when 1) you made a call and you shouldn't have made one; 2) you made a call that sounds nothing like the vocalization you were trying to duplicate; 3) you drop your call when a deer is close; or 4) you attempt to call a deer that simply isn't interested in responding. Like the late-season doe that flees at the mere sight of a buck or at the sound of his lovesick grunting, some deer may become panicky when they hear a particular call. The calls that are most likely to elicit frightened responses are the various buck grunts and other dominant or agonistic buck vocalizations.

Jim Holdenried uses his buck grunter to nail buster whitetails like this Illinois buck that scored in the low 170s.

The buck grunt is my favorite call. I've used bleats and blats with success, but for reeling a buck in, there's nothing like a grunt, in my opinion. Maybe I haven't given the bleat or blat the benefit of the doubt and experience; I don't know. What I do know is that in all the

The call industry is full of people who have paid their dues—like Missouri's Mark and Terry Drury.

years I've used deer calls, I've had more deer come in—and faster—when using the buck grunt than with any other call.

My first negative experience with this call took place several years ago while I was bowhunting the week before the opening of the Missouri firearms deer season. Until that time, I'd never scared a deer while calling other than the odd doe that would dart off unexpectedly. I'd applied some matrix scent to some draglines, then fastened the drag strings to my bootlaces. As I walked along, the drags bounced behind me, dispensing scent. I climbed up in the tree into my stand and waited.

Within fifteen minutes, a decent-sized buck came following my trail with his nose to the ground. He stopped and started nosing the ground where I had left the main trail and made my way to my tree stand. To get him moving in my direction,

I blew softly into my buck grunter. But rather than encouraging him to come closer, my call had the opposite effect. The buck turned around, arched his back, lowered his head, and then tightly clasped his tail between his rear legs as he slunk back across the trail and into a thick clump of sumac.

The buck would have been an 8-point, but was missing one antler. As I watched, he occasionally poked his head out of the thicket, stared first one way and then the other, then went back into the thicket to hide a little longer. After five or ten minutes of hiding, he poked his head out again, looked all around, then hid again. I was puzzled by this behavior until I realized that he must have had a run-in with a more dominant buck. The smaller animal probably had been pushed around, and possibly had gotten his antler knocked off in the process. The buck grunt brought back unpleasant memories of this experience. Since he was unwilling to run afoul of another bigger buck, he was both hiding and keeping a lookout for a bigger buck at the same time. This behavior prevented me from taking a shot at him, since he was out of bow range. It also kept him from ever coming back toward my tree stand. I later discovered that this type of behavior wasn't that uncommon for a more timid buck. But I also discovered that even the biggest, baddest bucks in the woods will sometimes go out of their way to avoid conflict when tending hot does.

Yet even after this unusual negative encounter, I have never hesitated to use either the aggressive buck grunt or the tending buck grunt in my attempts to call in deer. I've had super luck with it, and so have other hunters. Indiana's Billy McDonald was hooked on deer calling even before he experimented with commercially produced calls. He had heard bucks grunting in the woods and decided to try to call them in himself. He successfully did, too. His addiction to deer calling went over the top when, in 1988, he used a grunt call to lure in seventeen different bucks from four stand locations. One of the bucks he called in but didn't get included a whopper whitetail that would have scored between 160 and 170 Boone and Crockett points.

Randy Tillary of Kansas bow-killed a monster whitetail while using a buck tending grunt call. Tillary's trophy scored 223$\frac{7}{8}$ Boone and Crockett points as a nontypical and netted 199 points in the typical category.

As M.R. James, outdoor writer *par excellence* and editor emeritus of *Bowhunter Magazine,* said, "My calls are like my American Express cards: I never leave home without 'em. However, I often grunt with my natural voice. I've found it can be just as effective as using manufactured calls. At my Montana ranch, I found I could get a deer's attention with my voice grunt at distances of up to seventy-five or eighty-five yards. I also use that voice grunt to stop a buck just as he steps into an opening."

James hunts some prime Montana river bottoms. "A lot of the bucks that I shoot during the rut are on the move," he said. "One that's particularly memorable was trailing a doe. The doe continued along the fenceline past my stand. The buck was still on the other side of the fence. I voice grunted. That buck hopped over the fence and then wandered around, looking for me. I voice-grunted again to stop him. It did the trick, and I shot him."

Although partial to the buck grunt and rattling, James doesn't limit himself with regard to trying out other calls. "Early in the year, I'll bleat or grunt softly from time to time to try to pique the interest of deer within earshot," he said. "I call this 'curiosity calling.' I'll also use various doe calls to try to attract bucks I may see passing by my stand. During the pre-rut, I'll start and end each light rattling sequence with buck grunts. And I'll use the buck grunt occasionally when I'm hunting over a decoy. The biggest deer I've taken so far by calling scored about 150 Boone and Crockett points."

James enjoys calling in part because it allows him to see more and different bucks while hunting than he's seen while scouting. "I'm very familiar with the river bottoms where I usually hunt in Montana. I scout there and pay close attention to what's going on there. And yet most of the bucks I call in or kill are bucks I've never seen before."

The buck grunter works, no doubt about it, whether you're fortunate enough to be able to grunt with your voice, like M.R., or if you rely on an actual grunt call in one of its many guises. You may not always call hordes of deer, but you should call in more than a few. Both does and bucks grunt. Does, however, grunt all year long, while bucks grunt mainly during the rut. The best grunts to make are those of a rutting or tending buck or the grunts of a doe in estrus. Most hunters I've questioned replied that they see their best responses to various grunts between the end of October and the middle of November, and then again in mid-December. Grunting peaks when bucks are chasing does or freshening their scrapes just prior to and during the rut's peak.

Is it imperative to your calling success that you be outfitted with the most recent and up-to-date buck grunter on the market? Most definitely not, according to Mel Dutton. "I've been using the same three calls for the past ten years," Dutton said. "These are a Lohman buck grunt call from 1992 or 1993, a Hunters' Specialties buck grunt, and a Lohman doe bleat. They work as well now as they did when I got them."

Whether you want to have the latest available assortment of calls or you're satisfied with the tried and true is up to you. If you're in the mood to do some shopping, though, the most important thing to look for is good, realistic sounds. Calls that are well-constructed—made of sturdy materials, not flimsy one-shot components— will last longer. Check inside the call to be sure the reed is firmly installed and isn't likely to fall out or become displaced after prolonged episodes of calling. A few commercial buck grunters are extremely specialized. Not only will they make the buck grunt, the tending grunt, and the trailing grunt, they will make all of these calls well.

Other calls are even more versatile. Some produce any number of vocalizations—buck, doe, and fawn—with no problem. Many of the calls on the market can be easily adjusted to produce different grunt tones, both buck and doe, bleats, blats, snorts, and even fawn distress cries. Some calls operate when a person inhales on the tube or call end. Others work when exhaling or blowing through the call. Some products work either way. On a number of products tonal quality, frequency, and pitch can be adjusted by moving or repositioning the reed. To adjust others you move a flexible O-ring along the reed until the desired sound is produced. Some have "call chambers" that can be removed or repositioned for a wider array of sounds. Others can be adjusted with a dial that gives you the ability to completely control the call's tone. Some work merely by pushing a button.

Inflection chamber calls are made to emit the desired sound when you inhale or exhale, and merely twisting the barrel allows you to vary the tonal quality. Even better, inflection chamber calls work when you squeeze them, too, which means that you can position them on your stand platform or attach them to the trunk of a tree and then produce a call by pressing or leaning against the call with your foot.

Be sure that you test a call before you see a deer. A call maker's ability to produce handy, realistic calls apparently is limited only by the imagination. And, after viewing the huge range of great products currently available to hunters, I believe that this imagination is almost limitless.

One desirable innovation that exists in most of today's buck grunters is what Harold Knight termed *hyperventilation.* This is a word Knight coined some years ago to describe the sound of a truly excited whitetail buck. Such a buck, when he's hot on the trail of a doe, Knight said, "will often grunt both as he exhales *and* inhales—sort of a grunting in double-time, or hyperventilation." Hearing this sound led directly to the development of calls such as Knight & Hale's E-Z Grunt-R Plus®, which produces four tonal qualities of buck grunting. Such calls work whether the caller is inhaling or exhaling. As a bonus, a design like this, while not foolproof, is less likely to freeze when moisture comes into contact with the reed on frigid mornings.

The best way to describe hyperventilation as it relates to deer grunting is to compare it to a hen turkey's excited *cutting* in relation to the more usual mating yelps. Animals can get just as excited as people over various events in their lives. It pays to know when best to use this information in a hunting situation. A hyperventilating grunt is probably best suited to the peak of the rut.

Either buy calls made with reeds guaranteed not to freeze, or be sure they are constructed in a way that ensures that the reeds will not freeze. Should you have problems, and you might, protect your call from freezing by placing it inside your jacket or somewhere else where your body's heat will keep the call thawed and ready for use.

Jerry Peterson of Woods Wise Products in Franklin, Tennessee, designed one of the first dual-purpose double-reeded calls. Inhale on one end of the Buc-N-Doe® and you made a tending buck grunt. Inhale on the other and the result was a doe bleat. This call produced six basic calls, including contact doe and fawn calls and fawn distress bawls. Each reed cartridge—which means either removable end of the call—could be used without the tube for zero movement while calling or to free your hands so you could draw your bow. It was one of the first multipurpose calls.

Missouri's David Westmoreland first used the doe bleat in a hunting situation at the Buckmasters Classic. "Before then I didn't have much faith in any deer calls," Westmoreland said. "But during the Classic I saw one buck going directly away from me into some extremely thick brush. With no shot at all at that point, as well as nothing to lose, I made a doe bleat. The buck stopped. I waited fifteen seconds, then bleated again. The buck turned around 180 degrees and walked right back to me. I shot that 6-point at fifty yards."

Jerry Peterson graduated from college with a minor in wildlife biology. He believes that education has helped him immensely as a deer hunter. "I knew about the various studies in deer vocalizations made by various universities (e.g., University of Georgia and Mississippi State University in Starkville), but I wanted to find out for myself how many sounds whitetails can make. So far, I've catalogued more than thirty separate deer sounds, including a few whistles, proving, at least in my own mind, that wild deer are more vocal than penned deer. I then set out to determine which sounds would work best for calling deer."

Peterson, like Jay Cassell, presents some good arguments for the doe bleat or a doe contact call. "The buck's tending grunt became successful because bucks are so aggressive," he explained. "But because many bucks responded—and some weren't killed—those that survived became that much warier."

One hunter-outfitter who basically agrees with Peterson's assessment of the grunt call is Jerry Shively, of Flat Iron Outfitters, from Thompson Falls, Montana. "On a clear, windstill day, whitetails can easily hear deer calls from as far away as a hundred or two hundred yards," Shively said. "Whitetails can detect antler-rattling from an even greater distance. Hunters who wait in tree stands can and do call in curious whitetails each day of the various hunting seasons, but I truly believe any sound that originates high in the air could be one reason many deer approach calls cautiously. Whitetails aren't stupid. They realize such calls don't sound quite right, so they're not too eager to run right in. Since calls made such a huge splash during the mid- to late 1980s, overly enthusiastic hunters quickly educated many whitetails. That's one reason for something I've noticed during the past several hunting seasons: A whitetail hears a call, steps into an opening, and

Since deer can pinpoint sound with uncanny accuracy, rattling from the ground creates a more natural illusion than rattling from a tree stand. Credit: M.R. James.

then waits, its attention riveted on the place the call originated. You might not see this deer, but there's a good possibility it's able to see you, particularly in heavily forested country such as the areas I hunt. So, if you move to make another call, the deer will probably pin you. If you don't call, the deer loses interest. It's a no-win situation, but one that can often produce, if you're willing to hunt as a team with the caller on the ground and the hunter in a nearby tree. The deer won't be nearly as suspicious if the call is coming from ground level. Next, the hunter in the tree can, if he spots the deer, alert the hunter on the ground to the animal's position. The hunter on the ground may then begin to call quietly, barely loud enough for the deer to hear, or slip behind a bush or tree, somewhere the deer is unable to see him, and then call again."

Shively also recommends that if you're hunting alone, you buy a "no hands" call. "Be sure such a call doesn't interfere with your bowstring if you're hunting with archery tackle," he said.

Peterson believes doe bleats are underused by today's hunters—one reason they are so much more effective.

While developing his calls, Peterson listened to both wild deer and penned deer. "Whenever we separated the does from the bucks during the rut, the does bleated as if they were calling to the bucks. This reinforced what I'd seen in the wild when an estrous doe came into a scrape, assumed the classic stimulated posture [squatting, rubbing rear hocks together], and began to bleat loudly. It didn't take long for a buck to find her. From that observation and others, I believe if an estrous doe is ready to be bred but is not being tended by a buck, she'll try to find one on her own. One way of doing this will be by making either the doe contact call or bleat.

"A fawn's bleat is often called a 'mew' because it sounds like a cat," Peterson continued. "A doe bleats like a goat—*baaa*. And a doe's contact call is a longer, more drawn out, intense bleat that rises in tone as the doe becomes more stressed. The sound is *nee-yaat*—a flat sound with each syllable pronounced, and with minor emphasis on the last one. All of these calls are duplicated on our audiotape, 'The Vocabulary of Deer,' for anyone interested in finding out how deer sound."

Some hunters prefer using the fawn bleat like a predator call, making loud, insistent mews like a fawn in distress. They report that does charge in, feet flailing, looking for whatever is hurting the fawn. Some companies make fawn bleaters for this very purpose, but remember, if you shoot a doe that charges in like this, it's possible there's a late-born fawn still totally dependent on her. As stated earlier, though, there's nothing wrong with calling a doe in like this, then waiting for any satellite buck or bucks that may be trailing or accompanying her.

Jerry Peterson is a firm believer in the doe grunt, too. "The very first sound a fawn hears is the sound its doe makes when the fawn calls it to nurse," he explained. "When the fawn responds, it gets groomed and fed. It is rewarded with everything good in its life. From early on, deer are conditioned to come to a doe's maternal grunt. It means, 'Come here.' And since a doe's grunt isn't an aggressive call, you needn't worry whether a big buck, smaller buck, or a doe hears it. It won't frighten any of them."

According to Peterson, a doe's grunt is higher pitched than a buck's grunt and difficult, if not impossible, to duplicate on reed-

Mike Beatty, here with Buckmasters' Jackie Bushman, called in his tremendous whitetail while using Primos's The Can doe bleat canister. Courtesy Buckmasters.

type calls (those that are blown with the mouth). Peterson uses a sonogram to analyze actual deer sounds and then compares them to sonograms of his manufactured calls to determine just how realistic each is. "That's how we make all of our calls," he said. "We compare them to actual sonograms to see how they measure up."

A few call manufacturers prefer using doe grunts to call in deer. Dominant and subordinate bucks respond readily to doe grunts, and so do does. A buck's grunt sounds more piglike, with a distinct background clicking noise, while a doe's is somewhat higher pitched in comparison. Deer responding to a doe grunt come in either hopefully or casually. Such animals are neither worried nor fearful.

Will Primos of Primos Hunting Calls is one call manufacturer who is absolutely sold on the doe bleat as a way to take trophy whitetails. "You will not believe the photos I've received of deer taken with our doe bleater," Primos said. Mike Beatty's Ohio monster is one such buck. "There are more," Primos said. "Believe me. I've got a stack of photos here on my desk." The Can® is Primos's estrous doe bleat. This canister-type call is simplicity itself. Merely turn the canister over, and a quavering

The first time he used the bleat call, Kansas bowhunter Mike Rose took this huge preseason buck. Credit: Mike Rose

Jim Holdenried called this Boone and Crockett whitetail out of a Missouri swamp to start his trophy hunting career. Credit: Jim Holdenreid

bleat can be heard for several hundred yards in every direction. This is what Mike Beatty used to call in not only his trophy buck, but another good 8-point buck earlier that same afternoon.

"The Can® says, 'I'm ready, I'm here; where are you?'" explained Primos. "We have taken existing canister call technology and perfected it. The Can®'s estrous doe bleat is so complex it simply cannot be duplicated by mouth-driven air rushing over a normal reed. The inner workings of The Can® include a bellows-driven device that delivers air over an extremely thin reed to produce the slow, controlled *baaaaaaing* sound that gets weaker and then tails off at the end. It quavers and dies and is very similar to a sheep's bleat." Primos also makes and markets The Lil Can®, which makes the sound of an early season doe bleat, and The Great Big Can®, the call of choice to reach deer at long distances or on windy days.

In 1982 Mike Rose, a Kansas bowhunter, became one of the first advocates of the estrous doe bleat. It was Rose's first calling experiment. He blew once into the call and watched in amazement as a huge buck responded almost immediately.

"There's no doubt in my mind that my buck was looking for whatever made the sound," Rose said. "He crept down the path to my stand with every sense alert." The deer's rack ultimately scored 182 Boone and Crockett points and, at the time it was killed, ranked tenth in the Pope and Young record book. That lofty ranking has been whittled away over time. The most recent ranking places Rose's mighty whitetail at thirty-ninth, still a startling achievement for a bowhunter who really didn't know whether calling would work, but was willing to try it out to see for himself.

Literally hundreds of different deer calls can be found in catalogs and on retailers' shelves, far more than we could ever adequately cover in a book of any size. Rather than provide names and models of every call now on the market, generic descriptions of those calls now available will probably serve you more than adequately. As technology advances, calls will continue to be refined. And that means that model numbers and names will change, thus confounding any reader in search of a particular call. What we will say quite readily is that Louisiana's Eli Haydel may have been the very first person to market a buck grunter, well before anyone else ever thought such a device would work. Haydel's Game Calls is still in business. Herter's and Olt's Game Calls both made deer bleats well before other hunters believed in calling, and Bill Harper of Lohman Game Calls (now owned by Outland Sports) came up with a snort call

Literally hundreds of deer calls can be found on retailers' shelves and in catalogs. This Lohman Model 1122 Inflection Grunter® is just one of them. Credit: Outland Sports.

that almost everyone but Brad Harper was afraid to use back in the late 1970s and early 1980s. Lohman's Kmeer Deer® is still taking bucks decades after it first appeared on the market. M.A.D. Calls continues to confound with new and inventive calls, even after it was taken over by Outland Sports. Perhaps that's because

Mark Drury remains on M.A.D. Calls' pro staff. Credit: Mark Drury.

Outland has had the uncommonly good sense to keep clever Mark Drury on their staff as well as Brad Harris, one of the best deer callers in the business.

My advice is to stick with the names you know, whether game call manufacturer or pro staff member, and you won't be disappointed. And never be afraid to experiment. After all, all deer callers have, at one time or another, wondered why they were sitting in a tree making sounds like a pig or a sheep. Many of them are now staring fondly at huge bucks hanging on their walls—bucks that helped them answer that question.

And if the rest of you become as addicted to deer calling as I am, then you'll be trying every new deer call that catches your eye. Whitetail junkies—like me—are hooked on deer calling. Calling is in my blood, and it's a hard habit to break.

But then, why would I *want* to break a habit that brings in more and bigger deer than anyone ever would have thought possible just ten years ago?

DEER CALL MANUFACTURERS

Code Blue Game Calls
P.O. Box 1587
Fort Smith, AR 72902
Tel. 800-531-1201

Flambeau Products
P.O. Box 97
Middlefield, OH 44062
Tel. 440-632-1631

Haydel's Game Calls
5018 Hazel Jones Rd.
Bossier City, LA 71111
Tel. 800-HAYDELS
www.haydels.com

Hunter's Specialties
6000 Huntington Court Northeast
Cedar Rapids, IA 52402
Tel. 800-728-0321
www.hunterspec.com

Knight & Hale
P.O. Box 1587
Fort Smith, AR 72902
Tel. 800-531-1201
www.knight-hale.com

Lohman Game Calls
A Division of Outland Sports
4500 Doniphan Dr.
Neosho, MO 64850
Tel. 417-451-4438
www.outlandsports.com

M.A.D. Calls
A Division of Outland Sports
4500 Doniphan Dr.
Neosho, MO 64850
Tel. 417-451-4438
www.outlandsports.com

Philip S. Olt Company, Inc.
P.O. Box 550
Pekin, IL 61554
Tel. 309-348-3633

Penn's Woods Game Calls
P.O. Box 306
Delmont, PA 15626
Tel. 724-468-8311
www.pennswoods.com

Primos Hunting Calls
P.O. Box 12785
Jackson, MS 39206
Tel. 601-366-1288
www.primos@primos.com

Quaker Boy, Inc.
5455 Webster Rd.
Orchard Park, NY 14127
Tel. 800-544-1600
www.quakerboygamecalls.com

Pete Rickard, Inc.
R.D. #1, Box 292
Cobleskill, NY 12043
Tel. 800-282-5663
www.peterickard.com

Rocky Mountain Wildlife Products
P.O. Box 999
LaPorte, CO 80535
Tel. 877-484-2768
www.critcall.com

Sceery Outdoors
P.O. Box 6520
Santa Fe, NM 87502
Tel. 800-327-4322

Woods Wise Products
P.O. Box 1552
Franklin, TN 37064
Tel. 931-364-7913

9

Stands That Deliver

The rut's peak was still a week away, but bucks were on the move. Every year I wait for the day I call "the day of the bucks." On that day, I have seen as many as seven bucks, most in the 125 to 140 Boone and Crockett class. Some days I might be out walking, looking for fresh deer sign, when the bucks start moving. Other days, I'll be in my tree stand, hoping one will come to within bow range. I've had days when I've been in my stand and have seen many good bucks at a distance. Sadly, on some of those days I wasn't carrying a deer call. On one memorable day, though, I succeeded in calling in several nice bucks to the same stand.

The day dawned crisp and cool. Not a cloud dotted the cobalt-blue sky. As the sun rose, its rays warmed me as I waited inside a permanent tree stand Bob and I had erected many years before. This particular stand had a "porch" off to one side where we could wait outside should we see a buck coming in the distance. That way, the stand's wooden sides didn't get in the way of the bow, and there was be enough room to stand up at full height to shoot.

The first deer I called in took me completely by surprise. Since it was still cool, I was inside. I decided I'd make a few buck grunts to see if I heard or saw anything in the distance. After a short series of soft grunts, I stopped and listened. It was extremely quiet, partly due to the stand's location. Although oak forest surrounded the stand on three sides, within fifty yards I could see an open field where we sometimes pastured our horses. Straight in front of the stand, in the direction I was looking, was a sandstone glade

Whitetail hunters should practice to be proficient with both gun and bow whether or not rattling, calling or decoying are included in their hunting tactics. Credit: Bob Etling.

studded with small pine trees and cedars. After a few minutes of waiting, I thought I heard something, but I wasn't sure what. I grunted again, but then I heard the sounds of our horses trotting down a nearby hill to get to their water trough. I dismissed the noise as having been made by the horses and let my guard down just as a big 6-point buck walked out in front of the stand less than fifteen yards distant. He looked all around, searching for the "deer" that had beckoned with its grunt. I stood up, and the floorboards in the stand creaked and groaned. The buck looked up, but I don't think he saw me since he only stared my way for about fifteen seconds before turning his head downhill. He began walking that way as I tried to climb out of the stand and onto the porch. He must have heard me moving, because he clamped his tail between his legs and trotted away. That's what I get, I thought, for trying to be comfortable when the bucks are moving.

I grunted again, hoping, perhaps, to lure him back in. He wasn't through with me yet. He now circled in front of me, jumped the barbed-wire fence into the horse pasture, and came back toward the stand. There were now fifty yards of oak timber and understory between us, so there would be no shot in that direction. Suddenly, he turned his head and looked toward his backtrail. Then he leaped over the fence and raced down the fenceline and away from me.

I wondered what had scared him, so I continued to look in the same direction he had. I eventually saw a doe sprint out into the field and look behind herself. Her mouth was open, and she gave every appearance of being in estrus since she was holding her chinked tail straight behind her. I blew on the buck grunt and she quickly looked in my direction. Then whatever was behind her regained her attention. She spurted off across the field, and a big 10-pointer came charging out after her. I grunted for all I was worth, but either the buck was unable to hear me or he just didn't care. After all, he had what he wanted in his sights; why would he leave?

At that moment, I became aware of a tremendous racket in the leaves behind my stand. At first I thought it was a flock of turkeys searching through the leaves for acorns. Then the noise grew much louder. I straightened up, made sure the release was fastened correctly on my bowstring, and looked to the right. A doe rocketed through my shooting lane. She wasn't bounding, she was running, and a big 8-point buck was right on her heels. I grunted and grunted, but neither deer gave even the slightest indication that it had heard my pathetic sounds. I reached back into the main part of the deer stand and grabbed a small set of buck antlers I often carried to rattle with. I rattled as loudly as possible, grunting with the call as I did so. To tell you the truth, I really didn't expect anything to respond, so imagine my surprise when the 8-point appeared about 150 yards distant. He stood there, at full alert, staring in my direction. Then he started coming my way. As he did, I could see how aggressively he was behaving. His neck was swollen to twice its normal size. Adding to his already considerable bulk, he had bristled out his mane hairs so they stood straight away from his body. His head held high, with the whites of his eyes showing, he proceeded both slowly and deliberately directly to my stand. My heart was pounding as I watched a buck that would have scored well up in the Pope and Young record book make his way deliberately toward me, stiff-legged and sure. And that was my downfall. He did not rush. Rather, he proceeded slowly, staring around at every break in the woods. Had he stormed in, I might have had a chance. As it was, I was able to get a full head of steam built up behind a raging case of buck fever. When he paused eight yards away, I aimed and released the string. Unfortunately for me, I was so busy watching the buck's antlers that I missed his entire body by a good three feet. Score yet another point for the bucks on that long-ago morning. Only the knowledge that I'd chosen this stand site well made me feel any better. If nothing else, I had faith in my stand.

If there's one lesson I've learned from years of hunting whitetails, it is this: If you pick your stand carefully, there is no reason to ever give up until it is too late to hunt that day, the deer season is over, or you've tagged your deer.

The key to picking out the right stand is to realize before you even start that in any given area *some stand locations are vastly superior to others.* Identify one, and you'll soon stay on stand all season, too. One year not too long ago, I either spotted or called in thirteen bucks from my firearms stand before I finally shot a nice

10-point that scored 125 Boone and Crockett points—perhaps not the largest deer in the world, but still a great trophy, particularly here in the Ozarks, where bucks can be extremely unpredictable. But calling and rattling can make these animals less unpredictable. And so can a productive stand location.

Picking out productive stands has always come fairly easily to me, even when I first started deer hunting more years ago than I like to admit. While most other hunters rarely saw anything back when deer were scarce, I almost always saw something. Quite often that something was a dandy buck. Back then, I didn't always get my deer. But even so, I began to wonder why I saw deer while my fellow hunters didn't.

In hindsight, I'm sure a good part of it was tenacity. I just wouldn't give up

When picking out a stand, realize why some stand locations are superior to others. Credit: Jim Holdenried.

Whitetails are creatures of habit, particularly when it comes to their travel patterns. Credit: Mark Drury.

until quitting time, no matter what the weather. But another part was simply good luck. It had to be luck. I didn't know much about whitetails back then, and yet I was still pretty good at guessing where they'd eventually appear.

My first years of deer hunting were spent on a private farm. The landowner divided it into ten- or twenty-acre chunks, then assigned each of his hunters to his or her own area. We paid money for the privilege of hunting there, and hunters were forbidden to hunt anyplace but on their own little tract of ground. Within a few years, I knew every gully and bush on my twenty acres. Over time, I began to understand how whitetails used that piece of ground. I came to realize that they were creatures of habit, particularly when it came to their travel patterns.

When we bought our own land I was able to test years of whitetail observations on virgin hunting land. Being an outdoor writer helped too, since I could also incorporate ideas I'd heard from top whitetail hunters I'd talked to while researching articles. Because I'm so meticulous about choosing a stand, and since I'm willing to try most new tactics about which I've heard, including calling, rattling, and decoying, I've been tremendously successful at taking good whitetail bucks for almost forty years. Here's what you should look for before choosing your next stand location.

First, become well acquainted with the area's topography. A hunter can predict with startling regularity where whitetails will travel just by looking at the landforms in an area. Deer use some types of topography more readily than others. That's especially true during the breeding or rut period. Bucks like to establish lines of scrapes along the tops of ridges or next to creeks or streams. Favorite rubs or rubline locations will often be found in thick, brushy areas full of small, aromatic trees such as pines or cedars. Look closely, and you should be able to find the buck trails that connect these areas.

In addition, deer travel along certain topographical features all year long. In hilly areas, smaller bucks and does are notorious for choosing the easiest routes possible. Look for trails in hollows and for crossings where hollows rise to connect to one another at saddles or dips in ridges. Such dips make dynamite places to set up for calling, rattling, and decoying. The best such hollows will be those that are narrow and bordered by steep-sided hills. Narrow hollows like this will often funnel deer from many miles away.

In areas of crop fields or pastureland, deer will often travel brushy fencerows to take advantage of cover that may be scarce elsewhere. Whitetails don't like getting caught out in the open, not if they can help it. Likewise, when crossing unprotected areas like fields or power line rights-of-way, deer will usually stick to swales or small depressions that can help hide them.

As a hunter, there is not much you can do about the lay of the land. A farmer may put in a pond or do some bulldozing, but that's about the extent of human control over topography in most hunting areas. But even the most remote places may change from year to year, if only in minute ways. Savvy hunters scout before the season to learn what changes may have taken place and to consider how these changes might affect their hunting success.

Let's say a windstorm blew through and uprooted some big trees. Use such an "act of God" to your advantage. Deer, after all, can be lazy creatures. A tree or deadfall over a trail just might force them your way, and might even make them more receptive to rattling, calling, or decoying than they might ordinarily be.

Ditto for large rocks that roll out of a bluff or a new beaver dam that makes a favorite stream crossing inaccessible. Seek out the natural changes that take place in your area each year, and make them work *for you,* even if that means moving a stand to take advantage of them.

One of the best ways to determine where deer are most likely to travel is by scouting in late winter, just before the woods start budding out. This is when deer paths are easiest to spot. A good deer trail will literally stand out against the rest of the forest as you look at it.

Another point to consider early on in your stand selection process is whether the site is to be used for firearms hunting or bowhunting. While it's true that some stands will work for either, it's far likelier that you'll need at least two locations—and possibly more—if for no other reason than to keep one "fresh." That's because deer are as good or even better at patterning *your* movements as you are at patterning theirs. And the animal that's best at patterning humans is the buck that's attained two and one-half years of age or more. By the time animals reach that age they've seen just about everything, and have tricks for almost every circumstance you can imagine. Tricks include switching travel routes so they come nowhere near a stand they know was used recently.

When I'm choosing a firearms stand site, my first and foremost objective is seeing a fairly good distance, as long as part of what I'm seeing includes one or more types of deer-favored topography mentioned above. This is especially important for rifle hunters, and it's becoming more important for shotgun hunters as well, because these guns are getting more accurate at longer distances with each passing year. Seeing a reasonable distance is especially critical if you're a hunter, like me, who enjoys watching a deer's reaction to calls and rattling. You can throw your entire arsenal at him to see what works best, and learn while you're doing so.

Still, seeing a long way in itself isn't quite enough. I could sit in the middle of a hundred-acre pasture, for instance, even one with a nice swale, and stare all day at a lot of empty space, but it probably wouldn't be a productive deer stand. Ideally, you're looking for a spot where you can see a fair distance, one with some preferred terrain, but also one made up of as many different *ecotones* as possible—the more ecotones, the better.

What is an ecotone? It's simply the wildlife biologist's word for *edge*. An edge, as most deer hunters know, is a place where two types of habitat converge. Whitetails are edge animals. They spend much of their waking hours browsing for choice forage, often along edges. Whether edges produce more preferred types of forage, or whether whitetails instinctively realize they're less conspicuous there, I'm not sure. What I *am* sure of is that if you locate your stand near one or more prime edge habitats or ecotones, you'll probably find deer.

A crop field that ends against a stand of hardwoods; a fallow field that disappears into a thicket of small pines; a clearing on a brushy ridgetop; the distinct line where hardwoods meet evergreens; even where an overgrown meadow abuts a meandering creek—all provide excellent examples of edges or ecotones. Be certain that at least one preferred whitetail food, such as acorns, clover, honeysuckle, standing corn, and so on, is growing nearby. Since whitetails readily forage on many types of browse, that shouldn't be too difficult.

Now add what you know about an area's topography and deer travel patterns to the various ecotones you are able to see from a potential stand site, and you'll be well on your way to guessing where deer will be traveling, feeding, or congregating before you've spent even a single day in your new location. Such a place will be a natural hotspot, where calling, rattling, and decoying should all work well.

I once hunted such a stand, and it produced big bucks for me for many years. The stand was located along a major seventy-yard-wide power line right-of-way. One reason this stand was so productive was due to the wide array of edge habitat along each side of that right-of-way, where forest openings converged with timber. On

Apply what you know about an area's topography, deer travel patterns, and ecotones before choosing your stand sites. Credit: Kathy Etling.

our own property, there was also a place where a fallow field was visible beyond a grove of mature oaks. To my left a sizeable creek wound at the bottom of a steep bluff. I use my 10 x 40 binoculars constantly, because often all you'll see of a deer is a tiny movement through the trees. Glass all day and you'll be surprised how often you'll pick up the slight flash of motion from the hide or antlers of a deer. Without good optics you'd probably never see most of these animals. Nor would you get a chance to try out your call or rattling on them, should you be a hunter who likes to see an animal before trying to lure it in.

If you do find a good spot for a long-range stand, be sure to practice at varying distances with your firearm. Find openings through the trees where deer will probably be moving. If it is legal where you hunt, cut shooting lanes before the season. They don't have to be huge, just roomy enough so branches or brush won't deflect your bullet. Be sure to check forest regulations or get the landowner's permission before you begin.

Even though I now usually hunt from a tree stand, one of the best stands I've ever had was on the ground. When I hunted there, I sat above a large rock that was close to the top of a steep hill. Beneath the rock, a wooded hollow opened up for about a hundred yards before narrowing once more. This hollow was bisected by a small stream, about eighty yards below where I sat. I think I actually prefer ground stands. One reason is increased mobility. When you're hunting from the ground, not only can you move more easily in any direction, but it's easy to use your sling and brace your elbows against your knees. Since I always use a rest, that's an important consideration. Another worry in a tree is shooting while the wind is blowing. Any motion of the tree, however slight, can throw your shot off. Finally, I think it's easier to stay warm on the ground, and calling and rattling both sound much more realistic from the ground. Using one of the new camouflaged blinds that can be readily set up and some of the tips provided here, I wouldn't hesitate to call or rattle to deer from the ground. It's especially effective when a hunter or caller on the ground teams with another in a tree. Also, there are those perfect ground stands that will work better than tree stands for calling or rattling. Should you prefer hunting from such a locale, your most difficult chore will be finding it—difficult, but not impossible, particularly in steep, hilly areas with a number of good vantage spots.

When choosing a stand for bowhunting, the idea is to get up close and personal. My preference is to locate my stand at least ten yards downwind from a trail. I'll also try to leave some natural foliage or branches growing beneath my stand to help break my outline and the outline of the stand. This foliage will also help to obscure any calling or rattling motion from alert whitetails.

Bowhunters intent on bagging a trophy should try to place their stands downwind of the thickest, most rugged areas they can find. Big bucks love to hole up in impenetrable thickets. Often, even the slightest amount of human pressure will push them into the worst terrain in their entire home range. Savvy archers realize this and locate their stands accordingly.

As mentioned in previous chapters, whether you hunt from a tree or the ground, scent remains a tremendous factor. Find out as early as possible what effect wind and topography will have on scent dispersal in your area. Some stand sites may prove to be superb when the wind blows from one direction, but may work against you if the wind shifts. Other sites may work fine no matter which way the wind is blowing, but these sites are harder to find.

The sun has also been the downfall of many a deer hunter. If you're hunting in the South, where the sun may beat down viciously all day even well into the season, you'll want a stand that's shaded at least part of the time.

Farther north, a stand that will catch the sun's rays as early as possible, particularly when weather turns cold, will be desirable. That one small point can mean the difference between a comfortable day of hunting and one that's downright miserable.

Consider the sun for another reason, too. Let's say you've found the perfect spot, and you're out there opening morning. Everything is fine until the sun peeks over the horizon and shines directly into your eyes. The same thing can be true of the setting sun. Even the finest optics may work poorly when sunlight pours through the objective lens. And even if binoculars and scope work perfectly, human eyes simply aren't engineered to stand up to the sun's glare.

Once you find the perfect stand, there is no reason to quit hunting when it rains or snows. Whitetails are *always* out there, no matter how bad the weather. The most buck activity I've ever seen was on a day when it stormed sporadically all day long. The bucks simply went crazy, chasing does everywhere. Many of the best whitetail hunters believe that deer are *more active* during bad weather because, again, they've *patterned us hunters.* And most of us head in when weather sours. The only exception to the "deer are out and moving all day" scenario exists during all-day downpours or blizzards, when deer bed down—usually under thick conifers, if available—to wait out the storm. But as soon as the weather breaks, return to your stand, because the deer will be moving, and they'll be responding better than usual to calls or rattling.

To make it easier to remain on stand in bad weather, buy one of those inexpensive camouflage umbrellas that fasten around a tree trunk. They're easy to set up, and they work. All catalog sporting goods stores and many sporting goods retailers sell them.

Some hunting areas may hold more deer than others, but all hunting areas hold the secret to taking deer consistently. That secret is to stick with your constant analysis of whitetail movements and habits until you find the best stand sites wherever you are hunting.

10

Calling: Mixing It Up

So you've decided that perhaps you will use a grunt call. After all, grunting like a buck makes sense. So does imitating an estrous doe blat, particularly during the rut's peak. But is there anything else you can do to improve your odds of calling in a deer?

If one type of deer call works, why not try different brands of the same deer call? Indeed, why not try mixing it up even more by adding a completely different deer vocalization to the mix, or maybe more, to make the woods come alive with the sounds that deer make? Perhaps you might even team up with a hunting partner to create your own little whitetail drama, just to see what transpires. If nothing else is going on that day, mixing it up—using several types of calls alone or with someone else—may be just what the deer doctor ordered to pique the curiosity of one of earth's cagiest animals—the white-tailed deer.

We've already discovered that the reason calling works so well is that deer are highly social animals. Does, for example, inhabit the same home range for their entire lives, usually in female family groups consisting of a doe mother, her female offspring, and their female offspring. Such a group makes a point of knowing every other whitetail abiding in its home range.

Young bucks strike out on their own at eighteen months of age, when they're known as yearlings. These youngsters are highly mobile as they seek new home ranges—one that are underused by other bucks—where they can go about the business of someday becoming dominant bucks. These younger bucks will often travel great distances to find a new home range. The time of the year when most bucks attain yearling status, which is the age when does finally kick them out of the family unit for good, coincides roughly with either the pre-rut or rut periods. That fact is the major reason the majority of bucks bagged by hunters in any given year are eighteen months old. Such animals are extremely visible as they move about seeking new home ranges. Even if an animal finds a satisfactory area, it will be weeks before he is completely familiar with the territory. During those weeks, he will be more vulnerable as he acquaints himself with forage sources, bedding areas, and escape routes. A lonely young buck will be highly susceptible to the right deer call.

Older bucks may also, on occasion, be more vulnerable to calls. Should they be out during the preseason actively trolling for does, they will be highly interested in the sounds does make. This interest continues into and after the rut, but if a buck is already with a doe, he may decide a doe in the hand is worth two in the bush, so to speak, and ignore tempting doe sounds to stick with his lady love. Convincing the old boy to throw caution to the winds to come in or to see what's going on might mean creating a deer drama that includes doe sounds as well as those from a rutting buck, or even the sounds of two bucks behaving agonistically toward each another with grunt-snort-wheezes and aggressive grunts. Another factor working to a caller's advantage when deciding to mix up deer calls is that mature bucks seem to expand their ranges each year. Like yearlings, as these older bucks leave familiar territory, they become more vulnerable. Such a buck may be more curious about new surroundings than its old familiar digs.

Don't give up if calling seems like a lot of work for little reward, for sooner or later it will produce. Just remember, if you have ever fooled a buck at a particular location and did not kill it, that deer may remain highly suspicious and refuse to respond to a call made at or near the same location until the next season rolls around—or longer. If such is the case, it's probably time to change your calling position. Mature bucks are among the cagiest animals in the woods, and are also mostly nocturnal, especially during hunting season. They are the most difficult animals of all to call in. The "whitetail school of hard knocks" graduates students each year, some of whom, like the beginning caller, progress to bigger and better things.

As for teaming up when calling whitetails, one need look no further than Missouri's Jim Holdenried. "When my son, my friend Chris Murphy, and I team up to call deer, we usually have good luck," Holdenried said. "During the rut, I want to be out calling on my own. But during the pre-rut and post-rut periods, the three of us will often get together for some team calling. What works for us is for each caller to sit twenty or thirty yards away from the others. A favorite spot would be on the side of a draw right where it begins to narrow or funnel down, or close to any spot where deer naturally enter a fairly large thicket. Sporadic buck grunting emanating from two or three locations, like the three of us do, really inspires curiosity. Team calling works in another way, too. Say a deer is walking into another hunter's location, but the hunter is unable to see it. If one of the other team members can see the deer, this second hunter will grunt to try to make the deer turn to face the sound. When the deer turns, the first hunter is often able to see a deer he might otherwise have missed, or he may even be able to shoot at the deer."

Another way to call as a team is to position the caller in one location and the shooter somewhere else downwind. The shooter should see any deer that investigates from the downwind position first.

You can also try using a snort call in conjunction with a grunter to duplicate the sounds of bucks sparring. Just alternating the vocalizations of a couple of bucks facing off—their assorted agonistic snorts and grunts—is often all it takes to draw an audience of interested deer from the nearby woods.

One final caution: Try not to get too wrapped up in your calling. I've used the snort call, grunter, and rattling horns to mix things up on more than one occasion. While I have called in several good bucks like this, so far I've never bagged any of them. When I would move to put the antlers down or hang them in my tree to shoot, the bucks would see me. It never failed! Still, having deer come in like this—stiff-legged and with the hair bristling on the backs of their necks—is one of the most thrilling sights in nature.

Calling is exciting. It brings in deer you probably wouldn't have seen in the first place. It gives hunters who wait on a stand something to help keep their interest up all day. Anything that can help keep interest up—and you in the woods—will improve your whitetail success.

But beware: Once you make a call, anything can—and sometimes does—happen. Deer can come charging in, or they may sneak in so quietly you won't even hear them. You have to be prepared for almost anything—or for absolutely nothing. Like every other hunting technique, deer calling *won't* work every time you try it. It may not even work *most* of the times you try it. But it *will* work just often enough to keep it exciting. And it's this excitement that has sold so many hunters on the thrilling technique of mixing it up, whether with a team or by yourself, whenever you want to try something different to call whitetails.

The team concept is an excellent move for anyone thinking of mentoring a young hunter in the arts of rattling, calling, and decoying whitetails. Credit: Bob Etling.

11

Okay, I'm Sold on Calling! Now What?

All right! You've become a calling convert. You head out into the woods to try your hand at calling. You position your stand using all the tips provided in the previous chapters, and then you survey your brand new assortment of deer calls. Now what?

"Deer calling is the simplest form of wildlife calling," said Brad Harris. "If you can breathe, you can call. It's so simple, anyone can master it. The bottom line is confidence. Even those hunters who are already experiencing calling success will have even more success once they figure out how to adjust the calling to the conditions. If you use the proper call at the proper times—and you're not afraid of making mistakes, at least not in the beginning—you will be successful. I believe that I succeed because once I'm in control of a calling situation, I do what it takes to remain in control. Once I know a deer has heard me and is interested, I never let up. I reel it in until it's close enough to shoot."

Archers especially will want to buy mouth-grip deer calls both to minimize movement and to prevent bowstring or draw interference. Credit: Bob Etling.

Like most avid archers, Harris uses a mouth-grip deer call that won't interfere as he draws, aims, and shoots his bow. Alternative calls to those that are held in the mouth may be strapped to the wrist, the tree stand platform, even the tree itself, so that movement is minimized as the deer is coming in.

Harris swears that keeping a deer's interest high with calls is key to his success. On the opposite end of the calling spectrum is Jay Cassell. "I think most people call too much," he said. "I believe deer hear all this calling going on in the woods and soon figure out what's going on.

I took this big buck on a cold, overcast, windstill morning right at first shooting light. Credit: Bob Etling.

That's why the hunter who calls rarely and softly has a better chance. That's how I call, and I've taken quite a few good deer.

"This is especially true when you're hunting public land," Cassell continued. "If there are a lot of hunters out in the woods, and they're all using grunt calls or blats—anything—the deer are going to start avoiding those sounds, because they'll associate this sudden symphony of sounds with hunters.

"It's the same thing that's happening out West, where trophy bull elk are bugling less and less, because they know that a lot of the bugling is being done by hunters. Or with smart old turkey gobblers, who shut right up when they hear a lot of calling in woods that were a lot quieter right before the season. I wouldn't call turkeys smart, but the ones that have survived a couple of hunting seasons, and perhaps had encounters with hunters, they get extremely wary when they start hearing all that calling.

"To me, being in the right location is the key. Then a small amount of calling is all you need to do."

Of course, there are many other hunters who produce neither too many calls nor too few calls. They believe that they make just the right number of calls and at the optimum volume. The problem for the neophyte remains: How often should you call, and how loud should it be? Unfortunately, there are no pat answers to these tricky questions.

Many hunters want to know what experts see, when they're calling to deer, that makes them believe that a particular deer will respond. The first clue, of course, is when the deer stops, throws its head up, and looks intently in your direction. Another is when a deer suddenly appears, staring in your direction, where no deer had been just a moment previously. Any deer that is walking toward you, whether its eyes and ears are fixed on you or not, is likely to have heard your call. Brad Harris follows his hunches. "I believe that any buck you've been watching as he's moving along or working a scrapeline, even if he's at a distance, is vulnerable to your calling. That's certainly true if, when you see a mature buck walking, you

Only by staying perfectly attuned to your surroundings will you know whether you've triggered that certain something that will compel a buck to come in. Credit: M.R. James.

grunt and he stops and lays his ears back. Seeing a buck behave like this provides a solid indication that the buck is yours if you keep the pressure on him. So is seeing the buck bristle up." Bristling means that your calls have made that buck mad. An angry buck will be unable to resist the urge to find out for himself which young whippersnapper made him so angry.

"Listen for the sound of bucks grunting back to you," Harris concluded. "In my mind, that's the best part about calling; you're actually communicating with the animals. When you hear an animal grunt in reply, it's saying, *I hear you, I'm coming.* You might hear grunting without seeing the deer, so be sure you're listening for it at all times. Or maybe you'll just hear the sounds of a buck hooking brush, or of antlers thumping and scraping against the ground, or undergrowth snapping; or you might notice a nearby sapling being bent and beat all around. When the sounds of your call affect that buck in just the right way, the first thing he will do will be to take it out on something nearby. Nonvocal sounds help the buck to communicate his mood in the same way that vocalizations do. Listen for every sound the forest gives up. Only by staying perfectly attuned to your surroundings will you know whether you've triggered that certain something that will compel a buck to come in."

12
Why Rattle?

There is probably no whitetail hunter alive who has not yet heard about the almost mystical method of attracting deer that is known as **rattling.** When whitetails clash antlers, it's called either **sparring** or **fighting.** When hunters mimic the sounds of bucks sparring or fighting, this is termed rattling. It's called rattling because the first person who made those antler-clashing noises almost certainly did so by hitting or "rattling" one shed antler against another.

Think about the erratic noises produced by a baby's rattle held in a little tyke's fist. What is most distinguishable about these sounds is their randomness. An older child playing with the rattle might spice things up with a beat, or rhythm, and the randomness would disappear. Like babies playing with rattles, bucks fighting produce random sounds—antlers barely making contact or clashing violently. The random nature of these sounds means there is no right or wrong way to rattle as long as the sounds produced seem natural. The key word here is "random." Click antlers together like you are keeping time to your favorite tune, and that is the antithesis of proper technique. Rattling must be composed of natural sounds produced in a random sequence. Rattling's rhythm should be random, too. That's why *clash, 1 2 3,*

Calling and rattling brought this fine Montana buck in to M.R. James's stand location. Credit: M.R. James.

clash, 1 2 3, clash, 1 2 3, clash, 1 2 3, clash, 1 2 3, ad infinitum, isn't going to work. It's too predictable. Or if, by some strange chance, it does, it won't work as well as a series such as this: *tickle tips, pause, pause, pause, tickle harder, pause, pound on ground with antlers, grunt, clash loudly, grind antlers together, pull apart, snort, clash antlers hard together again, separate, pause, pause, pause, pound antlers on ground, pause, snort, grunt, clash as loud as possible, pull apart, wait.*

CREATE THE TOTAL ILLUSION

As Peter Fiduccia said, "To be successful when antler-rattling, you must always strive to create the *total illusion.* Consider what a deer might be doing while it's making a par-

Call manufacturer and big buck expert Will Primos uses synthetics in many situations. Credit: M.R. James.

ticular vocalization or preparing to spar or fight with another buck. Then try to duplicate the identical sounds, smells, and motions that attract nearby deer whenever the animals vocalize, interact, or fight. Deer aren't scared by such activity—far from it. They are familiar with the sounds of bleats, grunts, and snorts. Bucks with hardened antlers regularly hear the sounds of sparring or fighting. Movement

When you or your partner is rattling, whip saplings back and forth to simulate the motion created when a buck rubs its antlers. Credit: Bob Etling

becomes visible from afar as a buck rubs its antlers on a sapling. To some degree, rage or frustration is apparent when a buck is venting its anger on a tree trunk that's too large to be budged. Any hunter new to rattling must understand that anything goes when you are attempting to deceive a whitetail. Presenting a total package that fools all of a whitetail's senses may mean it will respond more rapidly and with less caution." And that, dear deer hunter, is a good thing!

Rattling falls into place with everything previously discussed regarding whitetail dominance and subdominance or subordination. Before bucks battle, they will lower their heads, paw the earth like enraged bulls, bristle the hair along the backs of their necks and spines, roll their eyes, grunt, and then sway side to side as if gathering the needed propulsion to blast themselves forward to meet their adversary. A sequence of fighting may also include the highest level of agonistic vocalization, the grunt-snort-wheeze. A liberal sprinkling of snorts and grunts is also common whenever bucks fight or threaten each other. It is literally impossible, as Bob Zaiglin has said, for any human to produce as much racket as two deadly serious fighting whitetail bucks.

Mel Dutton rattled in this buck to within twenty yards before it was shot by one of his hunters. Credit: Mel Dutton.

"Rattling is effective because the sound is already natural in the whitetail's society," added Mel Dutton. "In late summer, bucks have started sparring in South Dakota. By late August, once the velvet has been stripped off their antlers, they gather in bands of four or five to spar. Whenever two or more bucks get together, even for a friendly bout of sparring, the sound produced seems to arouse the curiosity of any other deer in the area.

By doing his best to duplicate the sounds, smells, and motions of two deer fighting, Stan Potts takes big Illinois bucks like these three. Credit: Stan Potts.

"I'm never afraid to rattle," Dutton continued. "I don't care if I believe a deer is twenty yards away, or even if I'm outside my blind or on the ground in plain sight. I never recall having spooked a deer while rattling unless an animal was extremely close without me knowing it, and then I unwittingly crashed the antlers together. As long as I abide by simple common sense, I don't spook deer."

Stan Potts of Illinois rattled this 193⅝ nontypical to within bow range. Credit: Stan Potts.

This discussion should allay at least some of the beginning rattler's trepidation. Okay, so it's difficult to frighten away deer when you are rattling. And rattling works—that's an undeniable fact. Another fact is simply this: Rattling works in *some* places—Texas, for instance—much better than in others. Why is this?

WHEN RATTLING WORKS BEST

Basically, rattling is more effective in some areas for the same reasons stated in previous chapters when discussing why calling works better in some situations than in others. The first item on your agenda should be finding an area to hunt with an optimal buck-to-doe ratio—somewhere in the range of 1:1 or 1:2. Don't worry if ratios are skewed farther apart, perhaps as much as 1:9, to provide an extreme example. Rattling will still work; it just won't work as well. When ratios are tremendously skewed, rattling will probably peak as an effective technique about one to two weeks before the start of the primary rut. Bucks will be too busy chasing estrous does later in the season to respond. A hunter rattling in an area with an excellent buck-to-doe ratio may attract as many as three or more bucks each day, while a hunter in an area where does far outnumber bucks may only rattle in one buck every four or five days. That still may be one more buck than a non-rattling hunter would have seen.

Should the buck-to-doe ratio be skewed far to the does' side of the equation, discuss taking more does with your hunting buddies. They may be reluctant to do so, but it will mean not only a better buck-to-doe ratio for future seasons, but improved success when rattling and calling. Harvesting does will benefit bucks in another way, too. Even in areas where buck and doe numbers are balanced, as many as 25 percent of the bucks may die from a phenomenon known as *post-rut mortality,* according to a study conducted by Dr. Charles DeYoung. DeYoung, the director of the prestigious Cesar Kleberg Wildlife Institute in Texas, discovered that bucks survive the rut in poor condition.

Rattling works best on well-managed ranches or hunting areas with a buck-to-doe ratio of 1:1 or 1:2. Credit: Mickey Hellickson.

Nature then throws another curve their way by making post-rut bucks lose their appetites. This may be an adaptation so that pregnant does have no competition for scarce winter forage. Since pregnant does rely on such forage to sustain their embryos, and thus, the species, the buck becomes expendable. A buck will be the last to eat and the first to die. Post-rut mortality particularly affects those bucks that

Texas hunter Murry Burnham is the dean of modern whitetail rattling. Credit: Murray Burnham.

were the most active as breeders. If there were fewer does and more bucks, breeding stresses would decrease, and more bucks would survive.

Native American tribes were probably well aware of the power of rattling. When Native Americans were pushed onto reservations, where they were discouraged from mingling with Americans of European descent, it is likely that most of their knowledge of rattling went with them. Antler-rattling was probably familiar to only a few white settlers. Word of mouth may have passed the technique down through generations of pioneers and hunters, until experts like Murry Burnham, of Texas, were finally able to inform other hunters about the technique through arti-

cles in outdoor magazines. Rattling as a tactic was slow to take off, probably because when hunters first started discussing it, deer were scarce in most parts of the country. But trickle out the news did, and when whitetail numbers eventually exploded in the twentieth century, rattling became a viable hunting tactic throughout the whitetail's range.

Texas whitetails historically have been more likely to respond consistently than deer from other states. But whitetails everywhere are susceptible to rattling. "I was bowhunting in Indiana around 1965, when I heard another bowhunter calling deer and rattling," M.R. James recalled. "That's what got me interested. I started talking to other

Bowhunter Judd Cooney rattled in and dropped this dandy Illinois whitetail. Credit: M.R. James.

108

hunters, read whatever articles I could find, and began to experiment. Most of what I know I learned through trial and error. As calling and rattling gained popularity, I made it a point to get to know pioneers such as Tom Flemming, Art Heinze, and Ted Lawson. I hunted with Dick Kirby of Quaker Boy, Will Primos of Primos Hunting Calls, Larry D. Jones of Jones Calls, and Jerry Peterson of Woods Wise, all of whom I watched, listened to, and learned from, and with whom it was easy to share ideas."

James has been rattling for years. He's had excellent results depending on the time of the year and the conditions. "During some seasons, I've rattled in as many as twenty to forty different bucks," he said. "During one memorable week in Iowa, I rattled and grunted in twelve bucks. Just last year in Kansas, I rattled in six bucks in as many days.

"One day as I was rattling, I looked down the fenceline and noticed a tree moving," James continued. "I thought, *That might be a buck.* Sure enough, here comes a buck, swaggering down the fenceline the way bucks sometimes do. His ears were back, his head was up, and his hackles were standing on end. He'd wander one way and then the other. His rack was somewhat deformed, so I didn't particularly want to shoot him. But then a little forked-horn came in. When that buck saw the forky, he chased him off 150 to 200 yards across an alfalfa field, then returned to me for the third time. He stopped beneath my tree again, so intent was he on finding that other buck.

"I rattled a one-horned buck in several times. That might have been the meanest buck I've ever seen. He'd use that one horn to draw blood whenever he'd fight other bucks. He was just a mean, aggressive buck. One day he and another buck started fighting. I shot the other buck, and I'll bet that one-horned buck thought he was the meanest, baddest buck around since *he* knocked the other buck down and it didn't get back up."

James is sold on rattling. So is Mel Dutton. "If I was allowed to use only one tactic for hunting whitetails, that technique would be rattling," Dutton said. "I'd read about Texas hunters rattling, so I decided to try it myself. I taught myself. Until I used it, I'd never heard of anyone in South Dakota using it. But I was quite successful right away. Since I started rattling in 1980, I've rattled in most of the deer I've taken. I've only been using a decoy since 1988. Even when I use a decoy, I'll be rattling to get the deer's attention."

"Rattling is the most forgiving of all the calling and decoying techniques I've used," said Peter Fiduccia. "A deer that is ready to come to it will come. Conversely, when a deer is not ready to respond, it won't. Rattling will sometimes work extremely well. Other times it won't."

Fiduccia discussed one New York hunting spot where, in the early bow season, he was once able to rattle in lots of bucks. But for some unknown reason, the honeyhole stopped producing. He returned this past season after not having had a single buck respond for the previous two years, just in case the area had become hot again. "This spot is unique because it's only an hour from New York City," Fiduccia said. "I'd been sitting on a ledge, doing some soft rattling sequences that involved nothing more than clicking and meshing the antlers together. I suddenly noticed a sapling waving back and forth below me. It was fairly obvious that a buck was taking out its frustration on that tree, yet wasn't quite aggravated enough to come to the antlers."

Fiduccia got out his doe blat call. He made several estrous doe bleats, one about every twenty or thirty seconds. He waited fifteen or twenty seconds, then lightly rattled for fifteen to twenty seconds. After that, he made another series of estrous doe bleats before repeating the entire sequence. "Each time I'd finish a sequence, the buck would move closer," Fiduccia said. "Another small tree started to wave around, then a branch snapped. I listened closer and heard the buck grunting—that distinct clicking noise obvious in the background. I stopped everything while the buck moved closer. After several minutes, I thumped the ground hard with the back of each antler. The sound I was aiming for was the sound buck hooves make when striking the ground. Then I tickled the antlers together again." Fiduccia had purposely thumped the antlers on the ground behind his stand to make the "hoof-stomping" sound more distant. It worked, too. "The buck thought the animals were leaving. He suddenly rushed in and stood broadside just twenty yards away." Fiduccia shot. That New York buck scored right at 150 Boone and Crockett points, not bad for a day of hunting along the eastern seaboard.

Fiduccia recommends using nonaggressive rattling techniques during the pre-rut period. "I always begin a sequence rattling in a less aggressive manner before moving on to more aggressive techniques," he said. "By starting out gently, I think I'm able to attract more bucks of every size. Less aggressive rattling appeals to almost every buck in the woods except the one that has just had his butt beat. The sound of antlers being lightly tickled together or lightly clacked, whether jazzed up with a grunt call, a snort call, or both, is almost irresistible to the highly social and curious whitetail. Not only will bucks respond, but so will does. And does may often drag a buck along with them." Fiduccia, as readers already know, isn't averse to throwing in some realistic touches such as grabbing a sapling and whipping it back and forth to emulate a buck raking it with his antlers.

Gary Roberson, the owner of Burnham Brothers Calls in Menard, Texas, has been rattling since he was fourteen. "Rattling will work anywhere," he said. "For it to work best, though, the area's buck-to-doe ratio should be 1:4 or better. The best time to rattle is a week to ten days before the rut's peak. Be aggressive, and use good equipment."

Iowa's Don Kisky will try to get as close as possible to a big buck's sanctuary

Iowa's Don Kisky tries to get as close as possible to a big buck's sanctuary or bedding area during the pre-rut period. Credit: Don and Kandi Kisky.

or bedding area during the pre-rut period. "During the pre-rut big bucks respond to rattling more out of curiosity than out of aggression," he said. "That's why I rattle lightly then. Try not to be too aggressive. When our bucks respond during the pre-rut, they generally walk in very slowly. Or they'll stand about eighty yards distant and survey the entire situation before coming any closer. If you move, you're had."

Some hunters always start their rattling sequences quietly because they don't want to startle a nearby deer. Through the years, more than one hunter has declared that loud rattling will scare deer away. Not so, says Mickey Hellickson, wildlife manager for the King Ranches in Kingville, Texas. "I authored a study [see Chapter 13] in which we compared results when we started rattling loudly or started rattling quietly. The study also compared short rattling sequences to long ones. We discovered that rattling simply doesn't scare bucks. It makes no difference if someone rattles loudly or quietly, rattles before the rut or after the rut. The idea that loud rattling frightens whitetails is a misconception, at least in my experience. We've documented the rattling in of hundreds and hundreds of whitetails and I don't remember scaring a single deer."

Hellickson, who moved to Texas from Iowa in the late 1980s, tried rattling—unsuccessfully—while still in Iowa. "The first time I tried it in Texas, I rattled in two bucks," he said. Hellickson's success illustrates the efficacy of the method when whitetail populations are balanced. Although rattling can work in Iowa, things must be perfect to inspire bucks to respond. Not so in Texas, where bucks are busy every minute competing for does. They will check out even the hint of a fight at a moment's notice if it is the right part of the season and under optimum weather conditions.

Jim Holdenried prefers calling to rattling. "I'll rattle, but I do so as a last resort after boredom sets in," he said. "When things aren't happening, I want to create action. Sometimes when you rely on grunting alone, deer are unable to hear it unless they are close. It seems like the sounds of rattling will carry much farther, and that's a tremendous advantage, particularly when under windy conditions."

Holdenried prefers to rattle aggressively just prior to the rut, rather than during the peak or post-rut periods. "If I find or hear of deer with their horns locked together it usually occurs anywhere from the third week in October to the last week," he said. "That tells me whitetails do their hardest fighting and pushing *before* the rut. That's why I clash the antlers together extremely hard during the pre-rut, then change during the rut's peak and afterward to tickling them lightly."

Holdenried uses every trick at his disposal, and that's a major reason he's so successful. "Last season I decided to hunt this one spot in Kansas even though the wind, which was quite strong, was totally wrong," he said. "I don't know what I was thinking. Other than the wind, the temperature that day was in the low twenties. The sky was clear and sunshiny. I was in my stand, grunting, when a buck responded. But before I could shoot, the buck scented me and ran away. I waited there, mentally kicking myself, until I noticed another buck crossing my trail about 150 yards away. I grunted, but the buck was too far away to hear me, especially above that wind. I picked up my rattling antlers and hit them just loud enough to stop him in his tracks. Then I grunted. I suppose the buck couldn't hear the grunt. After a few minutes, he turned to walk away. I tickled the antlers to stop him again. He turned and started coming toward me at a trot. He stopped again, and I tickled the antlers once again. He came in another fifty yards. He stood there about fifty yards away, looking around. I grunted. This time he heard me and started trotting toward my stand. As he walked beneath my stand I said, 'Hold it right there,' to stop him. He halted and I shot him." Holdenried's Kansas

Don and Kandi Kisky have their best success when rattling lightly, not aggressively. Credit: Don and Kandi Kisky.

buck grossed in the mid-130s using the Boone and Crockett scoring system.

PERFECT RATTLING WEATHER

Most of these hunters agree on the perfect morning to be rattling. "It would be cold and quite frosty," said M.R. James. "Those mornings are great because you can hear animals walking a long way off, and you don't have to compete with rustling leaves or wind. I rely a great deal on my hearing to tell if an animal is responding. Sounds carry better on such a morning.

"I remember one of the very first deer I rattled in," James continued. "I hadn't had much luck. I was hunting in Indiana toward the end of November. Now, mind you, I was stubborn. I'd read that rattling would work, and I'd heard from others that it would work, but I sure wasn't having much luck. So there I was banging my antlers together when I looked down and saw an 8-point buck staring up at me in the tree. Have you ever tried to bow shoot a deer when your hands are full of rattling antlers?"

My husband, Bob, has. One cold, clear, brisk morning during the pre-rut, before either of us really believed that rattling would work on our farm, Bob was in a tree stand rattling and snorting for all he was worth. We'd been inspired by Brad Harris, whom I'd interviewed for some project, and who afterwards had sent us some of Lohman's snort calls to try out. Try them out Bob did. "I was standing on my stand platform when a big 8-point buck appeared on my left," Bob said. "Its hair was all bristled up, and it was high-stepping closer and closer. The buck stopped and looked around. I fumbled with my stuff, managed to pick up my bow, but was so excited that I shot right over the buck's back. He jumped to the side, ran a few yards, then glanced back to where the arrow was sticking in the brush. He

Don Kisky is an avid shed hunter when he's not rattling in bucks like this Iowa monster that grossed 197 Boone and Crockett points. Credit: Don and Kandi Kisky.

sneaked over, smelled the arrow, and started to snort. With that, another 8-point buck came running in. I nocked another arrow, aimed, and shot under this buck while the other buck watched. Now, both bucks started running in circles, snorting. They finally both got out of Dodge while I stood there, pinching myself, wondering if I'd really just seen what I'd seen or whether my imagination had gone hog wild."

"One early November morning, about one and a half hours after first light, I noticed a huge buck crossing the ridge 150 yards in front of me while I was bowhunting," Don Kisky said. "I stopped him dead in his tracks with my rattling horns. The buck then turned and came right to me. When he was still eighteen yards distant, I shot, but missed. That buck would have scored in the mid-180s. I'll never forget that day. It was right at thirty-two degrees and spitting snow. Rattling is always better when it's cloudy and overcast, at least in my opinion."

Don and Kandi Kisky prefer to rattle on cold, overcast days. Credit: Don and Kandi Kisky.

Montana's Jerry Shively agrees with M.R. James, Peter Fiduccia, and Bob Etling. "Cool, crisp weather is what I like best when I'm planning to rattle or call," he said. "The colder and frostier it is, the better these techniques work. Not only does sound carry better under these conditions, but deer behave more aggressively. A good frosty morning or afternoon is what you're after. Deer already have their winter coats, and they are simply more active when it's cooler and they're more comfortable, not sweltering like they do on a warm, seventy-degree day."

"When it's really hot, I don't rattle much at all except during the very early morning hours," said Bob Zaiglin. South Texas, where Zaiglin does most of his hunting, outfitting, and guiding, can be brutally hot even when much of the rest of the country is experiencing frost and snow. "If it's hot in the evening, I'll just go sit somewhere and look for activity," he continued. "My favorite time to rattle is anytime there has been an abrupt weather change. If it was hot or warm and turned extremely cold, that's usually best. But it's only really good for about a day. It's almost as if deer move around so much after one of these changes that they wear themselves out.

"Deer normally shy away from moving as much during heavy rains, but not always. I've hunted during some major rainstorms and have taken some big deer then. A few years ago, I saw a really nice buck with a doe late one evening. As I was sneaking toward the oak patch where I'd spotted him, I spooked him out of there. That night the weather changed. It had been extremely hot, but a cold front moved through and brought rain with it. That next morning, I walked through a downpour to reach the spot where I'd seen the buck the night before. After about forty-five minutes, the rain stopped. A few minutes later, I began rattling. The first rattling sequence attracted a couple of small bucks. My next rattling sequence drew in four or five big bucks. The buck I'd seen the preceding evening was the last to appear. His 11-point rack had a twenty-five-inch-wide inside spread and scored 165 Boone and Crockett points. This is the type of weather situation I'm always looking for. I guarantee that under those conditions, the bucks will be ripe for the rattling horns."

ADVANCED RATTLING

Jerry Shively wanted to share one of his favorite rattling tips, one that most hunters—even those who rattle a lot—aren't aware of. After more than fifteen seasons as a whitetail guide, Shively has learned to regard this one as heaven-sent opportunity. "Let's say you remove a really good buck from an area," Shively said. "Rather than taking the next hunter somewhere else, start rattling right there. You might even want to set the hunter up right near the dead deer's gut pile. With one dominant deer down, the whitetail pecking order has changed. Bang your antlers around for a while and you're going to create some interest in local bucks trying to improve their social status in a hurry. This works extremely well. In fact, when I rattle under these circumstances, it's about the only time I'm 100 percent sure that I'm going to get some action. Of course, I'm hunting where I'm sure no one else

has been there to screw it up for me. It's not like hunting on public ground where anyone else might have been in there doing goodness knows what— and could still be in there, even as you're rattling."

RATTLING ON PUBLIC GROUND

Rattling will work on public ground, but remember that

Jim and Clarence Rickard were happy with this buck rattled in by Jerry Shively. Credit: Jerry Shively.

many other hunters may be using the same tactics as you are. The hunter who rattles on public land also runs a very real risk of calling in not only deer, but other hunters as well. For best results rattling on public ground, concentrate your activities in remote areas far from roads or other hunters. If this isn't possible, do the bulk of your rattling during the preseason and the postseason. Refrain from rattling during the firearms season, particularly when you don't know if the hunter on the next hill might just sling some lead in your direction simply because "it sure sounds like a deer over

there." If you are still intent on rattling on public ground during firearms season, paint your rattling horns fluorescent or hunter orange, or tie hunter-orange surveyor ribbon to each antler so that when it moves, the orange is clearly visible.

RATTLING DURING THE RUT'S PEAK

Bucks can be rattled in during the peak of the rut, but it just may be more difficult. After all, why would a buck that's probably trailing a hot doe leave his girlfriend to go to a fight? Again, it's not only the breeding frenzy that gets bucks into trouble. Curiosity can kill not only the cat, but the buck!

Jerry Shively used a Lohman Rattle-Box® to tantalize this 142^{2}/₈-point whitetail in for Steve Renock. Credit: Jerry Shively.

THE ART OF WHITETAIL DECEPTION

Hunters who believe and understand that one simple statement are well on their way to whitetail success.

"I've found that even the buck that's rutting hard can be pulled away from a hot doe," said Brad Harris. "What you as a rattler must do is work on that buck's feelings of dominance. In many cases, if a dominant buck hears the sounds of rattling, he simply won't tolerate it. Use louder, longer, more frequent grunts with your rattling during the peak of the rut. Throw in some grunt-snort-wheezes, too, particularly prior to your rattling or during breaks in your rattling sequences. I'll even use the grunt-snort-wheeze by itself if I see a mature buck with a doe. I attack his instincts, even if he's got what he wants. By asserting myself with loud grunts, snorts, and rattling, I'm challenging him for his doe, challenging him for his dominance, and if he *is* dominant, he isn't going to be able to stand it. He will have to come in and find out what is going on and what he can do to stop it." Which, of course, is what Brad Harris is hoping for.

POST-RUT RATTLING

Don't hang up your rattling horns just because it's late in the season. Every hunter surveyed has rattled in bucks during the last part of the season. "I think any buck close enough to hear rattling, no matter what part of the season it may be, will come in," said Mel Dutton. "Whether these bucks are responding from a sense of aggression or from curiosity doesn't matter. I just want to know that when I try a technique I'll have a good chance of seeing it work."

As long as there's a chance that an estrous doe remains in the woods, there's a chance that a buck will be looking for her. Bucks don't shed or cast their antlers until all does have been bred and are no longer entering estrus. Be forewarned, though, that bucks that have already been through the rigors of the rut may not have a tremendous amount of energy to expend on fighting. Many hunters seem to feel that success improves during the post-rut period with softer, less aggressive antler-rattling. Others, of course, feel the opposite.

No matter when you rattle or how, no words can quite describe the feeling that comes over you the first time a big buck comes at you, stiff-legged and proud, as you use your rattling horns in an attempt to beat him at his very own game!

13

A Scientific Approach to Antler Rattling

BY MICKEY W. HELLICKSON

Just as I pulled the shed antlers apart, I caught a glimpse of movement out of the corner of my eye. I slowly turned, but whatever had moved was no longer visible. I sat motionless for two to three minutes, staring intently in that direction. Although I saw nothing, I softly blew into the grunt tube hanging from a lanyard around my neck. At the sound of the grunt, a buck jerked his head up to listen to the sound.

The buck, a mature 9-pointer with tall tines and exceptionally heavy main beams, began trotting in my direction. He quickly moved to within thirty yards of me, then stopped and looked to his left. I looked in that direction, too. A second buck had also responded to my rattling. This buck, an 8-point, froze in his tracks when he noticed the first buck.

The two bucks then began sidestepping toward each other. Each bristled his hair to magnify his size. When neither buck seemed willing to back down from this initial encounter, each dropped his ears back along his neck. They continued to sidestep in half circles, one in front of the other, each with his head lowered and antlers extended. The larger buck finally called the smaller buck's bluff and charged him.

Mickey Hellickson's Texas research projects proved that loud rattling won't scare bucks away. Credit: Mickey Hellickson.

The smaller buck stood his ground for a few seconds and then the two locked antlers. But the larger buck quickly proved his dominance. The smaller animal broke free and raced back to the place where I had first sighted him.

I'd already had my fair share of excitement, but it wasn't over yet. Over the next twenty minutes, five additional bucks responded to my next two rattling sequences. At one point, three bucks stood within twenty-five yards of my makeshift blind under a mesquite tree. One buck walked past only five yards from where I was hiding.

Although two of these bucks were mature as well as within bow range, I was not hunting. Instead, this was part of my preliminary research toward a doctorate in wildlife biology at the University of Georgia.

Dr. Larry Marchinton, Dr. Charles DeYoung, and I had decided to examine buck breeding behavior as part of an intensive three-year telemetry study on movement patterns and behaviors of 130 different-aged radio-collared bucks. Bucks that respond to rattling offer a unique perspective to their breeding behavior. Whenever more than one buck responded, we were also hoping to estimate each one's relative dominance within the hierarchy. We decided to use rattling as a technique in our experiment, and would do so by measuring the responses of bucks to various rattling sequences. Rattling volume and length would be varied in each of four separate and distinctly different rattling sequences. Our goal was to determine which sequence, if any, would attract the greatest number of bucks.

Our rattling research was conducted at the Rob and Bessie Welder Wildlife Foundation Refuge north of Corpus Christi, Texas. This outdoor laboratory was an ideal study site for several reasons. The deer population at Welder is high, with one deer for every seven to eight acres. The buck-to-doe ratio is fairly balanced at 1:2 (one buck for every two does), and the age structure is balanced so that bucks of all ages are well represented in the population.

This meant we would have plenty of bucks of different age classes to study within the boundaries of the refuge's seventy-eight hundred acres. Seventeen thirty-foot-high observation towers located on the refuge provided another superb reason to conduct the study here. Each tower would be an ideal place from which to observe and videotape those bucks that responded to our rattling.

Most deer herds outside of south Texas are not well balanced in either age structure or buck-to-doe ratio. Most Georgia bucks, for instance, are between the ages of one and two. Relatively small landholding sizes, together with high hunter densities, limit the number of Georgia bucks that survive to the older ages commonly attained by Welder Refuge bucks. Overall buck responses to rattling will be lower in such areas simply because fewer bucks exist to respond to the rattling. We believe, however, that the rattling techniques most successful on the refuge will also work the best in other areas.

We devised four rattling sequences for this study. We randomly tested each of the sequences over three successive years during the pre-rut, rut peak, and post-rut periods. We began each sequence with a ten-minute segment that included one to three minutes of actual rattling followed by seven to nine minutes of silence. This sequence was repeated twice more during the next twenty minutes.

The four sequences were called SQ (short and quiet), SL (short and loud), LQ

To rattle in a fine Texas whitetail like this one is one of the most exciting hunting experiences imaginable. Credit: Mickey Hellickson.

Louder, more violent rattling imitates more closely the sounds made by two big, mature bucks battling each other for dominance. Credit: Stan Potts.

(long and quiet), and LL (long and loud). Each short sequence included one minute of rattling followed by nine minutes of silence. This pattern was repeated two times during the next twenty minutes for a total of three minutes of rattling in thirty minutes. Each long sequence included three minutes of rattling followed by seven minutes of silence. Again, this pattern was repeated twice during the next twenty minutes for a total of nine minutes of rattling in thirty minutes.

During the "quiet" sequences, we held our elbows close against our bodies to avoid making any loud antler clashes. But during "loud" sequences, we slammed the antlers together as violently as possible. During loud sequences we also broke nearby branches, rubbed bark, and scraped the ground to try to make as much "natural-sounding" noise as possible.

Two people then tested each rattling sequence at each of the seventeen observation stands. One person watched deer respond from the top of the stand, recorded data, and videotaped each buck with a camcorder. The second person rattled from the nearest clump of brush upwind of the stand. Both people were totally camouflaged and, when not rattling, remained motionless and quiet.

We estimated the age and gross Boone and Crockett Club (B&C) score of each buck that responded to the rattling. Prior to this study we viewed videos of bucks with known ages and known gross B&C scores. We also recorded the time each buck was first sighted, as well as in what direction from the stand the animal first appeared. Finally, wind speed and direction, temperature, and amount of cloud cover for each occurrence were also recorded.

The study began during the fall of 1992 and was completed in January 1995. We rattled 171 times. Sixty sequences were performed during the pre-rut, 60 during the peak of the rut, and 51 during the post-rut. Rut periods were determined based on harvest records of more than 900 does that were killed on the refuge during late winter. The pre-rut period was determined to be the three or four weeks prior to the rut's peak, while the post-rut was set at three to four weeks after the rut's peak.

One hundred eleven (111) bucks responded to our rattling. The two loud sequences (SL and LL) were performed 85 times and attracted 81 bucks. The two loud sequences attracted nearly three times as many bucks as the two quiet sequences (SQ and LQ). The two quiet sequences were performed 86 times and attracted only 30 bucks. The response rate was 95 percent for the loud sequences and 35 percent for the quiet sequences.

We found that as the volume of the rattling increased, the number of bucks responding also increased. Since the loud sequences carried farther, more bucks were able to hear the rattling. I believe that is why the response rate was higher for the loud sequences. Bucks also responded more quickly and more aggressively to loud sequences. On several occasions, bucks ran to within a few yards of the person rattling.

Louder, more violent rattling imitates the sounds made by two big, mature bucks battling each other for dominance and breeding privileges. Quieter rattling resembles the sparring sounds produced by

Mickey Hellickson studied the effects of rattling on whitetail bucks and now puts what he learned to use in his work for the legendary King Ranch in Texas. Credit: Mickey Hellickson.

two younger, less dominant animals. My favorite analogy is to compare the loud-volume rattling to a Mike Tyson–George Foreman heavyweight boxing match, while low-volume rattling is analogous to two teenagers having a light shoving match. Which fight would you most want to watch?

We found no difference among the response rates of the four sequences when they were combined according to the length of the rattling sequences. Short sequences (SQ and SL) had a rattling-to-bucks-attracted ratio equal to that of long sequences (LQ and LL). The short sequences were performed 88 times and attracted 57 bucks. The long sequences were performed 83 times and attracted 54 bucks.

When the data were grouped according to the timing of the rut, however, differences emerged. During the pre-rut, the LL (long-loud) sequence attracted the highest ratio of bucks. During rut's peak the SL (short-loud) sequence attracted the highest ratio of bucks. And during post-rut the SQ, LQ, and LL sequences attracted nearly the same ratio of bucks.

The majority of bucks responded to the rattling during the first ten-minute segment. The lowest response occurred during the third segment. However, the differences were not great. Forty-nine bucks (44 percent) responded during the first segment, 37 bucks (34 percent) during the second segment, and 25 bucks (22 percent) during the third segment. Someone who uses rattling as a hunting technique should consequently remain in the same location for at least thirty minutes to see all of the bucks that may respond.

When the data were grouped according to the period of the rut, we discovered that *the majority of bucks responded during the rut's peak.* The lowest response came during the pre-rut. During the rut's peak, 65 bucks responded to 60 sequences for a response rate of 108 percent. During the post-rut, 28 bucks responded to 51 sequences for a response rate of 55 percent. And during the pre-rut just 18 bucks responded to 60 sequences for a response rate of 30 percent.

The rut's peak is by far the best time to rattle if the goal is to rattle in large

Loud rattling is analagous to a Mike Tyson heavy-weight boxing match; soft rattling to two teenagers shoving each other. Which would **you** want to watch? Credit: Mickey Hellickson.

numbers of bucks. When rattling during the rut's peak, it's not unusual for more than one buck to respond at a time. Twice during this magic time of the whitetail's year, eight bucks responded during a single thirty-minute sequence.

Rattling during the rut's peak can be exciting, but the majority of bucks that will respond will be either young or middle-aged individuals. While a few mature bucks will respond, the overall response rate for mature bucks is lower during the rut's peak than during either the pre-rut or the post-rut. This is probably due to the fact that during the rut's peak, the majority of mature bucks fail to respond to rattling *because they are too busy tending, chasing, or trying to locate receptive does.*

In a well-balanced deer herd the vast majority of adult does enter estrus at about the same time. Mature bucks, because they are dominant over younger bucks, will do the majority of the breeding. During the rut's peak nearly all of these mature bucks are with does and therefore too preoccupied to respond to rattling. Younger, subordinate bucks, however, are usually not with does. These bucks are more available to respond to rattling during the rut's peak.

The highest mature buck response occurred during the post-rut, when an equal number of middle-aged and mature bucks responded to our rattling. During the post-rut most young and middle-aged bucks returned to bachelor groups. The mature bucks tended to be alone and were still actively seeking receptive does. Because mature bucks, more so than young or middle-aged bucks, were still actively engaged in breeding behavior, they responded in higher numbers to our rattling.

Since the majority of the adult does had been bred by the post-rut period, many mature bucks were searching for ever-fewer receptive does. Such does are often the yearlings and fawns that enter estrus later in the season than the adult does. Increased competition among mature bucks for the remaining receptive does stepped up their rattling response rate during the post-rut period.

When bucks were in bachelor groups, typically only one buck from the group responded to our rattling, even though all of the bucks could obviously hear the rattling. The buck that appeared to be dominant within the group was usually the buck that responded to the rattling.

The *second highest mature buck response occurred during the pre-rut,* even though most of the bucks responding at this time were youngsters. However, the overall response rate during this period was very low. Trophy hunters willing to sit and rattle for long periods without seeing many deer should try rattling during the pre-rut simply because of the increased likelihood that a mature buck will respond.

The highest number of bucks responded during morning rattling sequences. Sixty of the 111 bucks responding came in during the 64 sequences performed between 7:30 A.M. and 10:30 A.M. Thirty-three bucks responded during the 62 sequences performed in the afternoon. Only 18 bucks responded during the 45 sequences performed during midday.

When we examined this data according to the timing of the rut, the vast majority of bucks (83 percent) in the pre-rut period responded during morning rattling sequences. During both the rut's peak and the post-rut, a more balanced number of bucks responded during morning and afternoon rattling sequences.

As mentioned before, weather conditions were recorded each time we rattled. Not surprisingly, the highest number of bucks responded when wind speeds were lowest. As wind speeds increased, the number of bucks responding decreased, probably because fewer bucks were able to hear the rattling.

Sixty-seven of the 111 bucks (60 percent) that responded to our rattling were first sighted downwind of our stand. Bucks used the wind to determine what was making the rattling sounds. Mature bucks, surprisingly, were no more likely to approach from downwind than young or middle-aged bucks. Bucks seen upwind of the stand before rattling began would typically circle from their initial location to a downwind location as they approached the stand. Several bucks, however, did approach our stand from an upwind direction.

The highest number of bucks responded when cloud cover was 75 percent. Lowest responses occurred when there was no cloud cover. The highest response to rattling took place during periods of low to moderate temperatures. As temperature increased, the number of bucks responding to our rattling decreased.

In summary, loud rattling attracts more bucks than quiet rattling. Hunters shouldn't hesitate to slam antlers together as loudly as possible. Making as much additional natural noise as possible by breaking branches and kicking dirt and brush is also desirable. If hunters are not totally exhausted after completing the

As the volume of antler-rattling increases, so does the number of bucks responding, according to the results of a Texas study. Credit: Holly Fuller.

When someone is rattling for you, set up downwind of their rattling location so that if bucks circle in that direction, you'll be waiting for them. Credit: Bob Etling.

rattling sequence, they probably did not rattle loudly enough. Anyone who has had the good fortune to observe a true knockdown drag-out fight between two equally matched mature bucks realizes that it is almost impossible to make too much noise when trying to duplicate the sounds of such a battle.

During the silent periods between our rattling sequences we often used a grunt call to bring bucks in even closer or to temporarily halt bucks. During these silent periods we also simulated the sounds of a buck making a rub by rubbing the shed antlers on nearby tree trunks and branches. Bucks often lingered nearby after their initial response and often started making rubs of their own in response to our simulated rubbing.

The length of time someone rattles does not seem to be important. I would not rattle any longer than two to three minutes at a time simply to minimize the chances of a buck spotting you while you are thus engaged. I also would remain in the same location for at least thirty minutes to be certain that I saw any buck that might be late in responding.

Rattling during the rut's peak is the best way to see high numbers of bucks, but pre-rut and post-rut periods are better if the goal is to rattle in mature, trophy bucks. Although rattling can be productive during all hours of the day, mornings and afternoons are clearly the best times to rattle. Buck responses increase as cloud cover increases and as both wind speed and temperatures decrease.

Select stand sites where you have a clear downwind view, since bucks will typically approach from a downwind direction. Be sure not to neglect the upwind area, though, since a few bucks didn't seem to care about wind direction when responding. Rattle with a partner whenever possible. Have one person climb into a stand

and search for deer while the other person rattles. In our study the person rattling at ground level failed to see 63 of the 111 bucks that responded. If you plan to rattle alone, being in a stand should increase the number of bucks you will see even though these same bucks will have a better chance of spotting you, too. While I am sure that synthetic antlers can be used to attract bucks, I prefer to use the largest set of fresh shed antlers I can find.

I hope hunters will use our research to increase both their time afield and their success this fall. Antler-rattling is the most exciting

M.A.D. Calls Power Rattle® produces magnum sounds that carry a long distance. Credit: Outland Sports.

deer hunting technique there is. Not much in nature can compare to the sight of a big-racked, mature buck rushing into view in response to rattling, or having two bucks race in only to begin sparring with each another. The rush of adrenaline that surges through your body each time a buck runs in to your rattling horns seems to linger in your blood forever.

Table 1. Response rates of male white-tailed deer to four antler-rattling sequences by period of the breeding season and time of day during 1992-95 at the Welder Wildlife Refuge, San Patricio County, Texas (sample sizes in parentheses).

		PERIOD OF BREEDING SEASON			TIME OF DAY			NO. MALES RESPONDING
Seq.[a]	N	Pre-rut	Rut peak	Post-rut	0730-1030	1030-1330	1330-1630	(resp. rate)
SQ	43	0.13 (15)	0.29 (14)	0.43 (14)	0.50 (14)	0.36 (11)	0.06 (18)	12 (0.28)
SL	45	0.38 (16)	1.94 (16)	0.62 (13)	1.61 (19)	0.45 (11)	0.73 (15)	45 (1.00)
LQ	43	0.13 (15)	0.50 (16)	0.67 (12)	0.50 (16)	0.43 (14)	0.23 (13)	18 (0.42)
LL	40	0.57 (14)	1.50 (14)	0.58 (12)	1.00 (16)	0.27 (11)	1.38 (13)	36 (0.90)
Tot.	171	0.30 (60)	1.07 (60)	0.57 (51)	0.92 (65)	0.38 (47)	0.56 (59)	111 (0.65)

[a]*Rattling sequence abbreviations stand for short and quiet (SQ), short and loud (SL), long and quiet (LQ), and long and loud (LL).*

Table 2. Response rates of male white-tailed deer to antler-rattling by estimated age class and period of the breeding season during 1992-95 at the Welder Wildlife Refuge, San Patricio County, Texas (number of males responding in parentheses).

PERIOD OF BREEDING SEASON		ESTIMATED AGE CLASS			
	N	1.5-2.5	3.5-4.5	5.5+	TOTAL
Pre-rut	60	0.39 (7)	0.28 (5)	0.33 (6)	0.30 (18)
Rut peak	60	0.33 (21)	0.48 (31)	0.19 (12)	1.07 (64)
Post-rut	51	0.31 (9)	0.34 (10)	0.34 (10)	0.57 (29)
Total	171	0.33 (37)	0.41 (46)	0.25 (28)	0.65 (111)

Table 3. *Response rates (number in parentheses) of male white-tailed deer to different antler-rattling sequences by time segment and volume during 1992-95 at the Welder Wildlife Refuge, San Patricio County, Texas.*

TIME SEGMENT[b]	RATTLING SEQUENCE[a]						
	SQ	SL	LQ	LL	SQ+LQ	SL+LL	COMBINED
1	0.56 (5)	0.38 (17)	0.28 (5)	0.62 (16)	0.37 (10)	0.46 (33)	0.44 (43)
2	0.11 (1)	0.40 (18)	0.56 (10)	0.15 (4)	0.41 (11)	0.31 (22)	0.34 (33)
3	0.33 (3)	0.22 (10)	0.17 (3)	0.23 (6)	0.22 (6)	0.23 (16)	0.22 (22)
N	43	45	43	40	86	85	171

[a]*Abbreviations stand for short and quiet (SQ), short and loud (SL), long and quiet (LQ), and long and loud (LL) sequences.*
[b]*Time segment of response for 13 males not recorded.*

Table 4. *Response rates of radio-transmittered male white-tailed deer (N =18) to antler-rattling sessions performed within 200 meters during different periods of the breeding season and time of day during 1994-96 at the Faith Ranch, Dimmit and Webb Counties, Texas (number of sessions performed in parentheses).*

PERIOD OF BREEDING SEASON	N	TIME OF DAY			
		0730-1030	1030-1330	1330-1630	TOTAL
Pre-rut	5	0.0 (0)	0.50 (2)	0.33 (3)	0.40
Rut peak	14	1.00 (5)	0.67 (3)	0.67 (6)	0.79
Post-rut	14	0.75 (4)	0.75 (4)	0.83 (6)	0.79
Total	33	0.89 (9)	0.67 (9)	0.67 (15)	0.73

Table 5. *Estimated age and response (Y = yes, N = no) of 11 radio-transmittered male white-tailed deer to successive antler-rattling sessions performed during 1994-96 at the Faith Ranch, Dimmit and Webb Counties, Texas.*

MALE IDENTIFICATION NUMBER	ESTIMATED AGE	RATTLING SESSION			
		1	2	3	4
180	4.5	Y	Y		
602	4.5	N	Y		
1540	4.5	N	Y	Y	
1721	4.5	Y	Y		
1300	5.5	Y	Y		
1462	5.5	N	Y		
924	6.5	Y	Y		
1940	6.5	Y	Y	Y	Y
1326	7.5	Y	Y		
980	9.5	N	N		
1561	9.5	N	Y		

14

Rattling North and Rattling South

The rates of rattling success hunters can expect differ from one area to another. Yet there are plenty of places a hunter can go to tempt whitetails with the sounds of mock battle with a reasonable expectation of success. In Texas, ranches that offer hunting have such a variety of price ranges that most hunters can find several to accommodate their budget. Be aware, though, that on some ranches the average deer may sport only average racks at best. On the other hand, visiting a top South Texas ranch, one that can boast of balanced buck-to-doe ratios and balanced age classes of bucks, will set a hunter back some major dinero. Hill country ranches and outfits in the Texas panhandle, while often more reasonably priced, may provide just as much action but far fewer true trophy-caliber deer. It's the rare whitetail hunter who wouldn't be happy with one of the 125- to 150-point Boone and Crockett bucks it's possible to score on at one of these spreads. So little public land

Visiting a top South Texas ranch will set a hunter back some major dinero. Credit: R.E. Zaiglin.

exists in Texas that if you want to experience Texas rattling the way it's depicted in so many videos and TV shows, it's going to cost you. It may cost you quite dearly, too, depending on where in Texas you go.

Wonderful rattling opportunities exist in many other areas of the country as well. Eastern Colorado, if you stick it out by garnering an extra preference point each year you are unsuccessful in the draw or simply apply for points, has some truly tremendous whitetail hunting with excellent buck-to-doe ratios in many areas. Although much of eastern Colorado is private, hunters report good

Hunters can even book pack-in western hunts to experience the best of rattling, calling, and decoying for whitetails. Credit: Kathy Etling.

rattling success on Division of Wildlife landholdings as well as on the hundreds of thousands of private acres leased to the Division each year.

South Dakota and Wyoming are just two of the states with great whitetail hunting as well as plenty of walk-in areas, public easements, public hunting grounds, and cooperative agreements with private landowners. Many other states have similar arrangements, and these other states, quite possibly, will also provide some great rattling.

One state with which I'm extremely familiar is Montana. I've hunted whitetails there on many occasions. Montana is chock full of public land that's open to hunters. Although a Montana deer license is expensive, and you might not draw one, a do-it-yourself hunt where you can rattle in your own whitetails would be easy, particularly in the state's westernmost reaches. If you'd rather book with an outfitter, there are many excellent hunting outfits in the state. Two of the best—and ones with which I'm familiar—are Jerry Shively's Flat Iron Outfitters in Thompson Falls and Cheri DeBeau's Horizons West Outfitting in Dotson.

I wouldn't hesitate to plan a do-it-yourself whitetail hunt anywhere whitetails can be found. Idaho, Washington, and Oregon all have plenty of public land and a burgeoning population of whitetails. Be sure you check out winterkill rates before applying for licenses, though. If the winterkill was severe during any of the previous three, four, or even five seasons, deer numbers may be scarce, particularly trophy buck numbers.

Call the game department in the state where you would like to hunt. You already know the questions to ask: license fees; license application period; availability of public land; availability of state land and state-managed or leased land maps; buck-to-doe ratios; buck age class structure in the areas you are considering; the best trophy or quality areas; names of campgrounds or nearby motels; the type of weather you can expect at the time you'll be hunting; the approximate dates of the whitetail pre-rut period, the rut's peak, and the post-rut period.

To give you a better idea of what two different rattling hunts would be like in two completely different areas of the country, here is a comparison between a Texas hunt in the state's Hill Country and a hunt in Montana's rugged Cabinet Mountains, on the western slope of the Continental Divide.

TEXAS HILL COUNTRY

Several years ago, I hunted on a Texas Hill Country ranch owned by the Harrison Ranches and managed by Bob Zaiglin. Although this ranch has since been sold, it was there that I experienced, firsthand, the finest whitetail rattling of my life. My husband, Bob, and I hadn't gone to Texas to hunt the Harrison property. But when we discovered the outfitter with whom we'd booked had absconded with all the hunters' deposits—and his secretary—and that he'd hired no guides, we called Bob Zaiglin. Zaiglin kindly opened up this ranch even though it had been shut down for hunting only a few days previously. Zaiglin's guides were supposed to travel to another ranch in South Texas to help him there. Instead, they opened the ranch and its outbuild-

Bob tagged out the first morning of this Texas hunt after his guide rattled in several bucks to their position. Credit: Kathy Etling.

ings again, and rattled, called, and guided for us over the next three days.

A Texas whitetail hunt may be one of the most unforgettable experiences of your life. In some places whitetails are so thick they jump from behind mesquite bushes and bed down next to roads. You can't drive at night without seeing hordes in your headlight beams. Seeing so many deer boggles your mind as you recall hunts where, after days of futile waiting, you actually wondered if there were any deer left in your area.

Needless to say, with so many deer—and little hunting pressure, at least on well-managed ranches—the buck-to-doe ratio is right where it should be. Plenty of bucks are roaming the hills, ready to spar with willing contenders.

Experiencing rattling at this ranch was being exposed to a little bit of heaven. When I was there, finding a good buck was no problem. I just waited as deer charged in nearly every time my guide took me out. I was able to pick and choose from among more than ten bucks. Finally, in the misty grey light right after dawn on the third day of our hunt, a buck I knew was far better than any I'd seen before suddenly materialized through the fog. I shot and the buck fell.

Bob had tagged out the first morning when his guide rattled and several bucks raced in to their positions. He wasn't going to shoot, or so he said, but when one fine buck almost leaped on top of him, his reflexes responded and he fired. Bob's buck grossed a little over 125 Boone and Crockett points, while mine scored right at 130.

When we hunted the Hill Country we stayed in a trailer and cooked our own food. The largest deer taken that year went a little over 140 Boone and Crockett points. Although there were plenty of deer, there was little chance of taking a real trophy. Other Hill Country ranches advertise larger bucks, but the chance of taking an animal that exceeds 160 Boone and Crockett points on most Hill Country spreads is probably remote. The more a hunt costs, however, the more likely you will be to take a high-scoring buck. Otherwise, to simply sample the best rattling of your life, book with an operation that advertises its services as such. The rut usually peaks in the Hill Country during the first two weeks of November. We were there the first week in December. Previous groups of hunters had had hard hunting. Rattling wasn't working well, and calling was tough. But our flight arrived with a cold front. The next morning when we went out hunting, that cold front must have inspired the ranch's whitetails to be footloose and fancy-free and to be dead set on racing in to the sounds of rattling horns. On this occasion, Bob Zaiglin told us we were out hunting at the best possible time.

MONTANA'S WESTERN-SLOPE CONIFER FORESTS

Think of Montana and what most people imagine is an immense state of snow-capped mountain peaks. While Montana is often thought of as a great destination for trophy mule deer, only recently has it come into its own as one of the country's premier hunting spots for taking buster whitetails. White-tailed deer are so adaptable that they've moved into river bottoms and conifer forests all over the state. Believe me, little compares with a walk through forestland thick with Douglas firs that are so tall they almost block out the sun's rays. In these ancient northwestern rainforests, moss dangles eerily from the ends of tree branches, just as it does in a swamp. Tree limbs sometimes are woven so tightly together overhead you seem to be walking through a living tunnel. The forest's rugged,

Jerry Shively used M.A.D.'s Power Rattle® and the Grunt-Snort-Wheeze® to call this buck in for Kurt Kraft. Credit: Jerry Shively.

remote beauty and sweet conifer smell are reason enough to plan a visit. An even better reason, though, is to see the tremendous amount of big whitetail sign almost everywhere you look.

We hunted western Montana several times with the late Terry Kayser's outfit. Kayser, who was killed when he was thrown from his pickup truck while setting out deer stands, was a great whitetail guide. His operation has been taken over by

Easily accessed public hunting ground is plentiful in western Montana's conifer forests, and so are whitetails. Credit: Kathy Etling.

his wife, Cheri DuBeau, who now operates out of Dotson, Montana. Cheri outfits and guides for whitetails and other critters on Montana's eastern plains. She calls her outfit Horizons West Outfitters.

Sparring circles are commonplace in Montana. So are huge rubs, room-sized scrapes, and heavily used deer trails. Easily accessed public land is plentiful. Local hunters rarely stay out all day, so if you find a good place to hunt, you'll generally have it to yourself. In some areas, mainly those close to the roads, locals simply may park their vehicles, walk through the area, and then leave. If you can stay put, this extraneous activity doesn't seem to bother deer. I have noticed that Montana whitetails are more predictable—active—early and late in the day than deer I've hunted in other parts of the country.

Both Bob and I took good bucks in the 125 to 135 Boone and Crockett class while hunting western Montana near Noxon. Bob was being guided by Kayser when a big buck in the 150 to 160 Boone and Crockett class wandered by. From where Bob sat waiting in his tree stand, however, he wasn't able to get a clear shot at the buck. Kayser was rattling for Bob not far from where I was waiting when a dandy whitetail burst into the forest opening in front of me. I am not certain he was responding to the horns, but I wasn't about to give him a chance to race away to where Terry was rattling. I shot him and he dropped.

The next day, one of Kayser's guides rattled in a 160 Boone and Crockett class buck for another hunter. Although we were hunting during the peak of the rut,

I took this buck while on a rattling hunt to northwestern Montana's thick conifer forests. Credit: Bob Etling.

rattling was not yet producing fast and furious action. Temperatures were extremely frigid. On most days it would warm up to ten degrees below zero.

Kayser relied a great deal on his rattling skills. One of his favorite tactics was to skirt the edge of a recent clear-cut searching for fresh sign. We'd set up nearby, leaving an open area on our downwind side where deer would be able to dash out when lured by the sounds of Kayser's horns. Kayser always made certain that this downwind area was a place deer would naturally be drawn to. Several trails feeding into such an area were necessary for success. After we'd returned home, Kayser mailed us photos of the bucks his hunters had taken. Rattling always seemed to come into its own as soon as we boarded the plane for our return flight.

I wouldn't hesitate to return to Montana. Luckily, Jerry Shively outfits and hunts in an area not far from where we hunted with Kayser. Since Shively has a great reputation, he is the outfitter with whom I will book the next time I plan to hunt Montana's wild conifer forests.

The late Terry Kayser preferred to rattle and call from his location atop a slight knoll overlooking a recent clear-cut. Credit: Kathy Etling.

15

Getting Started Rattling

Does rattling sound like a hunting tactic you'd like to try, yet you're not quite sure where or how to begin? Does it make sense to wait until you get a deer this year, and then saw off its antlers? Perhaps you have a set of antlers from a deer you took last season, or before. Or, perhaps you can prevail upon someone you know for his or her next set of antlers. Should you wait until spring when you can go hunting for a nice, fresh set of matched sheds? And what's wrong with synthetics, anyway? Do they work as well as the real McCoy? Do sheds work as well or sound as realistic as fresh antlers? What about rattling devices? Surely whitetails must suspect that any "rattling" created by store-bought devices is phony, right?

Through the years I've interviewed many whitetail experts for the express purpose of learning what each believed was the most foolproof way of rattling in whitetails. While each expert's methods are amazingly similar to those of the others, and while even their preferred rattling sequences bear more than a passing resemblance to those of the other experts, and while the parameters they look for when they are preparing to set up are not that much different, it's clear that each of our

Not exactly a rattle bag, Lohman's Model 43 Dynamite Rattler® produces the type of sound a curious buck will want to investigate. Credit: Outland Sports.

experts has definite opinions about what another hunter should do and use to create the most realistic-sounding mock buck battles possible.

SYNTHETIC, REAL, OR SOMETHING ELSE?

I've used both synthetic antlers and real antlers, and I honestly have never been able to tell much difference between the two. I've rattled in deer using both types. If I were asked to put my feelings about the two antler types into words, I suppose I would say that real antlers sound more solid when clashed together. The synthetics I used seemed to be slightly higher-pitched, and they seemed to reverberate a bit more. I can't truthfully say this reverberation is a negative, though. The sound from the synthetic antlers might actually have carried farther because of it than the sound

Although Bob Zaiglin prefers to use fresh sheds to rattle in bucks, he has done quite well with synthetics, too, as evidenced by the buck in this photo. Credit: Bob Zaiglin.

from my real rattling horns. Were I to go rattling at this very moment, whether I would grab the synthetics or authentics would be a moot point. In fact, I'm so impressed with a few of the rattling devices I've recently seen that I just might use them instead. But more about them later.

Some hunters swear that nothing sounds like a fresh set of rattling horns. But if you bring antlers inside at the end of each day and rarely expose them to the elements, even a twenty-year-old set will sound identical to a set removed from a buck's head today. To get that so-called "fresh" sound, some hunters soak their sheds in water, no matter how new they may be, for several hours. Others rub their sheds down with petroleum jelly to seal in freshness. Still other experts prefer oiling or waxing their sheds with a scent-free product to preserve that "just-off-the-buck" degree of freshness.

Bob Zaiglin uses a large set of real antlers for his rattling horns. Mickey Hellickson looks for the heaviest, freshest pair of shed antlers he can find. "I've been using some massive horns lately," Hellickson said. "I cut off the brow tines and then shaved the surrounding area smooth to the beam so they're easy to grip. A large set of horns produces the greatest volume. My study revealed that volume is more important than any other factor to rattling success. The higher the volume, the greater the distance over which it will be heard. The greater the distance, the more bucks that will hear it. And if more bucks hear your rattling, more bucks are bound to respond."

Although he usually prefers using a Rattle-Box®, Jerry Shively used real antlers to lure this fine Montana buck in for Mark Easterling. Credit: Jerry Shively.

According to Peter Fiduccia, not only will smaller antlers rattle in bucks of all sizes, they're easier to pack around. Credit: Fiduccia Enterprises.

Proponents of using real antlers include other successful hunters, too, experts like Peter Fiduccia, Jay Cassell, and Jim Holdenried. "Using smaller antlers won't discourage smaller bucks from investigating," Fiduccia pointed out. "And smaller antlers are far easier to pack around." Cassell agrees. "I want to imitate the sound of smaller bucks fighting," he said. "By doing so, I hope to lure in a larger buck who's hoping to whip both their [smaller bucks'] butts."

Fiduccia noted that synthetic antlers usually don't have to be modified for safety's sake, but that if you don't modify real antlers you could be hurt in an accident while pulling them into your stand, climbing hills, or negotiating bluffs. "Always be cautious when using real antlers in a pub-

Modify real antlers before using them to rattle by cutting off the ends of tines; otherwise you could be seriously injured—or worse—if you fell on them while walking or climbing into a stand. Credit: Kathy Etling.

lic hunting area," he warned. Fiduccia modified his set of smaller antlers by trimming off sharp tines and drilling a hole through each base where he threaded a lanyard.

"I use real antlers for the most part," said Jim Holdenried. "I prefer a set of sheds the would score about 125 Pope and Young points. Smaller rattling horns don't do it for me, particularly not for more intense, 'hard' rattling sequences." Holdenried also removes sharp tines to keep them from cutting or jabbing his hands. "I've used a rattling bag, but I have better luck with real antlers," he concluded.

"I've used real antlers, synthetic antlers, and rattling bags," noted M.R. James. "I like actual antlers, real and synthetic, because of the sounds produced when I tickle the tines together or really grind the beams. Artificial antlers don't sound as true to me, but the deer don't seem to mind or notice. My favorite set of horns is a pair of sheds I found that score about 135 Pope and Young points."

For ease when packing into a hunting area and climbing into tree stands, James says it's hard to beat a rattle bag. "Rattle bags may have their drawbacks, but they're sure handy to tote," he said. "I prefer rattling bags full of ceramic dowels rather than wooden dowels. Ceramic just seems to work better, especially in wet weather when wood may swell and lose its crisp tones."

"I've heard it all, and the best sounds are produced by real antlers or good quality synthetics," said Gary Roberson of Burnham Brothers Game Calls in Menard, Texas.

"I won't even go into the woods without my Lohman's Rattle-Box®," stated Brad Harris. "It's so compact, it easily fits inside my fanny pack. A set of rattling horns is just so inconvenient and difficult to pack. I'd be so tired of dragging them around with me, or finding a place to hang them on my stand, which I hated doing, that I'd just leave them at home. That's where the Rattle-Box® has really paid off. I never go into the woods without it. The Rattle-Box® has enhanced my hunting and increased both the numbers of deer I've rattled in and the numbers I've harvested by rattling since I started using it. In fact, I took my very best deer while using

A nylon mesh rattle bag containing ceramic dowels is both easier and safer to carry than antlers, and sounds authentic enough to fool rutting bucks. Credit: M.R. James.

that little box. Better yet, I never forget to take it because it stays in my fanny pack." Harris believes the Rattle-Box® works so well because it is higher-pitched and crisper-sounding than most rattling horns. "I think that contributes to its success," he said.

Jerry Shively is another Rattle-Box® advocate. "You can use it with one hand, muffle it or mute it by rattling it against your leg, and it's much safer to pack around than real horns," he said. "Hunters don't realize how dangerous even a small set of rattling horns can be. Not only will you skin your knuckles while you're rattling,

you could impale yourself if you fell on them. Climbing into a stand with them is dangerous, too, even if you stash them in your daypack. If you fell onto any set of antlers, even if they've been stowed in your daypack, they could easily run you through. Walking through the woods with rattling horns can be a nuisance, too. They're always getting hung up if you sling them over your shoulder. I think

Lohman's Brad Harris won't venture into the woods without his Rattle-Box® (pictured here). Credit: Outland Sports.

Mick Hellickson uses the largest set of real antlers he can find to produce the loud rattling that attracts big bucks like this one. Credit: Mickey Hellickson.

I'll just stick with the Rattle-Box® or M.A.D. Calls' Power Rattle®. The Power Rattle® works well when you want to make a lot of racket."

A small sample of the great products on today's market would have to include the Primos Buck Board® deer call for both rattling and grunting, Sure-Shot's Rattlin' Antlers®, the Super Slam Rattling Bag® from H.S. Calls, Lohman's Dynamite Rattler®, Lohman's Model 36 Double Rattling System® (a.k.a. the Rattle-Box), and the Power Rattler® from M.A.D. Calls. Don't limit yourself to these choices, though. Any game call manufacturer is bound to have a good assortment of rattling products from which to choose.

NSF'S UPWIND RATTLING SYSTEM

Although I've yet to use one, I've heard great things about Norm French's Upwind Rattling System® (NSF Productions, 7672 Tidemill Rd., Hayes, VA 23072, phone 804-642-9529; www.deerrattling.com). When French, the device's inventor, heard that I was writing this book, he sent me a slew of trophy deer photos taken by hunters using his system. To use French's wireless remote-controlled rattling system, simply position it well upwind of the selected stand site. The system is controlled by a trigger on the radio controller. Pull the trigger and the resulting radio signal activates the device from up to seventy yards away. The Upwind Rattling System® is light years ahead of earlier, string-controlled systems. Although somewhat bulky, this waterproof system is light enough to carry in a daypack. The handy voltage indicator meter keeps tabs on battery levels so dead batteries should never victimize hunters on days when deer are responding well. The system runs on twelve AA batteries. French submitted his system for review to Virginia's Department of Game and Inland Fisheries. According to the department's Major Joseph K. Cooke, since the device features neither recordings nor electronic amplification, it is legal in Virginia. Although it is probably legal in other states and provinces, check either with French or with the game department in the state where you plan to hunt before buying an Upwind Rattling System®.

Steve Atkins, a Virginia hunter, was scouting a new piece of hunting ground not much past noon when he jumped a big buck along a ridgetop. The buck had been sniffing about a line of scrapes. Atkins, a friend of French's, called him to tell him about the buck he'd spooked. French suggested that he try one of his new systems, and Atkins did just that, setting up near the scrapeline, downwind of where the buck had been jumped. Thirty to forty minutes before dark, Atkins began using the system. (Although he was using the line-operated system, the effect is the same). He rattled for about sixty seconds, then stopped. Two minutes later, Atkins saw something on the opposite ridge. The hunter could tell it was a deer, but he could not see any antlers. He pulled the line for a few more moments to produce another short rattling sequence. The deer immediately headed toward the rattling, circling downwind of the rattler, which was upwind of where he was waiting. When the deer ventured to within fifty yards of him, Atkins knew it was the same big buck he'd jumped earlier. By the time the deer stopped to scent-check the wind, he was just twenty yards away and standing broadside.

Steve Atkins' big buck had a twenty-three and one-half-inch outside spread. One of the buck's brow tines measured eight inches long, and the other was nine inches. Atkins did not have his buck scored because he hunts for himself, not for others. Judging from the photo he sent to French, I'd guess his buck is in the high 140s, not bad for an hour's work on a piece of ground he'd never seen before. French has fielded letters and calls from successful hunters from all over the United States and Canada.

OTHER RATTLING "TRICKS"

Somewhat in the same vein, M.R. James will sometimes tie a rope to his rattling horns, then tie the rope to a bush or tree below his stand. He then lowers the antlers on this "haul" line so that they are resting in the bush or next to the sapling. When he jerks on the line, the antlers thrash about in the brush where they might attract a nearby deer.

One thing all of these hunters have in common is a high degree of originality and an ability to take tricks they've learned about and make them their own.

A rattle bag can be rolled against a tree trunk – or your leg—to create the sound of sparring bucks with a minimum amount of movement, as Wilbur Primos demonstrates. Credit: M.R. James.

"Some hunters will fasten a string to a sapling, then pull on it from their stand, high above, to create the illusion of a buck rubbing the sapling," Peter Fiduccia said. Fiduccia sometimes fills a third of a plastic zipper lock bag with fish tank gravel. He places the gravel-laden bag inside another plastic bag. He then makes a small hole through each bag, runs a long string through both, and attaches the bags to his ankle. In this manner he's able to rattle with his foot, with a minimum of movement, while he's waiting in his tree stand. As he rattles, he moves his foot back and forth to drag the bag over the undergrowth and forest litter beneath his stand. "This is just another way of setting the stage so that any buck listening will think a battle is going on,"

he said. "It provides a realistic sound, right down to the 'hooves' moving back and forth across the forest floor."

RATTLING FROM GROUND BLINDS

The argument about whether tree stands or ground blinds are better continues to rage among rattling experts. "I prefer ground blinds," said Fiduccia. "Ground blinds work better for breaking up your profile, or as something easy to hide behind. I've often made my ground blinds from stacks of cedar trees."

In agricultural areas, many hunters who rely on rattling report excellent success when set up behind a blind made of straw bales. The advantage here is that the blind is fairly stable, even during high winds, and it provides a great screen for hiding hunter movement. Being able to mask movement is vitally important to trophy bowhunters like Judy Kovar of Illinois.

SCOUTING FOR SPARRING CIRCLES

"What I'm looking for is an open spot that's surrounded by fairly heavy cover," said Jerry Shively. "The places that seem to work the best are those where I've watched bucks fighting over the years. Bucks seem to have very definite locales where they prefer to fight. You can identify one of these spots by the sparring circle evident on the ground. I've hunted this one piece of property for more than twenty years and I know all the bucks' favorite places to fight." As its name suggests, a sparring circle is a large, round area where you can tell animals were trampling the ground beneath their hooves. Grass may be flattened within this circle, or the earth may be mostly bare because bucks have fought there for many years. Brush and undergrowth may be battered and beaten, too. The ground may also reveal paw marks and antler gouges. The more such sign you discover in a particular location, the better your chances will be of rattling in a buck there.

"I don't really return to certain rattling locations per se," Bob Zaiglin said. "But I get these vibrations about a spot. I know, everybody laughs, but as I'm walking through the brush I really start feeling like *This is an area that I'd be in if I were a buck.* Or, *Man, this looks really deery. Look at all those fresh scrapes.* So, I move on to step two of my process: looking for a good place to station both my hunter and myself. I want to be in a spot where I can see in both directions. I really believe I rattle up more deer due to confidence than technique. I'm so confident when I think I've found a good spot that I'm almost positive that's why I've had such fantastic success." Zaiglin has rattled up whitetails everywhere he's hunted, even back home in Pennsylvania. In Texas, he's rattled up several hundred deer that have been taken by his hunters, and hundreds more that his hunters have passed up.

ONE RATTLER, TWO HUNTERS

Shively's favorite rattling tactic, when guiding hunters, is to position two hunters on stands two or three hundred yards apart. He then splits the distance between them and rattles. "My hunters usually see deer, but I won't," he said. "Since they're elevated they have a better view of the terrain. Since hundreds of yards separate them, one may see one buck while the other sees a different buck. I once had two hunters shoot at two different bucks at the same exact moment. None of us were aware of it until we got together afterward. '*I* shot,' said the one. 'No, *I* shot,' said the other. My head started spinning, but then I found out they'd both scored on really nice whitetails."

RATTLING FROM TREE STANDS

If you decide to do your solo rattling from a tree stand, choose a tree with a trunk that is large enough to hide you, should the need arise. "It's a good idea to always rattle from the side of the tree where you do not expect the buck to appear," Peter Fiduccia said. "Natural cover to break up your outline is a must. It's particularly helpful beneath your feet so that any deer looking upward will be unable to make out your human silhouette." Deer peering upward are a fact of life when rattling or calling emanates from the treetops rather than from down on the ground. You can sometimes mitigate that effect by rattling from the sides of steep hollows where the sound appears to be coming from farther up the hillside, even if you are in a tree stand. The risk in this maneuver is that a deer may come in higher up on the hillside, be on the same level as you, and be able to see you in the tree stand. "Another good ploy is to position yourself where you can whack your rattling horns against a leafy limb," Fiduccia said. "This simulates the sounds of a buck thrashing its rack in a bush or sapling. Don't be afraid to thwack the rattling horns against the tree's trunk, either. Doing so provides an even greater degree of realism."

A rattle bag can be rolled against a tree trunk – or your leg – to create the sound of sparring bucks with a minimum amount of movement, as Wilbur Primos demonstrates. Credit: M.R. James.

"I find it hard to get deer to commit to coming in when I'm waiting in a tree stand in an area where deer can see quite well," Don Kisky said. "One of my favorite tricks is to make them think that the rattling is going on just over the hill. Whenever deer can see well, they become extremely cautious. That's why I like rattling from the edge of a bluff or creek where it's difficult for them to circle downwind of me.

RATTLING SEQUENCES

"I'll always make a snort-wheeze before I start rattling," Kisky continued. "If I see two bucks in the distance, I'll use the snort-wheeze, too. When I rattle, I really

Don Kisky keeps his rattling sequences loud but short to pull in trophy bucks like this to within bow range. Credit: Don and Kandy Kisky.

go at it. I think it's impossible to make too much noise when you rattle during the rut. Of course, when you're busy flailing around rattling, it's easy for a buck to spot you. That's one reason I keep my sequences loud, *but short.* My normal sequence lasts just ten seconds. If you rattle too long, bucks may sneak in and spot you and you'll never even know they were there."

Don Kisky likes to play with a big buck's mind by making him think that the rattling—the "fight"—they hear is going on just over the hill. Credit: Don and Kandi Kisky.

Kisky has used rattling to take many of his biggest deer. These include bucks that were gross-scored at 197, 181, 179, 177, 171, 167, and 161, among others. To say that Kisky knows what he's doing with a set of rattling horns in his hand would be a major understatement.

"I do all my hard rattling from mid- to late October," Jim Holdenried said. "Prime time for me is from the eighteenth to the thirty-first and perhaps during early November, particularly if the action is somewhat dead. Those are the days when you might not be ready and suddenly, here they come at a dead run!"

"One thing you have to know about antler-rattling is that it's as much about what you're feeling as anything else," added Bob Zaiglin. "Say a buck is two hundred yards away—or maybe you only think he is. If you have the feeling that you are close to the buck of a lifetime and you want to bring him in, try just tickling the antlers at first. This is a great tactic to use during the cold, early morning hours following a warm spell. Some people like to clash those antlers together as hard as they can, but I can't help but think that this type of noise might inhibit deer from coming in. It's only on the second or third time I grind those antlers together that I begin to get louder and enhance my sequence so that it appears to any buck that may be listening that the ground and the brush are being torn apart by those 'two battling whitetails.' And that's what I want him to think."

"I'll start rattling right before the rut begins, around the first of November," Jerry Shively said. "We'll start with some light rattling and some get-acquainted grunts, nothing dominant or too loud. Our deer aren't yet fighting at this time. They aren't acting really aggressive. When you see them sparring, they're still just tickling

Kandi Kisky has taken deer as large as some of husband Don's, including this massive 170+ whitetail shot with a muzzleloader. Credit: Don and Kandi Kisky.

their horns. I rattle just enough to work on their curiosity."

Shively doesn't get serious about his rattling and grunting until about a week before the rut starts on November 15. "You can make a tremendous amount of noise out there if you're trying to mimic two deer seriously going at it," he said. "There is no way a single hunter can make enough noise to accurately duplicate it."

M.R. James begins his rattling sequences with buck grunts, and then starts raking a tree trunk with his antlers. "I start off slow, as if the 'bucks' are merely sparring," he said. "I'll mesh the antlers for several periods of ten to fifteen seconds with soundless intervals between the sequences. I let the action build in intensity as the 'fight' progresses, with prolonged grinding of the beams and clicking of the tines, but with occasional pauses. I seldom rattle for more than 90 to 120 seconds per sequence. I conclude by 'tickling the tines' one final time, then finishing off with three or four aggressive buck grunts."

As a bowhunter, James will seldom move on to a different stand site. Instead, he may rattle from the same stand site six to eight times during a four-hour period to attract any bucks that may be traveling through his hunting area.

"Do I vary my rattling sequences?" asked Brad Harris, rhetorically. "Yes, quite a bit. The way in which I vary my sequences intrigues hunters. I tell them that you have to get in tune with your surroundings. I rattle the way I feel, the way the weather makes me feel. On some days, it just seems like deer should be more responsive, so I'll rattle or call more often. On doldrum days, I'm more laid back, quieter, and I don't rattle as much."

One of Harris's typical rattling sequences will begin with one loud aggressive grunt in every direction. "That should get the buck's head up," Harris said. "He's now listening, so I pause a few seconds, then start rattling as though one buck has just confronted another, and then the battle begins. I rattle five to thirty seconds, just swiping the antlers together, and then I'll pause, listen, and wait, because you never know if a buck is just over the next ridge. I'll rattle, then pause, then rattle perhaps two times more while pausing and listening. I'll rattle, wait, and then maybe grunt. Even after I've quit rattling, I'll probably make a grunt every now and then in case the buck is coming but I'm unable to see him."

If it's windy, Harris will rattle loudly and more often. "You have to adjust to conditions," he said. "If I'm in an area where I'm able to see long distances, then

I'll probably rattle less. Cold, clear conditions usually mean rattling will be more productive than on warm or hot days."

Peter Fiduccia explained every detail he puts into his rattling sequences. "First, I find a good spot where I can set up," he said. "I'll start by dribbling some buck urine around the area. I then do my best to create the illusion I'm after. This means stomping my feet, stepping hard upon leaves and twigs, adding some aggressive grunts, hitting my horns against tree limbs, and then slamming the antlers against the ground or tree trunks. I'll do this for fifteen seconds, thirty seconds, forty-five seconds, or even an entire minute. I'll then pause to look and listen in all directions. You must stay alert. If you think it might work, shake a nearby sapling or stomp on the ground to entice any nearby whitetails into showing themselves."

Fiduccia then waits between fifteen and twenty minutes before rattling again. "The next time I'll wait thirty minutes," he said. "Some people move to a new area, but I prefer to stay put. Should a buck appear, try always to be positioned in a place where you're able to shake a sapling or grunt or do both. If you are unable to do this, then try to have a rattling buddy along who can. This simple motion or call may be the last nail in that buck's coffin. What you do is provide him with one final motive to rush in and see what's going on."

Fiduccia warns hunters who are new to the rattling game to remain at high alert for any sign of a nearby buck, including the sound of a snort or grunt, the slight movement of legs beneath nearby brush, sunlight glinting off an antler tine, a silhouette where you don't remember seeing one before. "Deer are shifty critters," he said. "Now you see them, now you don't."

THE BEST TIMES TO RATTLE?

Although all of our experts would rattle all day long, their consensus "best time" was early morning, particularly one that was frosty cold and windstill. Bob Zaiglin qualified his choice when he said, "I've rattled all day long, for many years. It doesn't matter where you might be rattling from—if it's not close to a deer you'd like to take, it will be for naught. Sunup is my favorite time to rattle, but you must be woods-wise enough to figure out where the buck you want is hiding, then decide how best to try to rattle him in. If you can get to within five hundred yards of where that is without disturbing him, your rattling and calling techniques will be perhaps 60 percent effective. If you can close that distance to two hundred yards, those techniques may increase in effectiveness to as much as 90 percent."

"I learned one time-management lesson the hard way," added M.R. James. "I owned this one place in the Indiana suburbs that had some great whitetail hunting. One morning I went in early and climbed up into my stand. It was still dark when I began rattling. I heard something, looked down, and saw a buck. It walked right under my stand. The only problem was it was still dark. I could see antlers, but it wasn't legal shooting time yet. I learned the hard way not to rattle too early or too late. It's difficult passing up a nice buck that you rattled in fair and square because you couldn't wait until it was time to shoot."

"Without a doubt, the first ten minutes of light and the last ten minutes are the very best times to rattle," said Don Kisky.

Jerry Shively reports having better rattling luck in the afternoons and evenings. Even so, he admitted, "There are days when I can't do anything wrong—but there are just as many days when I can't do anything right."

FROM WHICH DIRECTION WILL BUCKS COME?

Mickey Hellickson's Texas research study confirmed that bucks are more likely to approach a rattler's position from the downwind side. Surprisingly, as he stated in the previous chapter, mature bucks were no more likely to approach from downwind than younger animals were. A few bucks from all age classes broke precedent to come in from directions other than downwind. "I've rattled bucks in from all directions," said Bob Zaiglin. "They don't always come in from downwind. What will happen, though, is that the buck will usually circumvent the rattler to come in from the downwind side. That's why rattling with a team works so well.

"Say you have a north wind," he said, to illustrate his point. "One person is in a stand in a mesquite tree that's south of where the other person is rattling from the ground. The person in the stand to the south of the rattler will always see far more deer than the one who is rattling."

"I've rarely had bucks come rushing in except in Texas," M.R. James said. "The bucks I rattle in in other places usually approach my position slowly, their ears back, hair standing up on the backs of their necks, walking stiff-legged, and posturing. I've watched plenty of these bucks raking trees or brush with their antlers as they came closer to my stand. I've arrowed several that swaggered in and stopped directly beneath my tree. I really believe deer can pinpoint the exact location of any 'buck fight' they hear. It's a big thrill for me to rattle or grunt a good buck close enough to shoot at with a bow."

To which, I'm sure, the rest of our experts would add a fervent "Amen."

When rattling or calling, stay alert to any buck that might walk in stiff-legged and posturing, just waiting to work over a sapling with its antlers. Credit: Bob Etling.

16
Rattling: What To Expect

Okay, you're out in the field. You've started rattling. What should you expect to happen, and when?

To begin, remember that deer don't *only* vocalize. Nor do they merely tickle, mesh, or clash their antlers together in the sounds of battle, mock or authentic. Deer will also stomp their hooves to communicate with each other. Whether the stomping emanates from a doe that's trying to warn her youngsters or a buck reluctant to continue on the path it is taking, foot-stomping provides not only an aural warning via other deer's ears, but also a visual warning during periods of high winds. In the latter case, nearby deer may be able to see an agitated animal better than they can hear it.

Foot-stomping imparts a chemical message as well. A deer's hooves emit a pheromone—a chemical message—from the *interdigital gland,* a scent gland between the two parts of the deer's cloven hoof. A whitetail stomping on a trail, for example, is providing an olfactory warning to any deer that may follow that something wasn't quite right here. Whether it was the scent of a human hunter carried from afar or something along the trail that seemed out of place and, therefore, potentially dangerous, the interdigital gland does its work subtly and swiftly. Many hunters sweeten mock scrapes and mock rubs with commercial interdigital gland

Jay Cassell with a buck he rattled out of some heavy mesquite brush on a ranch near San Antonio, Texas. Credit: Jay Cassell.

Create the total illusion when rattling from the ground by using your antlers to rake trees, leaves, and brush and to thump the ground like a buck's hooves. Credit: M.R. James.

Avoid moving your rattling setup too frequently, because thick undergrowth can work to a whitetail's advantage and you might not see a deer approaching. Credit: Don and Kandi Kisky.

scent or with hooves frozen and preserved from previous seasons. Should a deer you decline to shoot discover your rattling setup and start stomping its foot because it suspects a human is nearby, your best recourse is to relocate. Any other deer that comes by will immediately be alert to the presence of danger. Move, but do so carefully. Don't stand up, believing that you haven't rattled in a buck, and then be startled to see a white tail bobbing off into the distance.

If an agitated buck races in looking for another buck, his pawing and stomping of the ground will not leave a negative olfactory warning for other deer. Although his hoof-stomping provides an auditory signal, if an olfactory threat or agonistic signal is communicated as well, biologists, at least as far as I know, are unaware of it. Should a buck race in and stomp prior to a "fight" that never materializes—and you miss your chance to take him—no olfactory warning will be given unless the buck

realizes that a human is there. If it fails to do so, you might even be able to rattle him in again. Should he run off unaware that a human was nearby, there's no reason for you to leave.

Moving your rattling location may work wonders, especially if there's a lot of great hunting ground and few other hunters, as in much of Texas and the West. Such a strategy may prove less lucrative in the East, Midwest, and South, where hunter densities are much higher. In states as scattered as Michigan, Missouri, Pennsylvania, and Georgia, staying in one place—even all day—is preferable unless you are hunting a large tract of private land with few other hunters. One reason to avoid moving your rattling setup too often is that thick under-

In most states, rattling from one place all day is preferable to moving, as archer Holly Fuller demonstrates. Credit: Holly Fuller.

growth can work to a whitetail's advantage by camouflaging its presence until the last possible moment. If you move and reveal your position, you're aiding the whitetail's cause. Stay put. Let *him* make the mistakes.

For every buck that bursts onto the scene in response to your rattling sequences, probably four or five others choose to take a wait-and-see attitude and remain hidden. These deer may be subdominants, their native caution holding them back to see what will transpire next. Or perhaps a dominant buck is biding his time, waiting for the best moment to charge into view. It's always possible that no buck has heard your rattling, but a buck is heading your way as you prepare to give up for the day. Should you leave the stand and risk spooking a possibly responsive

Successful rattlers like Iowa's Don Kisky agree that the one quality that will most help you succeed is patience. Credit: Don and Kandi Kisky.

buck? Granted, there are no guarantees that this theoretical "buck" will ever make its appearance. But it might also be the buck you bag.

A RATTLER'S MOST IMPORTANT QUALITY

Should you decide to give calling, rattling, and decoying a go, you must also work on the one quality that will help you succeed more than any other when using these techniques: patience. The more you rattle from any given stand, the more likely a buck will eventually investigate. Perhaps his curiosity finally maxes out. Perhaps he just traveled into hearing range. Perhaps he's finally bred the doe he was following, and he's looking for another. When he hears the sound of antlers clashing, he might think the "fight" is being waged over another hot doe and come storming in. Or maybe you've finally agitated him beyond all reckoning and he stampedes in to find out what in tarnation is going on. In any event, patience is a crucial part of the art of deceiving whitetails.

WHERE TO RATTLE?

If conditions are right, whitetail bucks—unlike turkey gobblers—will come in to almost any location. Bucks responding to rattling will race up hills and down, may storm across creeks, and will even race across bare fields, so great is their desire to view or participate in the "fight" now underway.

"I've experienced some of my best November rattling in eastern Colorado, along the Arkansas River," M.R. James said. "At this one ranch you could see deer at such a great distance you could actually watch as bucks ran across pastures or hopped

Bob Zaiglin team-rattles by setting up in a thicket that will disguise his movement well upwind of where his hunter is positioned in a tree stand. Credit: Bob Zaiglin.

M.R. James's whitetail hunting tools: rattling antlers, a rattle bag, and deer calls. He won't leave home without 'em. Credit M.R. James.

fences to reach the rattling. That was some of the most exciting rattling I've ever experienced."

Don't be reluctant to set up anywhere you feel there's a halfway decent chance of rattling in a buck. Just be sure there is a good place for you to hide until you or your hunting partner is able to make the shot.

Early in the season, rattle in areas where you have seen bucks moving about in their bachelor groups. Look for core areas where early rubs have been made on small, insignificant saplings and where platter-sized scrapes roughly mark the animal's semi-territorial boundaries.

As the primary rut approaches, remember that bucks will be traveling. They may return to core areas regularly, but they are more likely to check in only occasionally. No matter what size a buck's normal home range may be, once the rut commences, all home range bets are off. While some bucks may remain true to their annual home range, others may look for estrous does elsewhere. Some radio-collared bucks have been tracked thirty miles away from their annual home ranges, although this is the exception, not the rule. Don't waste your time targeting a particular buck that may no longer be in the area. Instead, set up close to an area frequented by one or more doe family groups. Whenever does are in estrus, bucks won't be far away.

STAY ALERT

Once when M.R. James was hunting in Illinois he set up his stand in a point of woods where three trails converged. "I climbed into my stand and began rattling," he said. "Now, I could see for a long way in every direction. I mustn't have been looking in the right place, because all of a sudden I saw something move out of the corner of my eye. This buck must have run all the way across the corn field in front of me without me seeing it. When I did, the buck was only fifty yards away. He walked in, licking his nose, and I shot him."

CAN YOU RATTLE TOO MUCH?

Too much of a good thing can sometimes work against you. That may be as true of rattling as it is of partaking of too many boilermakers on a Saturday night. Don Kisky believes too much rattling during past hunting seasons has worked against him more recently. "I've rattled so much in the past that I honestly think the five- and six-year-old bucks on our farm have become conditioned to the sound. Older bucks don't respond as readily as they once did. Yet I can hunt a farm where deer aren't used to the sound and rattle one right in. I've rattled in most of my larger bucks, but now, when they get to within seventy or eighty yards, I'll rely on grunting to bring them the rest of the way in. Three of my five largest whitetails have been grunted or rattled in."

17

Advanced Antler-Rattling

PART 2 OF A RESEARCH STUDY

CONDUCTED BY MICKEY W. HELLICKSON

Wham! I hit the shed antlers together as hard as I could and then quickly pulled them apart. Again, I slammed the antlers together with all of my force. This time I kept the antlers entwined and twisted the tines and beams against each other for several seconds. I repeated this several times. Two minutes into the rattling sequence I noticed movement and a flash of gray out in front of me.

The deer stopped out of sight behind a thick clump of mesquite trees. I continued to rattle, but tried to shield all of my movements from the deer. After several anxious moments, the deer stepped into view. His rack was huge. The main beams were over twenty inches apart and carried eleven typical points. The tines were also very tall and symmetrical. The only flaw, if there was one, was his lack of mass.

The buck had been sighted and photographed earlier, during the fall deer survey, by ranch owner Stuart Stedman. Based on these photographs and my sighting, we estimated the buck's gross Boone and Crockett Club score to be in the 160s. The only reason this buck was still alive was because of his age—he was only $4\frac{1}{2}$ years old!

Wearing a camo headnet or face mask and gloves when you rattle will help hide your moving parts from sharp-eyed—and suspicious—bucks. Credit: M.R. James.

The buck, #180, was one of 130 bucks that we had captured and equipped with radio-transmitting collars since my research started in 1992. We captured this buck in October of that same year. At that time, Dr. Charles DeYoung of Texas A&M University-Kingsville, had estimated the buck's age at $2\frac{1}{2}$ years.

Mickey Hellickson's first antler-rattling study proved that the post-rut and the pre-rut periods were the best times to rattle in mature, trophy-caliber bucks. Credit: Mickey Hellickson.

DeYoung, who has aged literally thousands of live deer, aged every buck we captured each fall based on the amount of lower jaw tooth wear. In 1992, this buck's rack tallied up a gross Boone and Crockett score of 89, with seven points and no brow tines.

It was now mid-November. I was collecting data for an ongoing study on buck responses to antler-rattling. Dr. Larry Marchinton, from the University of Georgia, DeYoung, and I had been studying this aspect of breeding whitetail behavior for three years. This project would satisfy part of my doctoral requirements at the University of Georgia.

The first part of this study was conducted at the Rob and Bessie Welder Wildlife Refuge, north of Sinton, Texas. Our primary goal was to determine which type of rattling sequence attracted the highest number of bucks. The results of this three-year study were reported in an issue of *The Journal of the Texas Trophy Hunters.*

RECAP OF EARLIER RESULTS

To refresh your memory from Chapter 13, we tested four rattling sequences on whitetails. These sequences varied by length as well as rattling volume. We rattled a total of 171 times during the three periods of the whitetail breeding season. Our rattling attracted a total of 111 bucks. We found that loud rattling attracted nearly three times as many bucks as quiet rattling, and that the length of the rattling sequence was not important. We discovered that the post-rut and pre-rut periods were the best times to rattle in mature, trophy-caliber bucks. The rut's peak was tops if the objective was to rattle in large numbers of bucks. Rattling sessions that took place between 7:30 and 10:30 A.M. attracted more bucks than sessions conducted either at midday or in the afternoon. Cloudy days with little wind and mild temperatures represented the most productive weather conditions for rattling.

A SECOND ANTLER RATTLING STUDY

The goal of this, the second part of our antler-rattling study, would be to rattle to specific radio-collared bucks, and then measure each animal's responses. Each of the 130 collared bucks was outfitted with a transmitter attached to a neck collar that produced a unique radio signal. We tracked each buck using telemetry for an entire year. We located each buck's position a minimum of one or two times each day.

To track the bucks, we used a radio receiver connected to a large antenna. We dialed the frequency of the buck we wished to locate into the receiver and then drove the ranch roads, stopping every quarter mile to search for the animal. At each stop, the antenna would be swung 360 degrees in an attempt to detect the buck's signal. Once we picked up the correct signal, we determined the direction from which the signal was strongest. A compass was used to plot a bearing in that direction. We then stopped two more times at locations farther down the road, where we repeated the process. When we had three bearings to use for triangulation, we drew each on a map. The intersection of these three lines represented the buck's approximate location.

Forty-three of the 130 bucks that we had captured and radio-collared had been equipped with special activity-sensing transmitters. These transmitters told us whether each buck was bedded or active whenever we located him, even though we were usually not able to see him. Each buck's collar produced a radio signal at a rate of one pulse per second if the buck was not moving and the collar around its neck was stationary. Whenever the buck moved, the collar would also move, which

Hellickson's study also revealed that cloudy days with little wind and mild temperatures were the most productive when rattling for whitetails. Credit: Mickey Hellickson.

would increase the radio signal to two or more pulses per second. Therefore, whenever we located one of these bucks, we could tell if he was not moving and bedded, or active, simply by the radio pulse rate.

One day I used radiotelemetry to map Buck #180's position. On this particular occasion I drove downwind of the buck and parked the truck. I eased in toward him quietly until I believed I'd closed the gap between us to no more than two to three hundred yards. At that point, I turned on the receiver and zeroed it in on the buck. In this manner I was able to detect his responses as I rattled to him by the pulse rate of his signal. I started the rattling sequence related at the beginning of this article.

Buck #180's radio signal became active almost immediately. As I continued to rattle, the pulse rate quickened even more, while the signal became louder. Based on this information, I knew not only that the buck was active, but that he was moving toward me. One minute into the sequence the signal had become so loud that I knew the buck would appear at any moment!

The buck stepped into the opening and almost immediately turned and disappeared back into the brush. I gathered up the telemetry equipment and returned to the truck. After I'd reached the truck, I waited thirty minutes and relocated the buck with three new bearings. I was thus able to determine how far and in what direction he had traveled after responding to my rattling.

Through the use of this cutting-edge technology, we were able to measure the individual responses of many whitetail bucks both during and after we rattled to them. We could tell whether or not each buck responded to our rattling, even if the animal did not move close enough for us to see him. Finally, rattling response rates were determined based on the gross Boone and Crockett scores of each buck as well as its age, which had been determined by patterns of tooth wear.

THE RESULTS

The results of the second part of our study were extremely interesting. With research assistants Fred Steubing and Justin McCoy aiding us, each autumn from 1994 to 1996 we located the same eighteen bucks. We'd previously collared them with the activity-sensing radio transmitters described above. During this phase of the study we located each buck, walked quietly to within two or three hundred yards of him, then created a long, loud rattling sequence. In all, we rattled 33 times near these 18 bucks. Five of the bucks were located and rattled to during the pre-rut period, 14 during the rut's peak, and 14 others during the post-rut.

During 24 of the 33 sessions (73 percent), bucks responded by becoming active and moving closer to the source of the rattling. In other words, *nearly three out every four bucks responded to rattling if they were upwind and within hearing range.* I doubt whether most hunters could have predicted that bucks would respond at such an incredible rate. Before I conducted this study, I personally believed that fewer than 25 percent of the bucks within hearing range would respond to our rattling.

During our 33 rattling sessions, the horn rattler succeeded only 11 times in spotting the collared buck that was the object of our rattling. Rattling during this second study was performed by one person situated at ground level. We realize that not having a second observer nearby in a 30-foot-tall tower significantly reduced the number of bucks sighted. And yet the 33 percent sighting rate during the second part of the study compared favorably with results from our first Welder Refuge study. During that study, the person rattling from the ground spotted only 48 of the 111 bucks (43 percent) seen by the observer in the tower.

This illustrates how critical it is for a hunter to be waiting in an elevated position. Rattling with a partner is probably the most efficient way to consistently see and take whitetail bucks. While the shooter climbs into a tripod or some other type of elevated stand, another person should rattle from the ground. Stand sites should be selected upwind of open areas to even further increase the number of bucks seen, since the majority of bucks respond from downwind.

Fewer bucks responded to rattling during the pre-rut than during the rut's peak and post-rut periods. During the pre-rut, 2 of 5 (40 percent) rattling sessions culminated in the buck becoming active and moving closer to the rattling. During the rut's peak, 11 of 14 (79 percent) bucks became active and moved closer, while 11 of 14 bucks (79 percent) became active and moved closer during the post-rut period. The rut's peak response rate was slightly lower than what

During thirty-three research study sessions, the horn rattler spotted the buck targeted by the rattling only eleven times. Hence the need for a rattling team. Credit: Mickey Hellickson.

had been observed during the study's initial Welder Refuge phase, while the response rate during the post-rut period was higher.

Buck response rates were highest during morning rattling sessions. Midday and afternoon sessions elicited identical response rates that were slightly lower than those registered after morning sessions. Eight radio-collared bucks responded to 9 morning rattling sessions (89 percent response rate). Six bucks responded to the 9 midday sessions (67 percent), while 10 bucks responded to 15 afternoon sessions (67 percent response rate). Midday buck response rates during this second

When this old Montana buck responded to rattling during the rut period, M.R. James arrowed him at fifteen yards. Credit: M.R. James.

phase of the study were higher than those attained during the study's first phase at Welder Refuge.

During nine sessions, bucks either did not respond at all or they became active but moved away from the person rattling. The average age of bucks that responded to our rattling was 5.8 years, while the average for bucks that did not respond was 7.4 years. This seems to indicate that older bucks may be less susceptible to antler-rattling.

Thirty minutes after responding to the rattling, a buck would move an average of almost a third of a mile. Two bucks traveled nearly three quarters of a mile. Two other bucks moved very little. We were able to relocate them in their original positions. After responding to our rattling, most of the bucks (73 percent) moved to an area upwind of where they had been originally, even though we had rattled from a downwind location. In other words, a buck typically first moved downwind toward the rattling. After responding in this manner, each buck then usually moved back upwind beyond the place where we'd originally located him. Buck movements away from our rattling site were highest during the post-rut and lowest during the pre-rut periods.

We rattled more than once to 11 bucks to determine if bucks learned to avoid rattling. In every case but four, bucks responded during either the second, third, or fourth rattling session in the same way that they had responded during the first. The four exceptions failed to respond during the initial rattling session, but responded during the second. We rattled to Buck #1940, a 6.5-year-old during the study's first year, four times. Each time he responded by becoming active and moving closer. Our results seem to indicate that bucks will continue to respond in a positive manner to rattling, even if they have already responded to a previous rattling session.

M.R. James rattled in this rutting buck less than 150 yards from his Montana home. Credit: M.R. James.

When the data were analyzed based upon each buck's known gross Boone and Crockett score, the results were surprising. Most hunters probably believe that trophy bucks are less likely than other bucks to respond to rattling. In this study, we found that the opposite was true. The bucks were separated into two groups. One group, which we called the "cull" group, included every buck with antlers that scored less than 130 Boone and Crockett points. All bucks with gross antler scores that exceeded 130 Boone and Crockett points were placed in the other, or "trophy" group. Sixty-seven percent of the trophy bucks responded to our rattling compared to only 50 percent of the cull bucks. In addition, bucks in the cull group moved, on average, nearly two and one-half times farther between pre- and post-rattling locations than did those bucks in the trophy group.

OUR RESULTS SHOULD IMPROVE HUNTING SUCCESS

Our hope is that hunters will use our research results to increase their chances of success during upcoming seasons. Antler rattling is perhaps the most exciting deer hunting technique there is. Little compares to the sight of a mature buck with an immense rack rushing into view in response to rattling—that much we know.

We thank the many individuals who assisted with our antler-rattling and data collection. Rob, Fred, Bronson, Brent, Don, Justin, Scott, George, and William happily volunteered their time to work on this project. We also owe a debt of gratitude to the Rob and Bessie Welder Wildlife Foundation and its staff, the Neva and Wesley West Foundation and ranch owner Stuart Stedman, the University of Georgia, Texas A&M University-Kingsville, and the Caesar Kleberg Wildlife Research Institute for financial support of this research. See results on the following page.

Table 1. *Radio-collared buck response rates to antler-rattling by time of day and period of the breeding season (number in parentheses is number of bucks that responded divided by the number of bucks that were tested).*

PERIOD OF BREEDING SEASON	NUMBER OF BUCKS TESTED	TIME OF DAY			
		0730-1030	1030-1330	1330-1630	TOTAL
Pre-rut	5	NO SESSIONS PERFORMED	50% (1/2)	33% (1/3)	40% (2/5)
Rut peak	14	100% (5/5)	67% (2/3)	67% (4/6)	79% (11/14)
Post-rut	14	75% (3/4)	75% (3/4)	83% (5/6)	79% (11/14)
Total	33	89% (8/9)	67% (6/9)	67% (10/15)	73% (24/33)

Table 2. *Age and type of response (Y = yes, buck did respond; N = no, buck did not respond) of eleven radio-collared bucks that were rattled to on more than one occasion.*

BUCK IDENTIFICATION NUMBER	AGE	RATTLING SESSION			
		1	2	3	4
180	4.5	Y	Y		
602	4.5	N	Y		
1540	4.5	N	Y	Y	
1721	4.5	Y	Y		
1300	5.5	Y	Y		
1462	5.5	N	Y		
924	6.5	Y	Y		
1940	6.5	Y	Y	Y	Y
1326	7.5	Y	Y		
980	9.5	N	N		
1561	9.5	N	Y		

18

Setups That Work!

Here are some diagrams illustrating rattling and calling set ups that have worked for our experts as well as for other hunters. Look them over and see if you can understand why each hunter positioned his stand the way he did, plus pay attention to other factors that could help as you set out to duplicate their success while using these techniques.

THE FUNNEL STAND

The Funnel Stand is one of M.R. James's favorite hunting situations. Here is his explanation of how to work this stand:

"The Funnel Stand is one of my Big Sky favorites. I've called in and arrowed several bucks while in place nearby. As with the Pine Tree Stand, I create a convenient fence crossing close to my stand tree by lowering the wooden rails of a fence well before the start of archery season. This site is located at a natural woodland funnel between a creek and a high bluff. I set up where two or more well-used trails converge. Two apple trees not far distant serve as an early season food source, but any deer moving through the area are naturally funneled past my tree. Bucks in the area can be attracted with rattling and calling sequences during pre- and post-rut action. When using a decoy, I set it up so any buck that approaches will have to offer me a close-range broadside or quartering shot at point-blank range. I typically approach my stand from the Southwest between the apple trees and thick brush, whether I'm hunting the morning or the evening. This route allows a minimum amount of scent and disturbance in reaching my stand."

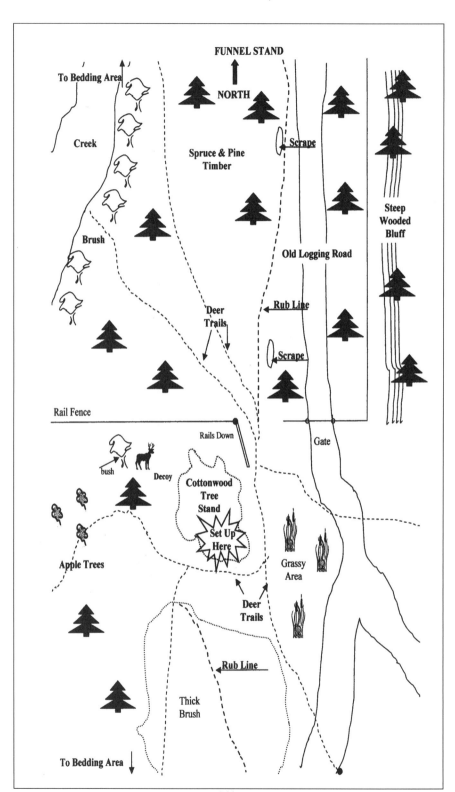

THE ASH THICKET STAND

This set-up comes to us from Mel Dutton. I call this the Ash Thicket Stand.

With the wind blowing from the Northwest providing the perfect entry to this ground set-up, Dutton moves in from the Southeast – into the wind – well before dawn to a dogleg corner of the ash thicket from which he plans to lure bucks. The thicket is located around a section of open prairie, as well as crosswind to a preferred whitetail feeding area. Bucks will be trolling that feeding area during nighttime hours as they are either searching for or accompanying estrus or pre-estrus does. There is also a chance that, if the wind is right, bucks may be lured into shooting distance as they move into the wind along the small finger draw to the east of the hunter. After rattling and calling for an hour or two with no action, Dutton will work farther into the wind before setting up again for another round of rattling and calling. If he uses a decoy, he will set it up near a small opening where an approaching buck will see it and move closer – through another opening – that will provide the bowhunter with a clear or mostly clear shot.

FIELD DECOY SET UP
FOR HUNTING LATE-SEASON BUCKS

When Jim Holdenried wants to score on a good buck during the late season, he takes his decoy to an agricultural field that's surrounded, on at least two or three sides, by forested woodlands. By setting up his decoy in the field where approaching deer are bound to see it, he is taking advantage of their eyes and sense of curiosity. When he adds some well-chosen calls, he's increasing the chances that they'll come in for a closer look. This would also be an ideal place to add movement in either the form of a tail-wagging rig, or a handkerchief. Always wear gloves when handling a decoy in such a situation, though. The wind is blowing in such a way that the hunter's scent should interfere with the fewest number of deer in the surrounding woods. This set up is ideal for either a rifle or muzzleloader hunter.

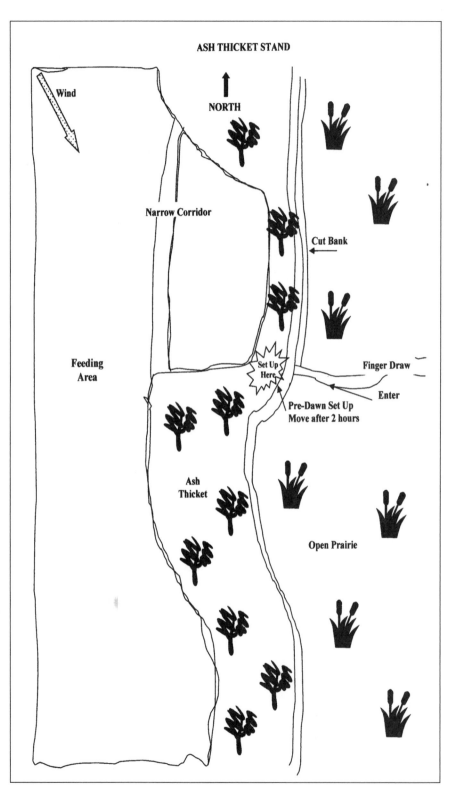

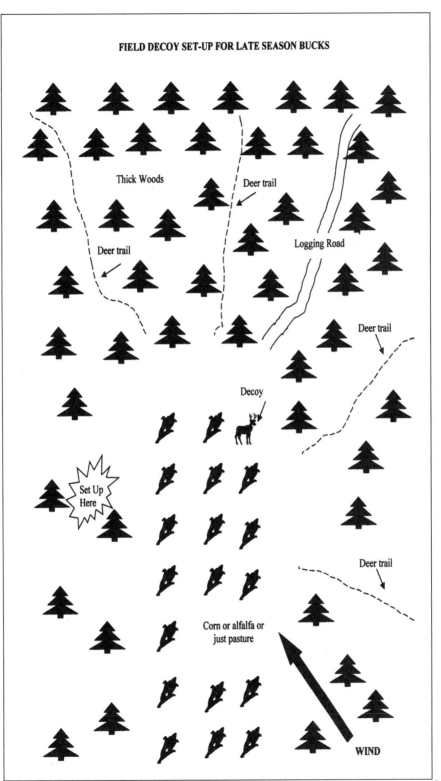

FIELD DECOY SET-UP FOR LATE SEASON BUCKS

Thick Woods

Deer trail

Deer trail

Logging Road

Deer trail

Decoy

Set Up Here

Deer trail

Corn or alfalfa or just pasture

WIND

THE RIDGETOP SET UP

Many of the places my husband, Bob, and I hunt are completely forested. Such a scenario should not present a problem, *if* you know where to set up. The Ridgetop Set Up was designed for such occasions, and is also ideal for team rattling or the use of a remote rattling device. Setting up downwind of a major deer trail, particularly in this situation where deer are forced to funnel between two sets of bluffs in order to cross from one ridgetop to another, can reap big dividends. The deer naturally travel either on or near the paths outlined. By rattling, you will attract the attention of any bucks bedding in the thick cover on the opposite ridgetop. The bluffs will impede these bucks from circling around behind you or downwind. That will force them into crossing the creek and approaching either from an upwind position – which, in this case, they usually do – or approaching from the path, in which case you will have an opportunity for several clear shots, or from below you. Since the woods are forested, but the trees are mature, during deer seasons you are able to see a good distance in all directions. No deer would be able to approach – except from behind you – without being seen. Since you have scouted out the bucks' favored bedding areas prior to your hunt, your odds are good of getting a shot at a buck whose curiosity or aggressive tendencies have gotten out of control.

THE FOREST COVER RATTLING SET UP

This set up is one that I've used with success. It takes advantage of a whitetail's tendency to circle around to try to catch the scent of 'deer' that are fighting. You set up near a field edge because a big buck will not want to enter the field–too dangerous during daylight hours–and will come in so that he shoud be in range when he appears. Notice the small opening between trees that is crosswind to the hunter's position and which many responding bucks must traverse. If you remain alert, you may catch the buck moving through this opening before he even gets into your decired shooting area. A team rattling effort could use the same set up simply by situating the second rattling team member either on the ground at the base of the tree (for a more natural presentation), or in a tree not far away. Make certain the team member whose turn it is to shoot has the best

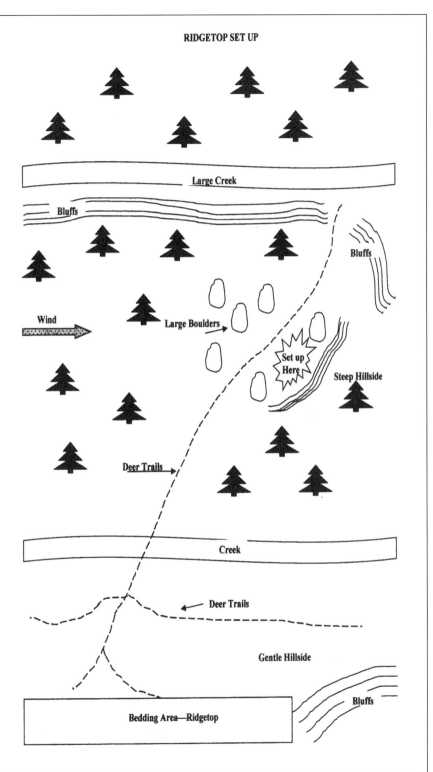

RIDGETOP SET UP

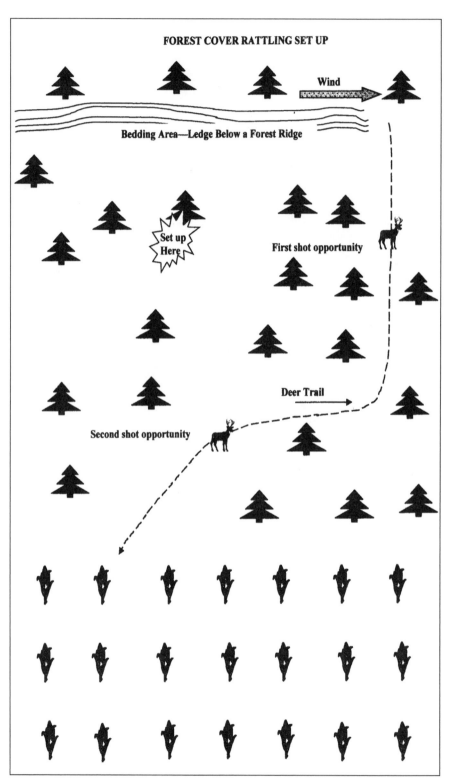

19

Team Rattling

If two heads are better than one, well, then two hunters hoping to strike white-tail gold should also be more successful than one—that is, if they use their heads to plot the very best way to approach a given situation. Team rattling is the single most effective way for two or three hunters, working in tandem, to capitalize on the curious or aggressive tendencies of a whitetail buck in general and a trophy buck in particular.

"One of the most exciting hunting experiences I've ever had took place while I was hunting with a friend on Anticosti Island [Quebec]," said Jay Cassell. "The two of us were both hunting on the ground, in an incredibly thick pine forest. We had found some fresh scrapes and rubs nearby, and could just tell this was an area that a buck called his home. I was the caller in this setup and had positioned myself in the brush. I started off softly, just tickling the tines of my antlers, but then

Jay Cassell admires a good 10-pointer he took on Anticosti Island. A combination of rattling and calling drew this buck into range. Credit: Jay Cassell.

I increased the intensity of the "battle." Soon I had a real ruckus going on—rattling, grunting, breaking branches, stomping on the ground, doing everything I could to imitate a serious battle between two bucks. My buddy, Dick, was stationed about twenty yards in front of me, hidden behind some deadfalls. Suddenly, we heard a deer practically screaming back at me—*whew, whew, whew.* One alarm snort after another—he kept up the snorts and was coming fast. As we watched, a really nice buck came rushing into view. At first, all I could see was his white rack sort of floating through the forest. Then I saw his body passing through the trees, headed straight toward me. He wasn't running, but he was moving fast. He was mad, and he was serious! I don't recall if he was an 8-point or a 10-point, but I was excited. I thought that all my hard work was about to pay off. It would have, too, but then Dick ended up shooting a sapling right in front of the buck—at maybe twenty-five

Rattling with a hunting buddy can be one of the most exciting ways to hunt whitetail deer. Credit: Jim Holdenried.

yards—and that buck was gone in a heartbeat. Man, that's exciting stuff!"

Brad Harris knows how deadly effective team rattling can be, even if it's used to increase the chances of buck encounters while stalking or still-hunting, whether with another hunter or a videographer. "I have had lots of success rattling from a ground blind, even during gun seasons while I'm decked out in fluorescent orange," Harris said. "I spent the second morning of the past Missouri gun season rattling and grunting from a ground blind. I'd started out in a tree stand, but I had a terrible cold. The hacking cough was especially annoying, since I was trying to get a buck to come in. The area was full of fresh sign, but I'd start coughing after several quiet minutes and couldn't stop. A half hour on any given stand was about all I was getting before I figured I'd ruined that spot, so we'd move about a hundred yards into the wind with my cameraman following close behind me. After I'd scope out the new area, we'd set up again. After the third such move, my cough was so bad that I was almost ready to give up. Before doing so, I decided to glass under nearby brush and through the trees for fresh sign or movement. I noticed a tine glowing through the undergrowth. I didn't know whether the buck was dogging a doe or not, but I started moving toward the tine.

"I broke out the grunt call when I no longer could see the buck," Harris continued. "The buck popped out of the brush and came running straight to me. I shot him at twenty yards on film and it was one of the more exciting hunts we were able to capture last season. I love calling or rattling from ground blinds in fresh, uncontaminated areas during rifle season. I love to

Team rattling is the single most effective way to capitalize on the curious or aggressive tendencies of a whitetail buck. Credit: Bob Zaiglin.

take hunters with me and use this very tactic."

While Harris's tale could not be strictly classified as team rattling, it does illustrate a degree of flexibility and "forgiveness" that most hunters don't realize they have. "If you've been calling and rattling from one location without success and decide to move elsewhere, that might be the smartest decision you make that day," Harris said. "A couple of years ago I was hunting in Kansas. One day I took another hunter with me. We saw fifteen bucks that day and were able to get three or four to come in to us. We'd spotted several of them while we were just

Double-teaming whitetails is one of the most effective tactics there is. Here, M.R James rattles on the ground while his partner waits in a nearby tree stand. Credit: M.R. James.

walking around. I saw one big buck with a doe, but couldn't convince him to leave the doe, nor could either of us get a clear shot at him. Most of these bucks were spotted while we were just covering new territory. I rattled and called one big buck in what was a perfect scenario. The deer moved right into an opening so the hunter could shoot at it, but the bullet missed its mark.

"Constantly moving to a 'fresh' area and hunting while you go makes good sense," continued Harris. "It's exciting to hunt like this with someone else, especially if you each take turns trying to call or rattle a deer in for the other guy. The thing about moving around like this is that each time you move, you're entering the 'zone of hearing' for additional whitetails. I'm not exaggerating when I say hunting like this is my absolute favorite way of hunting. Not only is it an exciting technique, it's extremely effective, too."

M.R. James concurred. "When I hunt with another person, we'll take turns," he said. "One hunter will rattle or call, while the other will be the shooter, should the occasion arise. My favorite setup is to have the shooter waiting in a tree stand, while the other person rattles or calls from the ground. A rattler on the ground can do so much more than one in a tree. He can use his rattling horns to rake leaves and brush, plus thump the ground with his boot or an antler butt. Rattling also sounds more realistic when it's coming from a person hidden on the ground."

James further stated that a decoy works especially well when set up for team rattling. "A decoy provides an interested buck with a focal point. As he's coming closer, the buck will usually focus his full attention on that other 'deer.'"

Mel Dutton says when he's being filmed while deer hunting, the team concept is the best way to obtain great shots. "When I work with a videographer, I usually do the calling," he said. "The bowhunter set up close to a decoy downwind about twenty yards from where I was rattling. That worked very well."

"The old 'switcheroo' will work no matter how it's set up," Harris added. "One hunter might rattle from a ground blind while the other takes a stand with his bow in either a ground blind or a tree stand twenty-five to thirty-five yards away. After a pre-ordained period of time, the partners switch to prevent one of them from getting all the action."

Harris likes rattling for gun hunters, but he wants to keep the hunter close at hand, "so I can see what he sees and vice versa. If I'm rattling from a tree stand for him, I want him sitting in the same tree or in the tree next to mine so there's no confusion."

When a hunter is rattling and calling, he sounds almost exactly like a whitetail buck. During the firearms season, whitetail bucks are on every hunter's mind. It doesn't take a rocket scientist to realize that a nearby hunter, upon hearing the sounds of two "whitetails" really tearing up the woods, might be inclined to slip in closer for a better look. The sight of a set of real antlers—or even authentic-looking synthetics—flashing about in the undergrowth might be more than this hunter can bear. He might not even wait to see antlers if his mind has suddenly gone AWOL from every principle taught during a course in hunter safety. Movement, coupled with the sounds of two whitetails really getting it on, may be all that's needed for the hunter to train his scope on you.

And don't ever believe that just because you and your buddy are bowhunting that you're immune to such rash judgment. Each season bowhunters are seriously injured and even killed by other bowhunters. Usually victims will say something to

To bag bucks like this, decide early on which team member will rattle—and for how long—and who will be waiting on stand. Credit: Terry Kayser.

the effect that being shot by another bowhunter never crossed their mind as being a possibility. It's better to be safe than sorry. Anyone thinking about calling, or, to a lesser extent, rattling whitetails should tell the hunters with whom they share a piece of property exactly what they will be doing and where. When using these tactics on public ground, it's best not to do so during the peak of the rut, when firearms seasons usually occur. Using such tactics can be just as dangerous during black powder seasons, too. Hunters should approach rattling, calling, and decoying with cool, level heads and do everything in their power to ensure that all parties involved—

174

This Montana buck was lured by rattling and calling, then halted just out of range. A decoy might have lured him in closer. Credit: M.R. James.

except the whitetail buck—go home in one piece when the hunt is over.

Before even heading out, formulate a plan. Decide which team member will rattle and which will be positioned on stand. If a buck runs in to the antlers but the hunter chooses not to take it, some teams immediately fall apart. Recriminations follow, with the net result that no one is happy. Deal with potential problems before they rear their ugly heads. Some questions that should be decided before agreeing to rattle or call as a team include:

How long a time period should a person rattle? Be sure you agree either on a set period of time or a specific number of rattling sequences.

If a deer responds and runs in to where the shooter can see it and he or she then misses the shot, does that hunter continue as shooter? Or do the rattler and shooter switch places once the shooter misses a shot?

If a deer responds but the shooter passes because it's not big enough, is the shooter justified in waiting until another, larger deer responds? Or should the rattler have a turn shooting?

What if someone gets a deer? After the deer is field-dressed and taken to the locker, will the successful hunter return to help other team members? Or will he or she leave the others to their own devices?

Will one hunter become jealous if another takes a larger deer?

What if, through luck, one hunter rattles in more deer than the other? Will the "better" rattler become upset with the one who isn't having as much luck?

These may sound like petty concerns, but plenty of hunters' ears are burning at this very minute from tales being bandied about by former hunting buddies. The rattler on one unsuccessful team was expected to create the sounds of mock white-tail battle for days on end as his buddy passed up first one buck, then several more. Each time a buck would come in—and the hunter would pass—the rattler tried to reason with the fellow that it was time to switch places. After two days, the rattler refused to rattle any longer. He insisted on switching places and promised that he'd shoot the first buck that came in. As luck would have it, area bucks suddenly became very difficult to rattle in. As you might have expected, the two are friends no longer.

Team rattling and calling can provide hunters with a thrilling method of hunting whitetails. Simply use some good, common sense, clear the air of possible misunderstandings before they occur, hunt safely and rationally, and you may see more—and bigger—bucks together than you would ever have seen alone. Team rattling is an ideal way of filming a friend or loved one's hunt, too. Finally, it's a great way to strengthen the camaraderie that so often binds hunting buddies together for their entire lives.

20

All about Decoying

We know that aboriginal hunters decoyed waterfowl, gamebirds, and game animals for many thousands, and perhaps even many millions, of years. Until fairly recently, however, decoying was neglected by everyone but waterfowlers. Dove, turkey, and crow hunters warmed gradually to the technique. They learned that to decoy—*to lure or to attract with either artificial or purposely deceptive situations or likenesses*—is to experience the immense satisfaction of fooling both a game animal's sense of sight *and*, more importantly, its native caution. When that animal is as wily as the white-tailed deer, decoyers must be prepared to spice up their sets even more.

A whitetail buck investigates one of Feather Flex's bedded does and goes berserk when "she" doesn't move in response to his antler prods. Credit: Bob Etling.

It's not uncommon for a person who decoys whitetails to work diligently to deceive not only its eyes but its sense of smell—and sometimes even its hearing.

Many of today's hunters remain unconvinced of the wisdom of decoying deer. Sure, some hunters have decoyed deer on occasion, but most have a tough time believing that it's a viable tactic.

Yet we know Native Americans sometimes concealed themselves beneath a bison's hide to slip closer to a herd of the animals. Why is it so much of a stretch to believe that they might also have hidden beneath a deerskin when stalking mule deer or whitetails?

The problem with decoying lies in attempting to convince more than the few believers already out there that this hunting technique is worth their consideration. Aboriginals decoyed animals because the tactic worked, plain and simple. But decoying goes far beyond setting out artificial likenesses of whitetail does and bucks near one's tree stand. Other, more subtle ways of decoying deer can also be successful. Mock rubs and scrapes, for example, can work like charms to attract curious or love-crazed whitetails. Mastering whitetail deception techniques means immersing oneself into discovering why such tactics work, as well as when, where, and how to use them.

THE FIRST MODERN WHITETAIL DECOYS

Tom Storm, a Montana archer, was one of the first hunters to toy with the idea of using decoys for whitetails. Storm began by making his own crude decoys, even including an early inflatable. His luck changed for the better when he discovered some incredibly lifelike deer decoys at a hunting show. These decoys–or "Deercoys®"—had been handcrafted of Styrofoam® by Missoula's Harry

A buck decoy set up near a fresh scrape may trigger local whitetails to respond in either a curious or an agonistic manner. Credit: M.R. James.

Brunnett. The decoy was far from cheap, but it had been constructed to last. Deercoys® were tough enough to withstand the charges of antagonistic whitetail bucks, and each was outfitted with a real whitetail's tail and glass taxidermy eyes, touches never seen on today's inexpensive decoys. "A deer looking into those glass eyes thought it was seeing a real deer," Storm said. The Deercoy® was molded with its head up, as if staring at some unknown object. That, according to Storm, is a major reason for its success. "Anytime a buck with slightly larger antlers glimpses the Deercoy®, it wonders why the decoy doesn't lower its head in submission. The Deercoy®, of course, can't behave submissively. So the real buck becomes curious and perhaps even enraged. He may move closer to find out why the 'newcomer' is behaving so badly. And that may place him within bow range."

"When a whitetail buck notices a new deer in its territory, it will usually become curious," Storm said. "The buck will want to find out who the 'new kid on the block' is. That's the exact reaction a hunter is hoping for."

Tom Storm recorded with his camera one big Montana buck's reaction to Harry Brunett's Deer-Coy®. Credit: Tom Storm.

Tom Storm hunts trophies. During one six-year period, he enticed more than a hundred whitetail bucks to within bow range. "Your decoy should have antlers slightly smaller than those of the buck you'd like to take," he said. "If you're after a 130-point Pope and Young buck, outfit your decoy with 120-point antlers, if at all possible." This isn't always possible, though, since most decoys sold come with a set of rather smallish antlers that seem to be the industry standard.

Louisiana's Dave Berkley became intrigued with the possibility of decoying whitetails at about the same time Tom Storm did. Berkley, who owned Feather-Flex Decoys before its acquisition by Outland Sports, developed a light, flexible, bedded doe decoy. "Deer perceive a bedded deer as being less threatening and more relaxed than one that is standing," Berkley said. "An alert decoy would arouse suspicion if it remained standing in the same position for too long."

Berkley first set up the bedded decoy in a thicket that served as a natural funnel between two fields. No sooner had the decoy been situated when a 6-point buck came in, pawed the decoy's rear end, turned it upside down, and gored it. Berkley later modified the decoy so that it could be used as either a buck or a doe.

"A decoy should attract a deer's attention," Berkley said. "When everything is done properly, a deer will become so intent on the decoy it will fail to notice the hunter. If a decoy has a whitetail's full attention, a hunter should be able to draw his bow or shoulder his gun with little fear of spooking the deer. That's its greatest advantage."

While Storm and Berkley believe in decoys, both also recognize that each wild deer is a unique individual. Neither believes a decoy will always work. "A deer may react positively or negatively to a decoy," Berkley said. "Remember, geese don't always decoy, and neither do ducks. The same is true of whitetails. But decoys can provide better shots, cleaner kills, and could even keep deer from noticing hunter errors that might bungle the hunt had no decoy been used."

WHY DECOYS WORK

"No whitetail hunting tactic is 100 percent surefire," said Dave Berkley. "If such a thing existed, we'd all be going on deer 'shoots' rather than deer 'hunts.' Scents may fool a deer's nose, calls may deceive its ears, and camouflage can play tricks on its eyes. With our weapons and our [generally] superior intellect, killing deer should be a snap, right? But we know that's not the case."

When explaining why decoy experimentation is important to a whitetail hunter, Berkley said, "Deer calls haven't been popular that long, yet it seems that some deer have become accustomed to them. Sure, a call may entice a deer to within forty

Many full-bodied deer decoys feature removable antlers and double as 3-D targets before hunting begins. This is Blueridge's Monster Whitetail Decoy®. Credit: Outland Sports.

or sixty yards, but what if he stops? That's when he wants to *see* something. Scents may help by reinforcing what the deer's ears are telling him. Camouflage can keep a hunter hidden. But when a deer has responded to a deer-like sound, it will *expect* to see a deer. In that, deer are like humans. We mostly depend on our vision, while our other senses merely reinforce what we're seeing. If a deer encounters a well-placed decoy after hearing a call or rattling, and it hasn't smelled human scent, it may be curious and relaxed enough to come closer."

WHEN TO USE A FULL-BODY DECOY

Hunters generally use decoys to lend realism to a particular situation. Whether a hunter is calling, rattling, or stand-hunting near a feeding or bedding area, a decoy can often pull a real whitetail in close enough for a shot with either firearm or bow.

A decoy will also usually stop a deer, even if it's heading toward thick cover. South Texas hunters, who often watch narrow *senderos* (roadways), know how quickly deer can disappear in such areas. A decoy will often provide an opportunity to shoot that might not otherwise exist.

Try placing a decoy in whitetail feeding areas during non-rut periods as well. Seeing another "deer" seems to calm deer. A decoy might also lure them out into feeding areas earlier than usual.

CHOOSING A DECOY

Should a hunter buy a stationary decoy or one made of fabric? A silhouette? How about a "stalk-and-shoot" model? Should you go for a bedded doe or a feeding buck, or vice versa? What about a decoy that can move? Remember, each decoy serves a purpose. Which one—or two or three—will work best for a particular hunter or situation will probably always remain a matter not only of conjecture, but also of chance.

A decoy can usually be converted from buck to doe, thanks to removable antlers. Deciding whether to use the buck or the doe—or perhaps *both* a buck and a doe—may mean the difference between success and failure.

"Don't use a buck decoy during the pre-rut if you're strictly a meat hunter," said Berkley. "Does with fawns won't approach a buck early in the season."

Positioning a buck decoy and a doe decoy together during the latter part of the preseason can sometimes work wonders. "Have the two decoys looking at each other, perhaps with the buck higher so he seems to be standing, and the doe glancing back over her shoulder at him," Berkley said. "Such a scene seems to relax deer and encourage them to approach."

Tom Storm believes that a buck decoy works best during the rut's peak. He also said that such a decoy will be more effective where the buck to doe ratio is balanced, particularly when it is outfitted with large antlers.

Storm recommended using a one-antlered decoy, too. "Bucks seem to respond to it faster, maybe because they believe they'll be able to whip this defective animal," he said. "Two buck decoys facing each other will also attract attention."

DAVE BERKLEY'S DECOYING HINTS

Dave Berkley has been decoying whitetails for years. Here are some of his personal tips for successful whitetail decoying:

1) Hang a fluttering rag, some toilet paper, or a white feather from a string nearby to provide some subtle, natural-looking movement. Movement makes a decoy appear more lifelike, and will attract deer more readily.

2) Position the decoy upwind from your stand. Face it in the direction from which your deer are most likely to appear. Any deer approaching a decoy head-on will be less suspicious than from any other direction.

3) Never face the decoy toward a hunter. Real deer will stare in the same direction in an attempt to discover what the decoy is looking at. The deer could spot the hunter and bolt before he has a chance to shoot.

4) Provide the decoy with something to "look" at, perhaps a turkey decoy or another deer decoy. Perhaps arrange a standing buck decoy so that it's looking at a bedded doe decoy.

5) Consider placing a bedded buck decoy atop a bush or bent-over sapling so that it appears to be standing. This makes the decoy more visible.

6) Twist a buck decoy's ears back into an aggressive position to really tick off larger bucks.

7) Be aware that real deer may interact with the decoy. Deer approaching from the decoy's rear will do so more cautiously than when approaching from the front. Deer between forty and sixty yards away may snort or paw to attract the decoy's attention. Since they will fail, they will either get nervous and back off or come in the rest of the way. If a deer approaches, it may paw, toss, bite, or gore the decoy.

8) Never leave your decoy in one spot for too long. Deer will become accustomed to it and ignore it.

Tom Storm places his decoys so that an approaching buck cannot move in from the rear. Credit: M.R. James.

9) Be aware that deer may destroy any decoy that remains set up overnight.

10) Rather than worry about danger from other hunters, buy a fluorescent orange decoy or paint your decoy (or part of it) orange. Rather than frightening deer, an orange decoy seems to encourage interaction and may make them madder than a more normal coloration.

11) Don't feel that you have to use rubber gloves or masking scent when handling decoys. I don't, and I've had many deer come in and never worried about scent other than wind direction.

12) Use calling and rattling—their proper use will attract even more animals to a decoy.

TOM STORM'S DECOYING HINTS

"One day, I set my decoy up at the edge of a clear-cut," Tom Storm said. "A big buck entered the cut about eighty yards away but didn't see the decoy. That's common, since most decoys don't move. I grunted, and the deer noticed the decoy. It strode over and started circling the decoy, walking behind the tree in which I'd placed my tree stand. Since I knew it would get my scent, I shot. Luckily, I made a killing shot at ten yards while the buck was still wrapped up in the decoy." The 144⅘-point Pope and Young buck was Storm's biggest one to date. The buck also proved that decoying is a great way to preselect trophy animals. "During one six-year period of bowhunting over a decoy, I passed up well over a hundred bucks," he noted.

Since deer think Mel Dutton's decoy is another deer, hunters can use it as either a blind or to provide cover when stalking closer to a whitetail. Credit: Bob Etling.

Here are Tom Storm's decoying tips:

1) Scout to locate rutting areas. Deer rut in the same spots each year. Placing your decoy in an adjacent natural funnel will increase its chances of being spotted.

2) Use rubber gloves when handling your decoy.

3) Use a scent eliminator on the decoy's body.

4) Apply a quality gel scent in an appropriate odor to the decoy's face and tail.

5) Squirt doe-in-heat urine on the ground around the decoy.

6) Consider wind direction and normal deer movements before positioning the decoy.

7) Never set up a decoy so that it looks toward you.

8) Place a buck decoy where it can be seen. Do not obscure with brush or trees.

9) Use larger antlers on your decoy to attract trophy deer.

10) "Crib" the decoy so a buck is unable to reach the decoy's tail. That means positioning the decoy's rear end close to a bush or in a thicket. Fifty percent of the bucks that get close enough to smell the tail will bolt; the other 50 percent will remain nearby. No matter how careful you may be, some bucks may still detect human scent on the decoy's tail.

11) When correctly positioned, a decoy should provide the bowhunter with either a slightly quartering away or broadside shot at any responding buck.

12) Shoot before the buck reaches the decoy. A buck might gore the decoy and spook when the decoy gets stuck on his antlers.

13) Use rattling and calling—they can attract even more deer to your decoy.

STALK-AND-SHOOT

Mel Dutton originated another use for white-tail decoys. Dutton developed a hard-shell, foldable decoy that is more like a decoy silhouette with antlers. Each decoy comes with a stake that can be stuck into the ground as the bowhunter sets up and prepares for a shot. It is also possible to use such a decoy as a "stalking" deer. The decoy provides enough cover for a hunter to make a stalk across open ground or through a forest. If a hunter is scrupulous about wind direction and human scent, a deer may be fooled into believing another of its own kind is approaching. "Whitetails see another 'deer,'" Dutton said. "They seem to be expecting some movement, so it's easy to move extremely close without spooking them." When a decoy is used in this manner, whitetails do not jump the string when he shoots his bow.

Mel Dutton's hard-shell, foldable decoy is both light and easy to transport. Credit: Bob Etling.

Dutton's decoys are made of vacuum-formed ABS plastic. The material looks reasonably realistic and is durable and light in weight. The decoys fold to make handling and packing them easier. The slot through the handle doubles as a peep-hole when you need to observe the deer's reactions. Once the decoy stake has been shoved into the ground, the decoy will pivot to continue to shield the hunter if animals attempt to circle him.

For safety's sake, use this tactic *ONLY* during archery season and *ONLY* when you are certain that *no one else is hunting nearby.*

HIGDON'S MOTION DECOY

I can write from personal experience about how effective Higdon's Finisher Motion Whitetail Decoy® can be. I used one while bowhunting in western Kentucky to lure six bucks in to my stand. I could have shot most of them, but I was holding out for a Pope and Young animal. I later killed a nice buck from the same stand with my rifle. When it stopped to gawk at my decoy, I was able to make a perfect shot.

The same year I bagged my buck, a friend of Mark Higdon (the brains behind the Motion Decoy) set up the decoy in an open field, then hunkered down in a nearby fence-line. Within a few minutes, a big 160-class Boone and Crockett materialized from nowhere to run over and challenge the decoy. Hunters from all over the country have taken superb bucks while using this clever motion silhouette. Justin Hillman, of Illinois, for example, had no sooner unpacked his Higdon decoy when he arrowed a 13-point Pope and Young buck that had paused just ten yards away from his stand.

Higdon's decoys are unique. The firearms or bowhunter can actually make them

The author shot this wide-racked Kentucky buck when it stopped to get a closer look at the Higdon Motion Decoy® she was using. Credit: Bob Etling.

move. Situate the decoy, climb into your stand, then pull on the line attached to the decoy to make its head nod. The head is connected to the tail, so the white tail also twitches. A substantial reel of Kevlar® line and removable antlers are included with each Finisher Decoy®. The decoy's body is made of rugged waterproof corrugated plastic.

Drawbacks? Well, if your stand or you aren't hidden well enough, or if your stand is situated low enough to be in the animal's line of sight, a deer may zero in on the hand movement rather than the decoy movement. Proper stand position, together with subtle and prudent hand movements, will minimize, if not eliminate, this risk once the animal's curiosity has been piqued. Results become almost uniformly positive once you learn when to move the decoy and when to lay off.

Seeing is believing, and in these cases, the animals' eyes sealed their fates. Higdon Motion Decoys (#7 Universal Way, Metropolis, IL 62960; phone 618-524-3385; www.higdondecoys.com).

ADDED DECOY ATTRACTIONS

A doe reveals a lot through her body language. When she holds her tail straight away from her body and perhaps slightly off to one side, she is indicating that she is in full estrus. When you position your doe decoy's tail similarly during the early or "false" rut period, as well as straight on through the post-rut period, this simple action could help attract the attention of roving bucks. Most successful users of deer decoys go to great lengths to make certain that their decoys' tails are signaling the proper mood for the particular moment.

Come-Alive Decoy Products makes a decoy that moves automatically. Big bucks can't seem to get enough of Come Alive's Tail-Wagger Rear®. Made of soft, flexible, UV-stable foam, this three-and-one-half-pound product makes no noise in action to betray its mechanical nature. Since it moves automatically, you don't have to make any movements that might reveal your presence, either. Simply choose either a fast or slow tail wag interval, install four C batteries, and you're in business. A new set of batteries should power the unit for about two hundred hours, although that time may decrease in cold weather. The Tail-Wagger Rear®'s realistic-looking foam tail is soft, flexible, and virtually indestructible.

Come-Alive also makes a Tail Wagger Motion® Kit, a tail-wagging unit that can be attached to most full-sized decoys or simply strapped to a tree. The kit includes a tail, circuit board controller, and DC motor. Other decoy companies may also sell models with tails that move, but to describe them here would make little sense, since members of the group may change from year to year. Check in catalogs and outdoor magazines or with your sporting-goods retailer before you buy to be sure you're getting the product you want.

One popular and economical jury-rigged version of a deer's moving tail is made by attaching a flimsy white rag or handkerchief to the decoy's rear end. The tail should move slightly in a wind, negating any need for a motion device. Simply apply some estrous doe scent and you're in business. (Be sure always to wear rubber or plastic gloves when you handle decoys and accessories.)

THE REAL McCOY?

Some hunters opt for a more realistic look to help them succeed. "Adding actual deer antlers and a tanned deer tail will help make any decoy appear more realistic," Tom Storm said. The tail seems to be the most important addition—as well as the easiest to make—if the aim is to further increase a decoy's appeal.

Some hunters even take a real doe's tail to the taxidermist to have it professionally mounted. Still others do it themselves. The easiest do-it-yourself method is to simply take an adult doe's tail, snap the last piece of cartilage in the tail, arrange the tail so that it resembles a question mark, and then freeze it.

This big Kentucky buck was racing past my stand when he spotted my Higdon Motion Decoy® and came to a dead halt! Credit: Bob Etling.

When the next deer season arrives, hang the tail on your decoy. You might also tie a line to the tail and hang it in a tree so that it is two or three feet off the ground but in clear view of any bucks that might pass by. For another variation on this theme, tie an additional fifty or a hundred yards of line to the tail and pull it into your tree stand or ground blind. When you spot a buck, yank on the cord to make the tail move. Be sure the deer can't see your movement, though. A buck spotting your frozen tail will come right in and start searching for the rest of the "doe." Since the tail isn't actually tanned, it probably won't last even a single season.

For a longer-lasting tail decoy, skin out a tail, make a slit on its underside, and remove all bone and tissue through the slit. Scrape off the fat from the underside, and then rub borax on the raw skin. Cut a piece of rigid wire (coat hanger wire works fine) to twice the tail's length. Wrap paper towels or newspaper around the wire until it assumes the same general shape and size as the removed bone, but slightly smaller. Wrap the paper-covered wire with masking tape. (Half the wire is wrapped with paper and tape and the other half is bare.) Stitch up the tail with heavy thread and tie the thread off at the end, but be sure to leave a small hole at the tail's upper end. Squirt latex caulk into the hole and then stick the wire-and-paper "bone" inside the tail so that the bare wire is sticking out. Set it aside until dry.

To mount the tail on the decoy, drill a hole in the decoy's rear end. Now slide the wire in, bending it when inside the decoy to keep it in place. In the wind, the tail will move just like a live deer's. If you want to make it move yourself, tie on a piece of fishing line long enough to reach to your stand or blind so you can tug on it. Sweetening the tail with estrous doe urine or scent can add to the decoy's appeal.

"I've used a real whitetail tail on a decoy, but I've added estrous doe scent to it," M.R. James said. "I've used tissue paper and also hunter orange plastic surveyor tape affixed to the decoy's tail or ears to add movement."

Check to see if your state or province allows the use of road-killed deer for decoy body parts. NOTE: Any decoy that emulates either a portion or all of a deer's body can be extremely dangerous when used during firearms season unless painted hunter orange.

OTHER DECOYING TRICKS

Peter Fiduccia has a long history of successfully decoying whitetails. "I started decoying deer before I rattled them," he said. "I learned about it from the owner of a farm where I hunted. As we were preparing for the hunt, this man handed each of us a deer's tail tied to a piece of white cloth that we were supposed to hang in a bush or tree.

"My decoying methods tend to be rather unorthodox. I've used a deer's mounted head, a bedded doe, and even red plastic apples in areas where apples don't grow. It doesn't matter. Deer are drawn to them by their scent. I first buy a dozen glossy, over-sized apples at a craft store. I put some apple cider or apple scent in a large plastic bag and then soak the apples in this. Add a Christmas-ornament hook to each apple, then toss three or four of them on the ground and hang the rest on nearby trees. Deer are drawn to apple scent. They'll come in, sniff the scent, and go right to the apples. Fake corn will draw deer, too. In fact, I think the biggest hunting fallacy there is is to stick to food scents that are indigenous to an area. Why use white acorn scent where there are lots of white acorns? I think it's better to use a new, intoxicating scent in an area where it's never been smelled before. It will pull more deer in, at least in my opinion."

ARE DEER DECOYS LEGAL?

Wildlife laws from state to state seem to change almost constantly. Be sure to check issues of legality with wildlife enforcement agencies in states or provinces where you will be hunting before you make plans to buy or use a full-bodied deer decoy. Do the same before removing whitetail parts from road-killed deer for use on a decoy.

ABOUT THE DECOYS

Products come and products go, but whitetail decoys are going to be with us forever. With that in mind, here is a brief rundown of some of the types of decoys a buyer might find at local sporting-goods retailers.

Two- or three-dimensional decoys made with polystyrene or polyethylene bodies generally pull apart (head from body, body from legs) for ease of transport. Every realistically painted decoy I've seen has also been sold with either a camouflage-patterned or hunter-orange carry-bag for safety going to and from the stand. If the decoy you're thinking about buying does not have such a carry-bag, you should find one that does.

Stalk-and-shoot decoys, movable-silhouette decoys, and standalone silhouettes are all popular. They are lightweight, some models seem to be extremely durable (make this decision after checking it out for yourself), and all are easily stored. Most fold for transport. When folded, they scarcely resemble a deer. These decoys are made of corrugated plastic or polymer plastic.

Decoys with a photorealistic image of a whitetail imprinted on some sort of tough, durable fabric surface are gaining popularity for a couple of good reasons. They are lightweight, reasonably priced, and are set up like a tent, with internal spring steel bands and fiberglass support poles. These decoys are also compact and flexible and can be stuffed into a daypack. Another plus is that a fabric decoy will move in even the slightest breeze. That quality, however, can also be a disadvantage: When it's really windy, it becomes difficult to keep a billowing deer from taking flight.

Carry-Lite's decoy is professionally sculptured, with lifelike detail down to its taxidermy-quality eyes and removable antlers. The ears and tail are moveable. The Carry-Lite breaks down easily and comes with its own mesh carrying bag and metal anchor stakes.

BEFORE MOVING ON . . .

If you are alone or on private land, decoying adds a brand new dimension to both rifle and bow hunting. But to stay safe, remember that any attempt to fool the ears or the eyes of an animal could result in the deception of a foolish hunter. Use decoys during rifle seasons only in areas where other hunters know precisely where these decoys will be positioned or if you are hunting alone. **NEVER USE DECOYS ON PUBLIC LAND DURING ANY FIREARMS SEASON.** No matter how many precautions you may have taken when hunting or bowhunting over a decoy, still be sure to position the decoy so that while you are in your stand you are not in danger. This means not only setting up the decoy so that it is behind a tree when you are viewing it, but also so that it is at a completely different elevation than your stand—either many feet higher or many feet lower. Another good tactic is to affix fluorescent-orange surveyor tape to the decoy or to position the decoy so that any rifle bullet mistakenly shot at it will strike an earthen backstop such as a hill or the side of a gully. Finally, when transporting decoys, **ALWAYS BE SURE TO CARRY THEM IN A CAMOUFLAGE OR HUNTER-ORANGE BAG** to eliminate the chance of mistaken identity by other hunters.

DECOY MANUFACTURERS

The list may change, but as we went to press here is the contact information for the major decoy makers:

Blueridge Decoys
A Division of Outland Sports
4500 Doniphan Dr.
Neosho, MO 64850
Tel. 417-451-4438
http://www.outlandsports.com

Carry-Lite Decoys
5203 West Clinton Ave.
Milwaukee, WI 53223
Tel. 414-355-3520
http://www.carrylite-decoys.com

Come Alive Products, LLC
4916 Seton Pl.
Greendale, WI 53129
Tel. 414-421-4474
http://www.tail-wagger.com

Mel Dutton Decoys
Box 113
Faith, SD 57626
Tel. 605-967-2031
http://sdibi.northern.edu/mel_dutton/

Feather-Flex Decoys
A Division of Outland Sports
4500 Doniphan Dr.
Neosho, MO 64850
Tel. 417-451-4438
http://www.outlandsports.com

Flambeau Products Corporation
Flambeau Outdoors
P.O. Box 97
Middlefield, OH 44062
Tel. 440-632-1631
http://www.flambeauproducts.com

Higdon Motion Decoys
7 Universal Way
Metropolis, IL 62960
Tel. 618-524-3385
http://www.higdondecoys.com

Tab Hinton Archery Targets
and Decoys
Tel. 601-947-2610
http://www.hintontargets.com

Montana Decoys
P.O. Box 2377
Colstrip, MT 59323
Tel. 406-748-3092
http://www.montanadecoy.com

Outlaw Decoys
624 N. Fancher Rd.
Spokane, WA 99212
Tel. 509-532-4624
http://www.outlaw.com

21

Decoying Tried and True

Decoying comes from the word coy, which means *flirtatiously shy or modest.*
The word coy has a long history. It derives from the Middle English, which in turn
evolved from the Old French word *quei, coi.* This, in turn, reaches back to the
Vulgar Latin *quetus,* which meant *quiet* or *still.*

That's your etymology lesson, and now for the straight scoop about the coy
way of hunting, or hunting in a *flirtatiously quiet* or still manner, a technique that
was used by Native Americans for thousands of years prior to European settlement.
Decoys, of course, are quiet and still because they are inanimate objects. Unless we
add batteries or pull on strings, they remain quiet and still. Yet decoys are made to
attract. And that's where the flirtation comes in.

Many hunters now believe that decoying is the third and final component of
what some term deer hunting's Big Three: calling, rattling, and decoying. If one
tactic works well on its own, doesn't it
follow that all three tactics used in conjunction with one another will work
that much better?

For example, to produce sheer
whitetail magic with decoying and calling, simply provide one or more of the
following special effects: the sounds of
a buck snorting, grunting, or both; the
sound of antlers clashing viciously; the
thud of hooves striking the ground; or
the snap, rattle, and pop of breaking
branches. These noises are natural to the
whitetail's world. Each is quite capable
of attracting deer in its own right. But
when you add precision audio effects
such as these to your calling and visual
deception, get ready. Whitetails won't
be able to resist.

M.R. James places his decoy in a shooting lane under
his tree stand to hold a buck's attention and allow a
point-blank shot with his bow. Credit: M.R. James.

Hanging a stand in a likely calling area is often the first step to calling/rattling success. Credit: M.R. James.

Combining a decoy with realistic sound effects works well enough for an individual, but when used in combination with one of the rattling and calling setups described in Chapters 21 and 22, the results can be awesome.

"I use a decoy to complement my calling/rattling setups," M.R. James said. "But let me warn you, the first few times I did, I had some negative responses. The deer would come in, see the decoy, then go into tail-tuck mode and slip around, sniffing the decoy. Of course, I knew nothing about decoying deer. I'd put the decoy under my arm and walked across three fields to my position. I didn't realize at the time that scent was giving me away. I knew better, too. Whenever I'd hang a hock or a scent pad I would always wear latex gloves, for example. I began to think that perhaps I should take such precautions when using a decoy.

"I now spread doe-in-heat scent around the decoy," James continued. "When transporting it, I put it in a garbage bag. I also wear rubber gloves when handling the decoy or setting it up. Things started to improve.

"I've only been seriously using decoys for the past six or seven years," James said. "I did so much of it on my Montana ranch without good results that people might say I'm a slow learner. That may be true, but I have learned what works for me. I try to position the decoy so that deer cannot approach it from the rear, and so that they must pass my stand in order to come face-to-face with it, which is a whitetail's natural inclination.

"Larry Jones, Dwight Schuh, and I got some great video shots of bucks coming in to decoys last year. One day, we spotted this buck about two hundred yards away. I set a buck decoy out in a field of half-picked corn, Larry dribbled some buck scent around it, and then we started calling and rattling. The whitetail buck came in to within fifteen yards of the decoy and pawed the ground right in front of it. The fact that we were able to get such amazing footage just reinforces my belief in decoying and the types of situations that can quickly develop when a hunter uses one properly."

James always rattles and grunts to add realism to his decoying setups. "I place the decoy within fifteen yards or so of my stand and situate it with its tail to a tree or thick brush," he said. "I've seen bucks attack decoys, sometimes goring them from the rear or side, so I will take pains to prevent this from happening.

"I think the sound of the antlers is what calls or draws the buck to you," James said. "The sight of the decoy then confirms what he's heard and holds his attention. The decoy acts as positive reinforcement since it is something—another deer—that the buck expects to see. In my experience, some bucks will hang up and not come in all the way if they can't see the deer they heard fighting or grunting."

"I've rattled quite a bit while bowhunting over a decoy," Mickey Hellickson said.

"Decoying works well to pull deer in closer to your stand, but I really think the decoy you choose should be as realistic as possible. I've used both Flambeau's Redi-Doe® and a full-sized McKenzie 3-D buck target as a decoy. Both have worked, but I've had more success when using the doe. I had one really nice buck happen past and see the doe. He walked right in between the decoy and my ground blind, never looking once in my direction. He came to within five yards of the decoy, and since he didn't stop or look my way, I was able to draw my bow and shoot him. When hunters use decoying with rattling, they're creating a situation that will attract a higher percentage of deer

M.R. James often shoots while seated so that his movements are kept to a minimum when a buck is responding to his calls or rattling. Credit: M.R. James.

close enough to shoot. I always keep a decoy in my hunting vehicle."

"I'll put my decoy in the same area of this one field on most days," Jim Holdenried said. "When deer emerge from the timber and enter the field, they'll see the decoy immediately and will usually come in. What makes this spot so good is that deer can see the decoy from several hundred yards in either direction. I must admit, though,

Mel Dutton arrowed this nice buck after rattling him in to his decoy. Credit: Mel Dutton.

I'll use a decoy primarily during the post-rut period. During the rut, I'll stick to the timber. Later on, I'll begin working the open areas in or near agricultural areas. My plan during the late season will sometimes shift to working whitetail feeding patterns. This is where crops and pasturelands become more important to me."

Brad Harris concurred, although he shies away from using decoys. "Decoys could work extremely well for anyone who hunts open country where deer rely more on their eyes. In those situations, when deer can actually see the thing that they thought they heard, I believe this often will seal the situation. Add rattling and calling, and I think it would become even more effective."

Harris remains decoy-shy, but admitted he hasn't given the tactic much of a chance. "I've had deer lock in on decoys," he said. "But then I've seen the decoys scare those same deer. I think I'll pass, but I know a lot of [firearms] hunters and bowhunters believe in decoys big time. These are the folks who have stuck with it and who have, over time, worked out the bugs."

Harris could have been referring to Mel Dutton, one of decoying's first proponents. "There are some situations just made to order for decoying," Dutton said. "A couple of years ago I'd been working on a tractor at our farm. It was snowy that day, and as I was returning to the house after work, I looked down the road and noticed a really nice buck browsing in an oat field not far from our equipment shed. I sneaked inside the house, put on some white camouflage, and grabbed my bow. Then I slipped back outside and headed to that equipment shed, making certain that the buck was unable to see my approach. When I got there, he was still feeding where I'd first spotted him. I belly-crawled with my decoy away from the shed and fifteen or twenty yards out into the field. Before getting ready to shoot, I stuck the decoy into the ground and then cracked my rattling horns together. The buck rushed at me so quickly I almost had to shoot it in self-defense."

Dutton's sneak attack buck just missed making Pope and Young. "I probably didn't even need the decoy except as cover, but then, you never know. The buck may simply have been intent on coming to the antlers." Regardless, Dutton's strategy for this situation turned out to be perfect.

What should hunters expect the first time a deer responds a decoy? As M.R. James said, "Reactions vary a great deal. One buck may approach without hesitation, then begin to posture as he nears the 'rival' buck. The next deer may seem unaccountably edgy and act suspicious, if not downright frightened. I've seen decoys scare off more bucks than calls or rattling efforts combined."

A good team-oriented approach to decoying involves positioning one hunter on the ground downwind of the whitetail's probable approach route. Another hunter should be waiting in a tree stand where he or she can get a good, clear shot at any deer that might come in. In an ideal setup, the ground hunter is in charge of special effects to provide a mock battle more realistic-sounding than any that could be created by a tree stand hunter.

Possible problems with decoys may arise simply because so many are so light. A stiff wind might topple a decoy not staked down extremely well. This is particularly true of rigid, flat-sided decoys positioned in loose or sandy soils at right angles to the wind. Try to find better soil for your stake. If this isn't possible, positioning the decoy so the wind is blowing parallel to the side with the greater surface area might solve the problem.

This problem can also wreak havoc with your stalk if, after you've crept to within range of a whitetail you'd like to bow shoot, you are unable to jab the decoy

Mel Dutton relies on his "system" of rattling, decoying, and calling to take big South Dakota whitetails during all periods of the rut. Credit: Mel Dutton.

stake deep enough into sand, soil, or rocks to keep it in an upright position. Dropping the decoy at such a delicate moment is, as you might imagine, a decoying *don't.*

Brisk winds might also disrupt someone hunting with a flexible, bedded-type decoy unless its edges are securely weighted down. Nothing is more frustrating than seeing your bedded Feather-Flex doe or buck tumble end over end while you're watching helplessly from twenty feet up in a tree.

Decoying as a whitetail tactic is coming into its own. Each year more hunters are trying it—and loving the results. "I'm always thrilled to call or rattle a deer in over a decoy," said Mel Dutton. "To me, that's the most exciting type of hunting there is."

22

Special F/X—The Big Three

When calling, rattling, or decoying are considered on their own merits, few would deny how effective each tactic can sometimes be. When used in tandem, however, their efficacy will often surge to the next level, which could be termed "unbelievable." "Deadly alone, deadliest together" could easily become the motto of anyone determined to find perfection as a whitetail special-effects artist. Knowing when to triple your threat with

Peter Fiduccia knows that to score on bucks like these you have to know your area and know the Big Three special effects of hunting: calling, rattling, and decoying. Credit: Fiduccia Enterprises.

whitetail hunting's Big Three will have a definite effect on your hunting success.

"Successful calling, rattling, and decoying depends on four basic factors: timing, hunting pressure, buck-to-doe ratio, and location," M.R. James said. "Based on my experiences, these techniques work best during the pre-rut. Success levels won't be as good during other times of the year.

"As far as pressure is concerned, if hunting pressure is heavy and deer are

M.R. James begins each rattling sequence by making several buck grunts on his deer call. Credit: M.R. James.

ultra-spooky from being pushed around since opening day, you'll be lucky to call or decoy whitetails.

"On the other hand, keen competition among breeding-age bucks helps improve calling, rattling, and decoying. If your hunting area is inhabited by only a few bucks, they won't have to compete with other bucks, so you'll be left high and dry with your bag of hunting tricks. After all, it's safe to assume these bucks would rather make love than fight. Anytime there are scads of willing, receptive does, calling and antler-rattling won't work well.

"Setting up in good spots is extremely important," James continued. "Be aware of prevailing wind currents and avoid places where deer are likely to spot your movements. Even so, the technique of rattling/calling and decoying will not be as important as the other factors listed above. The worst horn-rattlers and callers can enjoy good success at the right time of year if they are in a good location with solid buck competition for does. Conversely, the best caller/rattlers on earth won't do well if they try to buck the basic factors listed above."

Mel Dutton has perfected what he calls his "system." "My system works best during the first two weeks in November here in South Dakota," he said. "Maybe that's because rifle season doesn't start until the second weekend in November. All I know is that I've had great success right before rifle season. Sometimes I've used these three tactics to attract six, eight, and sometimes even more bucks in a single day. I think it works best right prior to the rut because bucks are extremely interested in does, but have not yet actually paired off with them. They're still moving about, searching for a hot doe, and that makes them susceptible to my system. I've had good success on smaller bucks during the remainder of November, too, but larger, trophy bucks are easier to call earlier in the month. Not that you won't sometimes call in or decoy in a larger buck later in the season. You can, but success will be more sporadic, probably because the tactics are attracting the odd buck when he is in between hot does."

Dutton's system during the first part of November involves first setting up his decoy, then retreating to a spot downwind about twenty yards away. He then cracks his rattling horns beam to beam. He grinds them together for thirty or forty seconds, then separates them while tickling the tines as he pulls them apart. "I don't hesitate to toss a buck grunt or grunts into the mix, either," he said. "A week or so earlier, though, in late October, I won't rattle aggressively at all. I just tickle the horns together to get any listening buck's attention.

"A few years ago I believed sequence composition and timing were very important," Dutton continued. "I no longer give either much thought. Now I may wait for four or five minutes and repeat my rattling and calling. I may go for another twenty-five minutes before doing it again. When I'm hunting from a ground stand, I may stay in one place and rattle off and on from there for one and a half or two hours before moving on. Of course, if I can see deer moving up ahead—or little flicks of movement through the brush or the timber—then I'm much more reluctant to move. Even if I can see only does, if the does are there at that time of year, the bucks can't be far behind.

"I mainly use my decoy like a blind," Dutton said. "That's one of the reasons I got the idea for a decoy in the first place. Since I hunt mostly from the ground, when I used to get into one of those large ash thickets, sometimes half a mile in

Mel Dutton rattled this dandy 6X6 whitetail in to the decoy, missed with his arrow, and then rattled the buck back in. He didn't miss the second time! Credit: Mel Dutton.

length, I'd have problems. I'd rattle as I'd begin slowly working my way through one of these thickets from the downwind side. Often, though, a buck would come right in and I wouldn't be able to shoot. Perhaps a limb would be in my way or maybe even the buck would even see me. But with the decoy, I just set it up in a little opening. The decoy provides enough cover so that I can crouch behind it and draw my bow. Plus, with the decoy, deer come in fairly relaxed. If they responded to calls and rattling and didn't see another deer, I think they would have been far more alert and easier to spook."

Dutton doesn't keep his decoy in a stationary position, not even as he's crouched behind it. "I move the decoy," he said. "I pivot it quite a bit. I *want* the deer to see it. I do this because not only do I want them to see it, I want them to get used to it moving. If it's perfectly still up until the moment you attempt your shot your movement *might* spook the deer. If you move beforehand, you will have better luck as you rise to shoot. I rarely spook deer when I'm using the decoy. In fact, on many different occasions I've shot, missed the buck, had my arrow deflect off a limb, and had the deer run away. Yet I've then been able to rattle the deer right back in. The nice 6 X 7 whitetail I shot this year? I missed him with my first shot. The arrow deflected off a limb and the buck bolted to about seventy yards away. I didn't let it upset me, though. Instead, I started rattling again and that same buck turned and came back within five minutes, to be shot at again. This time I hit him as he stood watching the decoy at twenty yards." Dutton's 13-point grossed 130 Pope and Young points.

"Right before I shot this buck I saw a couple of bucks a hundred yards ahead of me through the timber," Dutton said. "I'd just set up my decoy and was getting out my calls and my rattling horns. In fact, I was still on my knees, bent over, when I caught a glimpse of movement to my left. A deer had seen my decoy from the side and had come in. A nice 8-point was standing there about twenty-five yards away just looking at the decoy. I didn't have an arrow out yet, so I watched as the buck laid his ears back and stuck his head forward and came in to about ten yards away. I reached down and clicked together the tips of the antlers, which were still lying on the ground. The buck puffed out his neck, kept his ears back, and became infuriated. He came in closer. Now he was just three yards away from me. At this point, I seriously considered hurling my bow at him. That buck never did figure out what I was. He finally walked past, and when he got downwind he got a whiff of human scent and took off. This was a very aggressive buck. He meant to do some damage. If that decoy had moved, he would have done it, too."

Dutton explained that decoying can sometimes work even in situations where you might think it wouldn't. "A couple of years ago I was guiding a nonresident hunter," he said. "The night before, I'd seen a big buck herd a doe into this one pocket of timber. The next morning, I took the hunter into the downwind side of this pocket. I started rattling and calling at the crack of dawn. I stayed put, rattling and calling until 11:30 A.M., when the buck finally responded to the horns. Now, I know that that buck had a doe bedded no more than 100 or 150 yards from where we were set up. I think he finally became so curious he just had to come in to see what was going on. This just proves that a hunter can, in the right situation, lure a mature whitetail buck away from a doe in heat. But it isn't something you're going to do every day. I sat in that one spot much longer than I ordinarily would have, but I knew the deer were there, and everything felt right, so I stayed with it."

Dutton never hesitates to use rattling, calling, and a properly positioned decoy. But then he hunts thousands of acres where few, if any, other hunters are able to hunt during any given year. "I love to decoy big bucks in with calling and rattling," he said. "But maybe I'd be more reluctant to do so if I were hunting super-pressured deer that are called and rattled to a lot."

Still, you won't know until you try. And the best way to try is to examine your own personal hunting situation and decide what will work best and when. Only then will you be able to see for yourself the true value of the Big Three special effects.

23

Decoying with Mock Scrapes

Deer hunting was the last thing on taxidermist Terry Jenkins's mind on a November evening many years ago. One of his clients had just deposited an entire buckskin—reeking tarsal glands and all—on his shop floor. Until that moment, Jenkins had been considering the huge amount of work piling up in his Illinois shop. When he bent down, he got a whiff of the buck's ripening tarsals. "All I could think was—What could possibly be better for attracting deer?" Jenkins said.

Jenkins severed the glands from the skin. The next morning he took the glandular matter—which included the long, dark, urine-stained hair and the flesh underneath—to his bowhunting area. After he got out of his vehicle, he rubbed the glands over the soles of his boots. It was a dewy morning, the kind that's ideal for preserving a scent trail. He then made his way to his tree stand, which he'd placed in a hedgerow overlooking a forty-acre winter wheat field.

The night before, Jenkins had placed a stick in front of his stand to use as a thirty-yard distance marker. He now walked over and placed one of the tarsal glands on it. He climbed into his tree stand and methodically rubbed the other gland over tree limbs and exposed portions of the stand. He then hung the gland in the tree and began hunting.

Looking across the field at his backtrack, Jenkins could make out his path through the dew-laden wheat. Twenty minutes later, he watched a doe step into view. She was nowhere near his scent trail, but his hopes soared when a large 12-point buck appeared close behind her. A 10-point buck then popped into sight, intent on following the other two whitetails. The three animals left the field to enter the timber well out of bow range. Jenkins was sure he'd had his share of excitement for the day. But the best was yet to come.

"Twenty minute," Jenkins said. "Then I realized it was an 8-point buck. The deer stayed on my trail until it reached the marker stick where the tarsal gland was hanging. The buck became extremely agitated. It smelled both the stick and the gland, then started working them over with his antlers." While the buck was preoccupied, Jenkins drew back his bow and loosed the arrow. The 8-pointer ran a short distance and dropped.

When Jenkins looked up after he had shot the buck, he saw another buck, a 6-point. This deer also had its nose to the ground as it traveled the same trail the

Ernie Richardson has used mock scrapes to take huge whitetails like this Illinois monster. Courtesy Ernie Richardson.

8-point had followed and which Jenkins had walked on that morning. The smaller buck went straight to the stick and its gland.

"Bucks use tarsal gland scent to trail does and other bucks," Jenkins said. "When the rut's in full swing, every deer is going to the same party and nobody wants to be left out."

Jenkins made this discovery many years ago. Since that time, scent manufacturers have been quick to jump on the tarsal gland bandwagon with many formulations of tarsal gland scent.

Some years ago Russell Thornberry, the editor of *Buckmasters* magazine and a noted trophy whitetail hunter, also reported success with tarsal glands. " I'd been hanging tarsal glands on a bush downwind of my rattling location for many years," Thornberry said. " I realized that tarsal glands would probably work because they were so scent-laden and came so obviously from a real buck. What could possibly work better during the months when bucks are so curious about what other bucks are doing?"

Thornberry ties the two glands together so they are easier to handle and hang. When he's not using the glands, he keeps them in his freezer. "I've had good luck using the same glands all season long," he said.

Thornberry also noted that if a doe with darkened or tarnished tarsal glands passes your stand, be extremely alert. "That darkening reveals that she is in estrus," he said. "A buck should be along shortly."

Illinois's Ernie Richardson also swears by tarsal gland magic. Richardson has used tarsal glands for many years. When I last checked, Richardson was scrounging his gland supply from successful hunters at state check stations. After cutting the glands off, Richardson puts each in a plastic bag and labels it as either "buck" or "doe." To use a gland, he makes a hole with a leather punch through surrounding skin and threads a cord through the holes in each gland. He then ties the cord to his boot so that the glands drag as he walks to his stand.

HOW TO MAKE A MOCK SCRAPE

Before you start, you will need a few things: plastic gloves to wear when handling tarsal glands and tools, tarsal glands or scent, a garden claw, some twine or string to be used as hang lines, and, if you're not wearing rubber boots, a couple of gallon-size plastic bags to slip over your boots as you walk the last hundred yards to the stand and also after you're finished making your mock scrape. Also bring a small tarp to kneel on while making the scrape—it will keep human scent off the site. If you don't have a tarp, simply cut along one side and the bottom edge of a large garbage bag.

Spread the tarp on the ground where you will be making your scrape. Put on the plastic gloves and kneel on the tarp while you use the garden claw to rough up the ground. When the first rubs appear on saplings, prime the area you intend to target with some forehead gland scent (see next paragraph). This scent should include glandular material and secretions from the spongy sudoriferous gland, which can be found on a deer's forehead, as well as secretions from glands located at the corners of the deer's eyes.

To prime the area, wear rubber gloves and use a cotton swab to rub forehead gland scent on a couple of low-hanging branches. Return every other day and repeat this procedure. A week later, use your claw to slightly rough up the earth in a couple of places beneath these low-hanging branches. When freshening your location with scent, check to see if other deer are visiting it. Eventually, use your trowel or claw to bare about two square feet of earth. Reapply forehead gland scent to branches and tree trunks when you visit your mock scrape. When you're ready to start hunting, use an eyedropper to apply tarsal gland scent or doe-in-estrus urine to the bare earth of the scrape. You can also attach long draglines to frozen tarsal glands or rehydrated tarsal glands. Beat them into the earth with the trowel, attach the drag lines to your rubber boots, and walk well past your stand location so that any deer that follows this trail will walk past you broadside and out into an opening, giving you a clear shot. Hang the tarsal glands in a nearby tree, again making sure they're in a position so that any deer sniffing them will provide you with a good shot. Position the mock scrape so that an approaching buck will have to pass by your stand within shooting range. If you don't wear rubber boots, be sure that you continue to wear the plastic bags on your feet as you return to your stand.

Richardson once made a mistake that cost him a huge buck. "I'd been hunting near an old gravel pit," he said. "At the time I was still dragging the tarsal glands right to my stand. I hadn't been in my stand long when I saw a buck that would have grossed in the Boone and Crockett 180s. Instead of following the trail to me, he was working the scent *away* from me. I felt helpless as I watched him go over the hill. But he returned minutes later . . . heading right to me *and* the glands. I couldn't shoot because he was heading directly at me. When he got close, he saw me on the platform. He stuck his nose up, trying to scent me. I tried to draw my bow, as foolish as that sounds. The buck saw the movement and raced away. I felt sick."

One of the refinements Richardson now makes to his mock scrapes is to hang the tarsal gland in the spot where he wants the buck to be standing for the shot. Once he started hanging the gland in a small clearing upwind of his stand, his rate of success with this technique soared.

"I'll sometimes freshen older glands with either doe or buck urine, squirting it into the cuffs [openings] of the glands," Richardson said. "When I get where I'm going, then I'll often make a mock scrape."

Richardson takes a middle-of-the-road approach when it comes to freezing the glands. "While the weather is still warm I'll use a set of glands for no more than three days in a row before starting on a new set," he said.

MORE TALES OF TARSAL GLAND PRODUCTIVITY

Richardson once was invited to hunt some private land with a friend. "The area we planned to hunt had many isolated thickets full of brush and saplings. I helped my buddy find a hunting spot, then went to another spot. After looking around, I found a big scrape on the edge of a nearby wheat field. Since it had just rained, I could see that deer had already visited the scrape twice that day.

"In my pack were some old tarsal glands and a bottle of buck urine," Richardson continued. "I first dribbled buck urine in the scrape, then tied the glands to my boots to make a drag trail along the same route the buck had been using to reach the scrape. I found a good spot for a ground blind, hung the glands nearby, put plastic bags over my feet, and then walked twenty yards farther up a nearby hill. From there I could see the glands clearly.

"The buck appeared not long afterward. He was rubbing his antlers on a tree when he scented the tarsal glands. When he reached those glands, he sniffed them so hard he made them swing about," Richardson said. "But just as I drew my bow, the buck turned, probably because he'd scented the strange buck urine in the scrape. He was now quartering away. I drew and shot."

Richardson's buck weighed 187 pounds field-dressed and scored 130 Pope and Young points.

Terry Jenkins took another big 8-point buck from a five-acre patch of woods that he called the Hell Hole. The woodlot was surrounded by open fields and was virtually impossible for a hunter to approach without warning every deer hiding within the thicket.

"I first rubbed tarsal glands on the soles of my shoes," Jenkins said. "I'd already placed my stand there while I was scouting earlier in the season. I now traveled along a small creek west of the woodlot in an area were I thought the buck might be hiding. I climbed into my stand and hoped the buck would soon discover the scent trail I'd just put down. When the buck finally came in, he was trailing the tarsal glands with his head to the ground." Jenkins's shot was good.

Jenkins believes the best time to use tarsal glands is about one week before the rut begins. "Use them right before the does are ready to breed, when bucks are looking for action," he said. "Tarsal glands have never failed me at that time. I'm convinced that using tarsal glands has definitely helped me become a better white-tail hunter."

T.R. MICHELS'S MOCK SCRAPE METHOD

Here's the method Minnesota trophy whitetail outfitter T.R. Michels uses to make mock scrapes both for himself and his clients:

1) Wear rubber gloves.
2) Find a tree with an overhanging branch, or cut a branch and nail it to the tree where you plan to make the mock scrape.
3) Break off the end of any branch that will be left dangling above the scrape.
4) Apply Dr. Juice Deer Attractant® to the end of the branch.
5) Make a mock scrape using either a detached real deer hoof or the heel of a rubber boot.
6) Drizzle a good-quality interdigital scent on the bare ground of the mock scrape.
7) Use a scrape dripper filled with quality buck urine over the mock scrape. T.R. prefers the Ultimate Scrape Dripper® (from the Wildlife Research Center, 4345 157th Ave. NW, Anoka, MN 55304) because it drips only during the day. He feels this is important if you want to attract bucks during legal shooting hours.
8) Drip doe-in-heat urine near the scrape, not in it.
9) Use a different bottle or brand of interdigital scent when you leave a scent trail from the doe's urine to yet another scrape dripper, which should be filled with doe-in-heat urine.
10) Add a bedded doe decoy for further realism. (When T.R. guides bowhunters, he uses a bedded doe decoy and attaches a piece of tissue paper at the tail to simulate movement.)
11) While on stand, grunt, bleat, and rattle to help get a buck's attention.

24

The Bare Truth about Mock Rubs

The bowhunter waits in a tree stand high above the ground, intently watching a deer trail. Along this trail, he knows, are many fresh buck rubs. Along this trail is one additional rub, too. But while this other rub looks real and smells real, it isn't real. Instead, it was made by a human being.

The bowhunter waits, hoping the buck responsible for the many real rubs will come walking down the trail. Before too many minutes pass, his patience pays off. A big 8-point buck ambles down the trail, travels past the cluster of real rubs, and heads straight for the fake, or **mock**, rub. The buck reaches it, pauses, sniffs the mock rub, and then licks it. The animal is standing broadside not twenty-five yards from the hunter's position. He draws his bow, releases his arrow, and is soon tagging his deer.

With deer hunters everywhere hard at work making mock scrapes, imitating whitetail grunts, bleats, and snorts, thrashing antlers together and luring deer in with decoys, it was just a matter of time until some hunter, somewhere, decided to see if mock rubs might work, too.

Scouting for sign and interpreting that sign is an art, one that separates serious hunters from casual ones. Whitetails don't tell us what they're doing every hour of every day. Neither do they reveal why they do what they do. We must figure these things out for ourselves by interpreting clues left by deer. The whitetail rub provides us with a fine clue, albeit one that is consistently underrated by most hunters.

Many hunters look at a rub and think, *Yeah, a buck's been through here, so what?* Then the rub is forgotten while the hunters kick about nearby, minds and eyes focused on finding something really important, like a scrape. But a few astute individuals have been paying more attention to rubs than to scrapes, and their hunting has improved as a direct result. What these individuals have learned has been mostly the result of trial and error. But there is plenty of scientific knowledge about the whitetail rub to learn from as well, information that's been documented by some of the country's finest white-tailed deer biologists.

RUBS AS SIGNPOSTS

Larry Marchinton, Karl Miller, and the staff of expert whitetail biologists and researchers at the University of Georgia School of Forest Resources have long been fascinated with whitetails, and in particular, with whitetail *signposts*. A signpost is a visual and olfactory clue that deer make for other deer to find. Deer use signposts to inform other deer that they have been in a particular spot. Scrapes and rubs both are considered signposts. But while scrapes have been studied and hunted extensively, rubs are just coming into their own, especially among the hunting community. As they do, hunters are beginning to realize that for too long rubs have been either overlooked or given short shrift. In other words, rubs can and do produce. But before we consider some of the best rub-hunting techniques from hunters who

Jim Holdenried relies on big rubs to let him know a big buck is nearby. Credit: Jim Holdenried.

believe in them, here's an overview from University of Georgia studies of what rubs are all about.

From the work of Drs. Marchinton and Miller and their associates, the rub puzzle is slowly beginning to make sense. It's no great secret that antlered bucks make rubs. But it's not common knowledge that a dominant buck, when confronted by another buck, often will rub in direct response to this second buck's presence, as if the act of rubbing verifies his own dominance, or perhaps to put fear into his opponent's heart. Another interesting rub fact is that whitetail bucks often pause while rubbing on a tree to sniff and lick at the portion of the tree on which they're rubbing.

A rub sends a strong signal to deer in a couple of ways. When antlers fray or peel

Count on rubs this size to lead you to a whopper like the one M.R. James arrowed near this one two days after this photo was taken. Credit: M.R. James.

bark off a tree, this newly whitened area of the tree is seen more easily—even at night —than the rest of the tree trunk. As a buck rubs, its sudoriferous (forehead) glands deposit glandular secretions full of pheromones, or chemical signals, onto the tree. He may then lick the tree, which complicates the olfactory signal because of the additional pheromones that are present in saliva. If a buck has been licking its tarsals, he will deposit residual tarsal gland and urine scents on the rub. This hodgepodge of scent is so potent that hounds are still able to detect it several days after a rub was last visited; whitetails should be able to do so, too.

Licking the rub tree or the branches overhanging a scrape will further complicate an olfactory signal with the buck's salivary pheromones. Credit: Kathy Etling.

A rub found near a pawed-out area on the ground or next to a scrape adds complexity to the signpost function since the scent signature now also contains interdigital gland scent, deposited when the whitetail pawed the ground.

PRIMING PHEROMONES

Biologists say that rubs not only serve as territorial markers, but they may perform another important function as well. The earliest rubs, with their identifying buck pheromones, may actually help to promote estrus in whitetail does. Studies conducted on domestic sheep and goats have proven that *priming pheromones* from males actually bring females to estrus by causing them to ovulate. There's an excellent chance that the pheromones that bucks deposit on rubs and scrapes perform the same function for white-tailed deer—and for good reason.

The sooner a whitetail doe enters her estrous cycle, the sooner the buck can breed her. If an area's buck population is sufficient to breed all the does within a month's time, the rut is easier on the bucks. Post-rut mortality, when bucks die of natural causes brought on by the stress of a three-month breeding season, kills a fairly large percentage of animals each year. Three-month breeding seasons aren't nature's way. But when buck-to-doe ratios get out of whack, does will go into estrus every twenty-eight days until they are bred, and bucks will rut until the job is done. In some places, there are ten or twelve does for every one buck, and when a good number of the bucks are yearlings, there's going to be trouble. Oh, a doe will stand for a youngster; but if she knows there's a big, heavy-horned dominant in the area she's going to gravitate to him. If most of the does prefer older and larger bucks, the result can be high post-rut mortality rates as the bucks wear themselves out with strenuous breeding activity. Since a buck will chase a doe until she's ready to breed, and will defend her from all interlopers wanting a cut of the action, even the strongest animals can quickly be worn down.

Early one-month-long breeding periods are good for another reason. Fawns born early in the year have more time in which to gain weight, so they are larger and have more body fat when they enter their first critical winter period.

RUB NUMBERS AND SIZE

Even with minimal scouting at the end of August, it's still often possible to calculate whether or not an old mossy-horns is around by the number of *early* rubs you find. A big, old buck may rub on larger trees later in the rut, but the very first rubs you find—no matter how small they are—very likely belong to Boss Hawg. *He* remembers the rut from last year, and he's raring to go. His testosterone levels increase faster than the hormone's levels in less dominant animals do. These early rubs are warning every doe in the area to get ready because *he's* ready.

If you're hunting in an area that doesn't have many rubs, no matter what part of the rut it may be, chances are that there aren't many mature bucks in that area. In fact, areas with many rubs, and many large rubs, will be those with the best buck-to-doe ratios *and* the largest bucks. Younger bucks usually have neither the hormonal levels nor past experience that impels them to make large numbers of rubs.

DOES AND RUBS

Hunters primarily interested in getting some venison for the freezer should learn more about rub-hunting, too. Recent studies have proven that does will often respond to antler rubs when they see them. They will do so by first moving to them, and then smelling and licking them. Scrapes and licking branches are no longer thought to be the only methods of communication between the sexes. The area's dominant doe, when she approaches a new rub, will rub her forehead on the tree, sometimes on the exposed bark portion. This forehead rubbing is *always* combined with sniffing, licking, or nibbling of the rub tree. Dr. Marchinton and his colleagues also found that does were more likely to react to fresh rubs—those less than two days old—than to older rubs. All three does in the study responded to the rubs, while only two responded to scrapes.

WHITETAIL DOMINANCE AREAS

Rubs are usually clumped together. But rather than being made by a single buck, as was once believed, rubs on one tree will sometimes be made by several

Local deer know—before the rut begins—which buck is the biggest, baddest deer in the forest. Credit: Kathy Etling.

bucks. Biologists now feel that since the same tree (or trees) is often rubbed during subsequent years, a rub may be used by one or more local bucks to mark the boundaries of what may be called a *territory* or a *dominance area.* Or, as Marchinton theorized, the rubs themselves may serve as an expression of a buck's dominance since there are often several well-defined rub areas—dominance areas—within any buck's home range.

The plot thickens. The dominant buck in one area may not be the dominant buck in a nearby area. But whitetails appear to be extremely tolerant of each other, even during the peak of the rut, as long as proper dominant/subordinate behaviors are followed. Since buck home ranges overlap considerably, particularly in areas with high buck populations, this tolerance is a good thing. If whitetail bucks were more rigid about dominance and territoriality, they would also become more aggressive toward each other. Few bucks would survive from one year to the next.

Most dominance battles are decided by foot-flailing when bucks are still in velvet. Serious fighting, when bucks have hardened antlers, is both dangerous and uncommon. Biologists now believe that the worst battles take place when a dominant buck, one that is unknown to resident deer, intrudes on territory where he hasn't ventured before, particularly when in pursuit of an estrous doe.

Local deer know—long before the rut begins—which of them is the biggest, baddest buck in the woods. They also know which bucks are fairly evenly matched. And while 99 percent of all bucks may yield to Mr. Big, other, more evenly matched bucks also may yield to one another *depending upon where the confrontation occurs.* In other words, Buck A may yield to Buck B *only* when Buck A visits Buck B's dominance area. But Buck B, when visiting Buck A's dominance area, may then yield to Buck A.

Locating your tree stand or ground blind in an area replete with rubs can pay huge dividends when rattling, calling, decoying, or using all three techniques. But savvy hunters no longer rely solely on natural rubs made by real whitetails. These hunters now sweeten the pot by making rubs of their own. These mock rubs reveal yet another advance in whitetail hunting strategies.

MOCK RUB THEORY

So what happens when a hunter moves into an area of buck rubs to make his own mock rub? Local bucks are thrown into a quandary. Suddenly, a strange new "buck" has moved onto their turf and is making rubs. Deer smell these rubs and don't recognize the scent. Make such a rub in a buck's dominance area—identifiable by a cluster of similar real rubs—and you can bet he'll be interested, if not downright perturbed, at the impertinence of the new kid on the block.

EYEWITNESS ACCOUNT

A few years ago I was out shooting photos when a really nice 8-point buck came wandering along. I was on the ground when I suddenly heard a deer grunting nearby. As I turned and spotted the buck, I noticed that he was grunting with each step he took. He continued to move closer, then bristled up like a porcupine. The hair down his back and behind his ears stood on end as he stopped to survey the terrain. I could tell that his attention was riveted on a group of small rubs. Stiff-legged and with bowed neck, the buck walked to the rubs and sniffed them up and down, his eyes rolling, as if trying to identify the buck that made them. When he'd satisfied himself as to the scent signature (at least, that's what I think he did), he proceeded to make his own rub over the preceding rub. He then thoroughly anointed the rub with his forehead glands so that his own scent would predominate.

USING MOCK RUBS

Greg Bambenek, an avid hunter from Duluth, Minnesota, is better known as "Dr. Juice" for his expertise in the field of deer scents and attractants. Bambenek earned an M.D. degree, so the title is appropriate. One day, while scouring published scientific papers for anything that might be helpful in his work with white-tailed deer, he read that the whitetail's sudoriferous glands enlarge significantly during the rut period.

Bambenek also knew the relationship between rubs and the deer's sense of sight and smell. As mentioned earlier, deer prefer to rub on trees with a distinct smell, such as pine, cedar, sourwood, cherry, and sassafras. Scented wood probably enhances the scent portion of the rub's function.

Bambenek realized that if the whitetail's forehead glands enlarged during the rut, they must do so for a purpose. From there it wasn't long before he had developed Dr. Juice's Forehead Gland Scent® with a chemical structure that would emit its deer-appealing odor over a period of time—not all at once. "I enjoy observing deer," Bambenek explained. "After watching many of them make rubs, I thought I might be able to attract a buck to a particular tree simply by applying forehead gland scent to it. I started out with a tree species whitetails naturally seem to prefer. Minnesota deer rub mainly on sumac, aspen, pine, or cedar trees, especially those with no low-growing branches. I first applied forehead

The Wrap-a-Rub®, sold by Walker's Game Ear, is ideal for those who want to make mock rubs on public land or who are reluctant to deface a tree. Credit: Walker's Game Ear.

gland scent to trees of these species on the sides facing established deer trails. I then applied the scent to 'mock rub trees' from which I'd shaved off the bark on one side to resemble a whitetail's normal rub."

If Bambenek made his mock rub during the pre-rut period in an area where a buck was already making rubs, that buck would return to scope out the mock rub within a week. Bambenek also discovered that deer would visit his mock rubs whether bark had been stripped off or not. Under ideal circumstances, the buck would be back within two days. Bambenek could tell if a buck has visited since it rubbed on nearby unrubbed trees, where its new activity was clearly be visible. Bambenek also left a thin, sharp edge sticking up on all artificially-rubbed trees, both those with and without bark removed. He'd know when a buck had visited these pre-rubbed trees simply by observing whether that sharp edge had been smoothed down or rubbed over.

Bambenek proved to himself how important rubs are in the whitetail scheme of things. "Hunting is simply playing the percentages," he said. "A mock rub increases the chances of luring a buck back to a particular area. A mock rub close to where a whitetail's already been rubbing will arouse his curiosity. He doesn't know what buck made the rub, so he'll want to find out. He'll return, hoping to discover which buck is horning in on his area, and that may lead him right to you."

Bambenek took a good 8-point Wisconsin buck one year using this very technique—with a slight variation. Instead of cutting or rubbing the bark off the side of a tree already growing nearby, Bambenek chopped down an aspen from another locale, peeled the bark off one side, and then took it to the area where he wanted to place his stand. He pounded it into the ground, creating his own rub tree precisely the right size and exactly where he wanted it to be. "Do something similar to position a mock rub where no suitable tree is growing," he said. For this application, Bambenek used an aspen about four inches in diameter. He wears rubber gloves when handling rub trees or potential mock rubs to eliminate as much human scent as possible. He applies forehead gland scent to the side of the tree facing the deer's trail at about the same height a buck would normally rub. He then erects a tree stand where he will have a good shot at any deer that might visit the mock rub. Right before hunting season opens, he freshens the forehead gland scent one last time. He even used a muzzleloader at sixty yards to bag another mock rub buck.

BEEN THERE, DONE THAT . . .

Bambenek is far from alone in creating mock rubs. "I use a medium to coarse wood rasp, the kind you can buy at any hardware store, to make mock rubs to attract whitetails," stated Chuck Adams, noted Montana bowhunter. "Finer-toothed files take too much time. I make my rubs near scrapes to visually distract any deer that visit or scent-check that scrape. I don't make small rubs; I work on saplings about the size of my wrist. I use the rasp to rub about three-quarters of the way around each sapling. Then I squirt a small amount of doe-in-heat urine or rutting-buck urine on the rub and get ready.

"These rubs work in the same way a doe decoy will," Adams continued. "A decoy, though, can sometimes become a major distraction, one that might even spook a deer on occasion. Mock rubs are subtler. A buck noticing my rubs will zero in on them and come straight to my stand location. He'll be so interested in the new rubs that he won't notice me. That gives me a great opportunity to draw my bow."

Adams said deer are conditioned to look up in trees for hunters where he hunts in western Montana. He welcomes any distraction that will work to his advantage. "Mock rubs work very well," he said. "During one six-year period, I know about two dozen bucks have come to my stand because of them."

Adams knows another hunter who creates an entire rubline along an existing deer trail. "When bucks see these rubs, they're drawn along the trail," he said. "As they travel along, they seem compelled to make their own rub on top of each mock rub. This guy has taken several good bucks like this."

"I've had a tremendous amount of success in areas with just a few rubs," Peter Fiduccia said. "Once I find a rub in a good location for a stand, I'll look the rub over closely to see how it's made, then go about thirty-five yards off to the side, find a slightly smaller tree, and make my own similar rub. I'll then mark the mock rub with buck urine. This second rub acts like a buck magnet. It activates in the responding buck what I call the *spider syndrome*. When a buck sees a rub he didn't make, he'll go to it as if on a string. Most bucks will usually trot in. Larger bucks will usually be slower in responding. I believe this works on a buck's instincts. He sees the rub, knows it isn't his, and has to leave his own calling card so that no doubt exists in another buck's mind that the responding buck belongs in that particular territory."

Fiduccia advises hunters who want to try out mock scrapes to carry a small ruler in their pack. "You can look at one of your mock rubs and mistakenly believe no deer has visited it," he said. "But if you know you made the mock rub twelve inches high, and it's fourteen or fifteen inches when you measure it with a ruler, then you know a real buck has come by and touched it up. Without a ruler you never would have known that it had already attracted a buck's attention. This proves that a rub is being used." Fiduccia does disagree somewhat with Chuck Adams. "In my personal experience, my larger rubs are usually ignored," he stated.

A WORD TO THE WISE . . .

Before making mock rubs anywhere but on land you own yourself, be sure you check with either the landowner or the governing authority to find out whether it is okay to do so. On public areas especially, defacing or destroying flora or vegetation is usually prohibited. If this is the case, consider wrapping a piece of white, light gray, or pale-tan flannel or other cotton cloth around your mock rub trees and tying it in place with a string. Neither the cloth nor the string will harm a tree, and the fabric provides an ideal wick for the application of scent. Should you not want to help out another hunter with your mock rub, simply remove the material at the end of your hunt. Be sure to take it home with you to properly dispose of, or store in a zipper lock bag to use the following season.

THE T.R. MICHELS 3-S SYSTEM: SIGHT, SCENT, AND SOUND

So now you're interested in making mock rubs. But before you begin, consider the following step-by-step method contributed by Minnesota trophy whitetail outfitter T.R. Michels. This method is labor-intensive, because Michels leaves nothing to chance. Although he sometimes uses mock rubs alone, he often combines them with mock scrapes for a potent one–two combination. While he or his hunters are in their stands, Michels may toss in antler-rattling and buck-grunting for good measure.

Michels calls his hunting system the 3-S's of Sight, Scent, and Sound. Mock rubs form an integral part of his system:

1) Always wear rubber gloves.
2) Use a wood rasp to scrape bark off a likely-looking tree near an existing cluster of rubs close to a trail with a good spot for a tree stand.
3) OR, cut two- to four-inch-diameter poles, use a wood rasp on them, then position them in the ground near a trail or rub cluster to create your own mock rubs.
4) Pour Dr. Juice's Forehead Gland Scent® or another forehead gland scent on the rub.
5) Position mock rubs so that responding deer are close enough for a shot.
6) Be sure there are no obstructions between you and where the deer should be standing.
7) For the best of all worlds, make a mock scrape, combine it with a mock rub, and add some calling, rattling, or a decoy.
8) If you're bowhunting, add a bedded-doe decoy for extra realism and attach a piece of tissue paper at the tail to simulate movement.
9) While on stand, grunt, bleat, and rattle to get a buck's attention.

Always keep in mind that mock rubs are being used to pull a buck *back* into his own area. The point of a mock rub is to arouse a buck's curiosity about another unknown "buck" possibly infringing on his dominance area. The buck might already be nearby. Your aim is to lure him into shooting position.

For the keenest edge of all in your quest for whitetail hunting success, consider the rub. Not only do rubs reveal a whitetail's presence in the past, a few mock rubs tossed into the mix can even help predict his future—and *yours,* too!